B2B Brand Management

Philip Kotler · Waldemar Pfoertsch

B2B Brand Management

With the Cooperation of Ines Michi

With 76 Figures and 7 Tables

 Springer

Philip Kotler
S.C. Johnson & Son Distinguished
Professor of International Marketing
Kellogg School of Business
Northwestern University
2001 Sheridan Rd.
Evanston, IL 60208, USA
p-kotler@kellogg.northwestern.edu

Waldemar Pfoertsch
Professor International Business
Pforzheim University
Tiefenbronnerstrasse 65
75175 Pforzheim, Germany
waldemar.pfoertsch@pforzheim-university.de

ISBN-10   3-540-25360-2 Springer Berlin Heidelberg New York
ISBN-13   978-3-540-25360-0 Springer Berlin Heidelberg New York

Cataloging-in-Publication Data
Library of Congress Control Number: 2006930595

Springer is a part of Springer Science+Business Media

springeronline.com

© Springer Berlin · Heidelberg 2006
Printed in Germany

Hardcover-Design: Erich Kirchner, Heidelberg

SPIN 11408604   43/3100-5 4 3 2 1 0 – Printed on acid-free paper

Foreword

Brands are an important part of all cultures across the planet, as well as in the business world. Brands help people make decisions, small ones, as well as big ones. They enable you to trust the *Bordeaux* you drink, the *Mercedes* you drive, and the *GE Jet Engine* that lifts the plane you count on to take you places. Brands are the ideas, perceptions, expectations and beliefs that are in the mind of consumers, your potential customers or any individual who can effect your enterprise.

We live in an interconnected world, made more transparent by the proliferation of new communications technologies. Today, a person, a company, a brand, even a nation, is increasingly accessible and exposed to the observation of the citizens of the world. Strong brands go far beyond just creating awareness; they accurately expose the corporate soul and brand promise for all to see. I believe consumer understanding dominates everything in the business world. Today, consumers have greater access and control over the information from which their perceptions about a brand are created. The ideas and impressions we might hope the consumer to have about our brands are subject to the competing ideas, which are available for consumer perception.

This is a new age of consumerism, one that has evolved into a higher order of brand relationship and accountability. It is a business world where examples like *Enron* have resulted in greater consumer mistrust of the information coming from brands and companies. It is a business environment I call ecologism – where a brand, a company or its leaders cannot hide behind inaccurate pretenses. The truth about your company will always be discovered. It is simply no longer an option to be silent about exposing what your company values, mission or relevancy is. While there are only local consumers, the accessibility of information, this transparency, makes all brands globally susceptible to scrutiny.

The **best brands** consistently win two **crucial moments of truth**. The first moment occurs when customers choose, select or sign the contract to buy after having evaluated all other offerings of the competition. The second moment occurs at the customers' homes, offices or production sites when they use the brand, when they experience it and are satisfied or not satisfied. Brands that consistently win these moments of truth earn a special place in the customers' minds and hearts. These brands are remembered and the re-buy occurs more readily and more profitably. The value of trust earned between the brand promise and the brand experience realized has always been the simple foundation in any sustainable commercial endeavor.

Some **industrial brands** focus intensely on winning these moments of truth. They do this by being in touch with their clients and customers, and by understanding not only their engineering and application requirements but also their brand expectations. We have learned that brands like *IBM* don't stand only for mainframe computer servers or IT software, but for operating a bank or airline 24 hours and 365 days. *Apple* is more than its technology; it is a brand that continuously thinks differently. P&G goes beyond making everyday household and personal care products, by touching lives, improving life. Nissan shifts things – a person, a life, the world, or simply the way you move through it.

It's no coincidence that many of these brands are thriving after their management has listened to the speeches or lectures of Philip Kotler or Waldemar Pfoertsch. Many have read the books and articles of the authors and come back to their workplaces inspired to apply their management principles. Their passionate belief in marketing and brand management is inspirational and effective. It is helping reinvent how we think about creating and fostering our own B2B brands.

This first comprehensive book on B2B brand management will provide even the most experienced business manger with a new way of looking at B2B branding. It provides proven case studies that bring B2B brand management to life. It will provoke the reader to think about a systematic approach to branding, based on facts, rather than personal judgment. Focused branding moves you closer to your customers. Professors Kotler and Pfoertsch encourage us to look for more differentiation without neglecting the competition and they encourage us to get top management attention for the branding decisions on a continuous basis.

In short, this is the ultimate book for managers and customers in the B2B2C value chain.

Tim Love   June 2006
Vice-Chairman *Omnicom Group*
New York, NY, U.S.A.

Adel Gelbert
Managing Partner *BBDO Consulting*
Munich, Germany

Preface

Brand building goes far beyond creating awareness of your name and your customers promise. It is a voyage of building a corporate soul and infectiously communicating it inside and outside the company to all your partners, so that your customers truly get what your brand promises.

Although one of the authors wrote this statement many years ago, we are all still committed to it. The world around us has changed and is constantly changing – every year, every month, and every day. Technologies/products and services/marketplaces emerge, evolve, and disappear. Along with globalization and hyper competition has come the explosion of choices in almost every area. Business-to-Consumer (B2C) companies have identified and applied branding and brand management decades ago to adapt to these changes. Many Business-to-Business (B2B) companies still regard such effort as irrelevant for them. Recently though, B2B brand management has been given more and more attention by researchers as well as practitioners all over the world. Following up on this recent development, we offer the following central tenet:

> **Brand management for industrial goods and services represents a unique and effective opportunity for establishing enduring, competitive advantages.**

Whether you are selling products or services, a strong brand is the most important and sustainable asset your company can have. Your brand strategy should always be the guiding principle behind every decision and every action. This book aims to put B2B brands and branding into their actual context. It describes current thinking and best practice, draws comparisons and highlights differences to B2C, and ventures thoughts about the future of B2B.

Branding is not only about creating fancy names and logos. To equate branding with such superficial cosmetic effort is like judging a book merely by its colorful cover. It is absolutely crucial to understand that there is more to brands than meet the eye. Just take one moment and try to imagine a world without brands. There would be no *Porsche, Mercedes-Benz, BMW, Volvo, Chrysler,* and no *Ford,* just a variety of automobiles that are more or less alike. Which would you buy? Which company would you trust? On which attributes would you make your purchasing decision? Such a world would lack much more than just fancy brand names and logos – it would lack one of the most important factors that simplify our life in an increasingly complex environment: **Orientation**. Brands differentiate, reduce risk and complexity, and communicate the benefits and value a product or service can provide. This is just as true in B2B as it is in B2C!

Philip Kotler   June 2006
Evanston, IL U.S.A.

Waldemar Pfoertsch
Pforzheim, Germany

Acknowledgements

Our cumulative experience with marketing, branding and brand management amounts to more than 70 years. Nonetheless, this book wouldn't have been possible without the help and guidance of various people. When we started work on this book, some people asked us why we wanted to write a book on **branding**, an area already inundated with many valuable publications. When we clarified that our focus would be on business-to-business and not on business-to-customer brand management, a few surprised seconds of silence were followed by a storm of questions. Judging from the nature of these questions, we realized that there was a great need from managers to understand this area in a practical way without reducing the complexity of the subject matter.

Our understanding of marketing and branding, acquired through years of research, teaching and listening to people, forms the foundation of this book. Additional reading, and even more research was necessary to come up with a running theme for this book. Thanks to Jim Collins' most successful book *Good to Great – Why Some Companies Make the Leap … and Others Don't*, we got the inspiration to create **guiding principles**, a step-by-step approach for achieving or maintaining a successful brand management for B2B companies.

Creating this book has been a demanding task: the subject is a complex and moving one, drafted in a global environment, researched on three continents: America, Asia, and Europe, and produced in real-time through Internet platforms or constant e-mail communication. *Microsoft Word* reached its limit many times and drove us up the wall many times – if they are interested, we have some good advice to contribute.

We would like to recognize and acknowledge the valuable insights and observations contributed by the following individuals: At the publishing company *Springer*, Dr. Martina Bihn, Dr. Werner Mueller, Heidelberg, and Paul Manning, New York, who enthusiastically supported this project from the beginning and helped us to go through the various high and low phases of this project. There are a number of people who have inspired and supported our work; some have even reviewed the manuscript and have provided their commentary to help improve it. We want to thank them wholeheartedly for their valuable time and counsel. They are: David T. Krysiek, Managing Director, *The Brandware Group, Inc.*, Atlanta GA, U.S.A.; Dr. Karsten Kilian from *markenlexikon.com*, Lauda-Koenigshofen, Germany; and Paul Hague, *B2B International Ltd*, Manchester, U.K. for unconventionally providing us with valuable information.

We are also want to express deep thanks to our colleagues and friends at Kellogg Graduate School of Management: Alice Tybout, Harold T. Martin Professor of Marketing, Chair of the Marketing Department; James C. Anderson, William L. Ford Distinguished Professor of Marketing and Wholesale Distribution; Mark Satterthwaite, A.C. Buehler Professor in Hospital & Health Services Management, Professor of Strategic Management & Managerial Economics; Ed Zajac, James F. Bere Distinguished Professor of Management & Organizations; Daniel F. Spulber, Elinor Hobbs Distinguished Professor of International Business, Professor of Management Strategy, and Professor of Law at IIT Illinois Institute of Technology; Jay Fisher, Director, Ed Kaplan Entrepreneurial Studies; and M. Zia Hassan, Professor and Dean Emeritus and acting Dean at Stuart Graduate Business School IIT. At UIC: Shari Holmer Lewis, Dean and Director, University of Illinois at Chicago College of Business Administration Office of Executive MBA Program; Joan T. Hladek, Coordinator Executive MBA Program; Doug Milford, Associate Director of Academic Services; John McDonald, Dean of the Liudat Graduate Business School UIC; and Joseph Cherian, Professor Marketing and e-Commerce; Chem Narayana, Lecturer and Professor Marketing University of Iowa (Emeritus). At Pforzheim University: Prof. Dr. Joachim Paul, International Business; Prof. Dr. Konrad Zerr, Marketing; Prof. Dr. Gabriele Naderer, Market Research.

We had many fruitful discussions with business leaders, friends and colleagues, some late into the night. In particular, we would like to mention John Park, ex CFO Orbits, now CFO *Hewitt Associates Inc.*, Lincolnshire, Ill.; Scott Bruggerman, Partner, *Innovation Center*; Michael Kalweit, Principal, *EMK Advisory Group*, Chicago; Gisela Rehm, *BoschSiemens Appliance*, Munich; Simon Thun from *Noshokaty, Döring & Thun*, Berlin; Helmut Krcmar, Professor at the Technical University Munich.

Special thank you goes to companies and individuals who provided us with information or wrote the foreword for the first edition, Tim Love, Vice-Chairman from *Omnicom Group*, New York; Burckhard Schwenker, Chief Executive Officer, *Roland Berger Strategy Consultants*, Hamburg; Adel Gelbert, Managing Partner *BBDO Consulting*, Munich, and Isabel von Kap-herr; Torsten Oltmanns, *Roland Berger Strategy Consultants*, one truly B2B Chief Marketing officer (CMO); and Christiane Diekmann. We appreciate the support of the various capacities which provided us insight in their companies for the write-up of the case studies. This includes: William J. Amelio, President and Chief Executive Officer, and Mark McNeilly, Program Director Branding & Marketing Strategy of *Lenovo*; Dr. Klaus Kleinfeld, Chief Executive Officer of *Siemens* and his team; *Lanxess* CEO, Dr. Axel C. Heitmann; José de J. Alvarado Risoul, Corporate Brand Director, *Cemex*; *Samsung* Vice Chairman and CEO, Jong-Yong Yun. The Mexican success story of *Cemex* wouldn't have been possible without the valuable insights contributed by Alberto Oliver Murillo. Many thanks also to Gunjan Bhardwaj, who helped to put together the Indian case study about *Tata Steel*, as well as Oliver Kong, for helping with the *Lenovo* case.

We believe that although far from being perfect, this book makes a meaningful contribution to increasing the knowledge of B2B **branding**. We hope you share this opinion.

Contents

CHAPTER 1

Being Known or Being One of Many

"It is a capital mistake to theorize before one has data. Insensibly one begins to twist facts to suit theories, instead of theories to suit facts."

Sir Arthur Conan Doyle (1859-1930), Sherlock Holmes

When talking about brands most people think of *Coca Cola, Apple, Ikea, Starbucks, Nokia,* and maybe *Harley Davidson*. These brands also happen to be among the most cited best-practice examples in the area of **Business-to-Consumer (B2C)** branding. For these companies their brand represents a strong and enduring asset, a value driver that has literally boosted the company's success. Hardly any company neglects the importance of brands in B2C.

In **Business-to-Business (B2B),** things are different – branding is not meant to be relevant. Many managers are convinced that it is a phenomenon confined only to consumer products and markets. Their justification often relies on the fact that they are in a commodity business or specialty market and that customers naturally know a great deal about their products as well as their competitors' products. To them, brand loyalty is a non-rational behavior that applies to breakfast cereals and favorite jeans – it doesn't apply in the more "rational" world of B2B products. Products such as electric motors, crystal components, industrial lubricants or high-tech components are chosen through an objective **decision-making process** that only accounts for the so-called hard facts like features/functionality, benefits, price, service and quality etc.[1] Soft-facts like the reputation of the business, whether it is well known is not of interest. Is this true? Does anybody really believe that people can turn themselves into unemotional and utterly rational machines when at work? We don't think so.

Is branding relevant to **B2B** companies? *Microsoft, IBM, General Electric, Intel, HP, Cisco Systems, Dell, Oracle, SAP, Siemens, FedEx, Boeing* – they are all vivid examples of the fact that some of the world's strongest brands are **B2B brands**. Although they also operate in B2C segments, their main business operations are concentrated on B2B. Then why are so many B2B companies spurning their fortune?

Take for instance the *Boeing* company. Only a few years ago a very interesting incident happened at the *Boeing* headquarters in Seattle. Shortly after Judith A. Muehlberg, a *Ford* veteran started as head of the Marketing and Public-Relations department, she dared to utter the "B" word in a meeting of top executives. Instantly, a senior manager stopped her and said: "Judith, do you know what industry you're in and what company you've come to? We aren't a consumer-goods company, and we don't have a brand."[2] Since then US aerospace giant *Boeing* has come a long way. Nowadays, branding and brand management do matter in a big way to them. In 2000, the company's first-ever brand strategy was formalized and integrated in an overall strategy to extend its reach beyond the commercial-airplane business. Today, the brand spans literally everything from its logo to corporate headquarters. Even the plan to relocate its corporate headquarter from Seattle to Chicago has been devised with the *Boeing* brand in mind.[3] In 2005, *Boeing* introduced its new flagship aircraft. In a worldwide campaign with *AOL*, they searched for a suitable name and invented the *Dreamliner*, which was inaugurated by Rob Pollack, Vice President of Branding for *Boeing Commercial Airplanes Marketing*.[4]

What is branding all about anyway? First of all we can tell you what it is not: It is definitely not about stirring people into irrational buying decisions. Being such an intangible concept, branding is quite often misunderstood or even disregarded as creating the illusion that a product or service is better than it really is.[5] There is an old saying among marketers: "Nothing kills a bad product faster than good advertising."[6] Without great products or services and an organization that can sustain them, there can be no successful brand.

Now you may wonder what branding really is all about. Scott Bedbury, author of the book *A New Brand World* puts it as follows:[7]

> **"Branding is about taking something common and improving upon it in ways that make it more valuable and meaningful."**

Brands serve exactly the same general purpose in B2B markets as they do in consumer markets:

> They facilitate the **identification of products, services** and businesses as well as differentiate them from the competition.[8] They are an effective and compelling means to communicate the benefits and value a product or service can provide.[9] They are a guarantee of quality, origin, and performance, thereby increasing the perceived value to the customer and reducing the risk and complexity involved in the buying decision.[10]

Brands and brand management have spread far beyond the traditional view of consumer-goods marketers. Brands are increasingly important for companies in almost every industry. Why? For one thing, the explosion of choices in almost every area. Customers for everything from specialty steel to software now face an overwhelming number of potential suppliers. Too many to know them all, let alone to check them out thoroughly.

For example, *Pitney Bowes*, one of the winners in Jim Collins' book *Good to Great*,[11] has recently introduced a new branding campaign. After being on the success track for more than 15 years, they felt it necessary to educate their customers about all their new products. Chairman and CEO Michael J. Critelli explained on *Bloomberg Television* how *Pitney Bowes'* new business-building brand campaign will fuel the company's long-term growth strategy and his Chief Marketing Officer Arun Sinha elaborated that a brand is more than a product – it's a shorthand that summarizes a person's feelings toward a business or a product. **A brand is emotional, has a personality, and captures the hearts and minds of its customers.** Great brands survive attacks from competitors and market trends because of the strong connections they forge with customers. And that is what *Pitney Bowes* wants to achieve with its B2B customers.

The Internet furthermore brings the full array of choices to every purchaser or decision maker anywhere with just one mouse click. Without trusted brands as touchstones, buyers would be overwhelmed by an overload of information no matter what they are looking for. But brands do not only offer orientation, they have various benefits and advantages for customers as well as the "brand parents", the originating company. They facilitate the access to new markets by acting as ambassadors in a global economy.[12]

Another important aspect of B2B branding is that brands do not just reach your customers but all stakeholders – investors, employees, partners, suppliers, competitors, regulators, or members of your local community. Through a well-managed brand, a company receives greater coverage and profile within the broker community.[13]

Other than the **biggest misconception** that branding is only for consumer products and therefore wasted in B2B, there are other common misunderstandings and misconceptions related to B2B branding and branding in general. One frequently mentioned branding myth is the assumption that "brand" is simply a name and a logo. Wrong! Branding is much more than just putting a brand name and a logo on a product or service.

Take one moment and try to think about what "brand" means to you personally. Without a doubt certain products, brand names, logos, maybe even jingles, pop into your head. Many people think that this is all when it comes to defining brands. But what about the feelings and associations connected with these products, brands, companies? What about the articles you read about them? What about the stories you've heard about them? What experiences have you had with those products, brands, companies? We could go on and pose more questions like these. **A brand is an intangible concept.** To simplify it and make it easier to grasp is quite often equated with the more **tangible marketing communications elements** that are used to support it – advertising, logos, taglines, jingles, etc – but a brand is so much more than that:[14]

- A brand is a promise.

- A brand is the totality of perceptions – everything you see, hear, read, know, feel, think, etc. – about a product, service, or business.

- A brand holds a distinctive position in customer's minds based on past experiences, associations and future expectations.

- A brand is a short-cut of attributes, benefits, beliefs and values that differentiate, reduce complexity, and simplify the decision-making process.

Keeping all this in mind makes it clear that brands cannot be built by merely creating some fancy advertising. If you internalize the concept of "brand" as a promise to your customers it is quite obvious that it can only come to life if you consistently deliver on that promise. Of course, your brand promise needs to be clearly defined, relevant and meaningful, not to be mistaken with exaggerated marketing promises.

A further misconception of branding is that it is seen as a small subset of marketing management. Wrong again! Since a brand is reflected in everything the company does, a **holistic branding approach** requires a strategic perspective. This simply means that branding should always start at the top of your business. If your branding efforts are to be successful, it is not enough to assign a brand manager with a typically short-term job horizon within company.[15]

Building, championing, supporting and protecting strong brands is everyone's job, starting with the CEO.[16] Active participation of leaders is indispensable because they are the ones who ultimately will be driving the branding effort. Brands and brand equity need to be recognized as the strategic assets they really are, the basis of **competitive advantage** and **long-term profitability**. It is crucial to align brand and business strategy, something that can only effectively be done if the brand is monitored and championed closely by the top management of an organization.[17] To appoint a Vice President of Branding, someone who is responsible solely for brand management would be an important step. No matter what the actual title, this person should be the one person taking the required actions for keeping the brand in line.

Strong leaders demonstrate their foresight for the brand, make symbolic leadership gestures and are prepared to involve their business in acts of world statesmanship that go beyond the short-run, and therefore require the sort of total organizational commitment which only the CEO can lead. Consider *Nucor*, America's largest steel producer today. In 1972, about 5 years after facing bankruptcy, F. Kenneth Iverson as President and Samuel Siegel, Vice President of Finance, renamed their company and announced "*Nucor* sells steel to people who actually care about the quality of the steel". This announcement and all steps that followed propelled the company to the top of its industry.

But do brands really pay off? Are they worth the effort and time? Evaluating and measuring the success of brands and brand management is a rather difficult and controversial subject. Moreover, it is not always possible to attribute hard facts and numbers to them which most marketers certainly prefer. As a result, there are only a restricted number of research project and analysis dealing with the actual return on investment for brands.

Current results by *BBDO Consulting Germany* highlight the power of branding. To visualize the effect of brands and branding on share price, they compared the financial market performance of 23 of the 30 DAX companies. The obvious result of the enormous difference in performance accentuates the general importance of brands. Companies with strong brands have recovered significantly faster from the stock market "slump" in the wake of the 9/11 terrorist

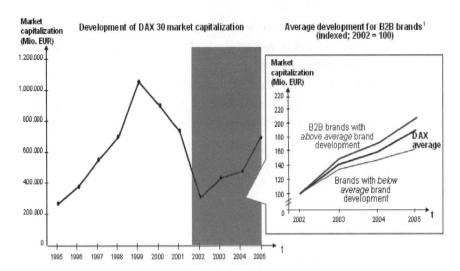

Fig. 1. Branding's effect on share price[18]

attacks than weaker brands. Strong brands provide companies with higher return.

Companies that once measured their worth strictly in terms of tangibles such as factories, inventory, and cash have to revise their point of view and embrace brands as the valuable and moreover equally important assets they actually are (along with customers, patents, distribution, and human capital). Companies can **benefit tremendously from a vibrant brand** and its implicit promise of quality since it can provide them with the power to command a premium price among customers and a premium stock price among investors. Not only can it boost your earnings and cushion cyclical downturns, it can even help you to become really special.[19]

The definition, benefit, and functions of brands embrace every type of business and organization. In order to create and maintain the sustainable competitive advantage offered by the brand, companies need to concentrate their **resources, structure and financial accountability** around this most important asset. Businesses with a strong brand positioning are benefiting from clarity of focus that provides them with more effectiveness, efficiency and competitive advantage across operations.[20]

B2B brand advocates underline that the real importance of brands in B2B has not yet been realized. *McKinsey & Company* is one of them. Together with the *Marketing Centrum Muenster (MCM)*, a German marketing research institute, they investigated and analyzed the importance and relevance of brands in several German B2B markets. They revealed that the most important brand functions in B2B are:[21]

- Increase information efficiency

- Risk reduction

- Value added / Image benefit creation

Since these functions are essential determinants of the value a brand can provide to businesses, they are crucial in regard to determining **brand relevance** in certain markets.[22] The above mentioned brand functions are also vital to B2B markets. They will be discussed in connection with brand relevance in chapter 2.

We cannot guarantee that a business will realize immediate benefits after implementing an overall brand strategy. Since branding requires a certain amount of investment, it is more probable that it will see a decline in profits in the short run. Brand building is aimed to **create long-term non-tangible assets** and is not meant for boosting your short-term sales. Michael J. Critelli, CEO of *Pitney Bowes* is aware of this and plans to run the current re-branding efforts over a period of many years.

In the 1980s, personal computers gradually entered the homes of consumers. At that time the highly recognized brands in the industry were those of computer manufacturers like *IBM*, *Apple*, and *Hewlett-Packard*. Back then, only the most sophisticated computer users knew what kind of micro processing chip their machines contained, let alone who made them. All that changed in 1989, when *Intel* decided to brand its processors. Because of the accelerating pace of technological change as well as constantly growing sales rates in the consumer market, the company decided to focus on end users. They realized that **establishing a brand** was the only way to stay ahead of competition. Today, *Intel* is a leader in semiconductor manufacturing and technology, supported and powered by their strong brand, an almost unbeatable competitive advantage.

Along with the Dot Com boom came companies that seemed to prove the opposite – they managed to establish strong and successful brands within a very short time. Many mistakenly saw the shooting star-like success of *Yahoo!* and *AOL* as a sign of enduring changes in marketing management and practices. Some even argued that this "is the new reality". We maintain that they were just exceptions to the rule. Establishing brands does take time. There is no worse mistake one can make than to expect immediate and fast results from branding efforts. Brands are built over time.

It is also not our intention to claim that B2B branding is the answer to all your company's problems. We are not trying to create just another management fad that is going to disappear in a few years. Just as there are limitations in the B2C branding world, limitations also exist in B2B. These restrictions will be identified and examined thoroughly in the following three chapters as we substantiate the importance of B2B brands accompanied by numerous examples from various industrial areas.

To lead you through this book we have created a **Guiding Principle** in chapter 4 that illustrates visually different stages on the branding ladder.[23] It can literally be seen as the path you have to follow in order to achieve brand success. You will see that there are many things you have to consider in order to successfully climb the ladder to success.

The beginning of the path is marked by the decision whether or not to brand your products, services, or business. If a company, especially the people at the top, is not convinced that it is the right thing to do, it doesn't make any sense to continue. After making the decision to brand, you have to figure out how you are going to do it. But deciding on the best brand portfolio that fits your respective business/industry is not enough to ensure your company's brand success. Therefore, the next stage addresses all the factors in practice that make branding successful.

What would a book on **brand management** be without presenting a number of success stories showing the potential rewards of holistic branding efforts? Chapter 5 provides illustrative brand success stories. At the same time it is important to be realistic and acknowledge that there are many things that can go wrong – so be aware of branding pitfalls! Chapter 6 focuses on five pitfalls of branding. Finally, the future perspective will be dealt with in chapter 7. Key trends and developments related to B2B branding and branding in general will be discussed.

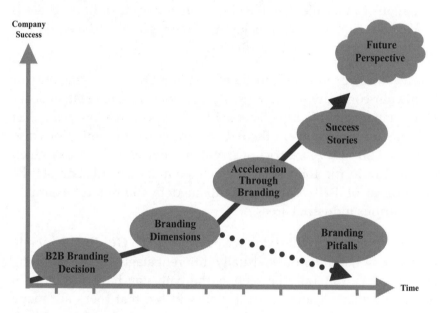

Fig. 2. Guiding principle (structure of the book)

B2B Branding Decision – First of all, we are going to bombard you with arguments and evidence that clearly highlight the importance and relevance of brands in B2B markets whether you already have brands or if you are looking for guidance with the decision to brand. Brands cannot be created over night. The decision to brand a product, line of products, or company needs to be based on evidence that brands do actually matter in the respective area. The environment for establishing and managing brands is complex and dynamic. Brand management is challenging – whether you are in the consumer goods, services or industrial products sectors. Therefore, we will provide you with insights about actual brand relevance in your area.

Branding Dimensions – Since nothing can be done without knowing the fundamentals, this stage is to give you an understanding of the general branding dimensions especially aligned to cover the B2B area. Furthermore, we will point out factors that are necessary to accelerate the success of a company through branding efforts. As a foundation, you need to know the basics and understand what a holistic branding approach can accomplish if soundly realized.

Acceleration Through Branding – This is finally the "How to do it" chapter in this book. Here you will learn how to plan, create, implement, and manage your brand strategy. Moreover you will find examples of the first branding steps of other companies.

Success Stories – No book on branding is without success stories neither is this one. Without the living proof that branding efforts in B2B can be successful some business companies would probably never think of creating brands themselves. In this chapter we will provide you with some insights into strongly branded B2B companies from various industries. Although no company can be successful by imitating the brand management of another business it can gain valuable information and hints for their own brand. Important questions related to the point of differentiation, factors of success, and even similarities can be answered.

Branding Pitfalls – Branding in general is a delicate matter. Branding in B2B can be even more delicate if one doesn't understand what it is all about. There are some general pitfalls generated by common misunderstandings related to branding. We deliberately dedicated a whole chapter to branding pitfalls in order to demonstrate the importance of taking careful and well considered actions related to brand management. Brands are just as fragile as they are profitable if well managed.

Future Perspective – In this chapter we will try to provide you with some outlook into the future. We will concentrate on depicting general implications rather than making specific predictions of the future. Future trends towards Corporate Social Responsibility and Design emphasis for instance are important developments that can change and redefine brand management of the future.

The essence of this book is to infect B2B companies with the branding-virus – empowering them to make the leap to becoming a brand-driven and more successful company. There are many ways to measure overall company success: sales increase, share value, profit, number of employees, mere brand value (index), etc. To keep it simple and to limit alterations that may have been influenced by various other sources than the actual brand, we chose sales over time as measurement for a company's success in our Guiding Principle. The transition point represents a company's rise to the challenge of building a B2B brand.

Summary

- **Branding is just as relevant in B2B** as it is in B2C. Brands like *Microsoft, IBM, Intel, Dell, SAP, Siemens, FedEx, Boeing* are vivid examples of the fact that some of the world's strongest brands do exist in B2B.

- Branding is not about stirring people into irrational buying decisions – it is rather an **effective and compelling means** to communicate the benefits and value a product or service can provide.

- Branding is about **taking something common and improving upon** it in ways that make it more valuable and meaningful.

- **Trusted brands act** as touchstones, offering orientation the flood of information, and many other benefits and advantages to buyers.

- **A brand is much more than a product**, a brand name, a logo, a symbol, a slogan, an ad, a jingle, a spokesperson; these are just tangible components of a brand – not the brand itself!

- "Brand" comprises various aspects. **A brand is a promise, the totality of perceptions** – everything you see, hear, read, know, feel, think, etc. – about a product, service, or business. It holds a distinctive position in customer's minds based on past experiences, associations and future expectations. It is a short-cut of attributes, benefits, beliefs and values that differentiate, reduce complexity, and simplify the decision-making process.

- **Branding should always start at the top of a business**. Building, championing, supporting and protecting strong brands is everyone's job, starting with the CEO.

- **Brands do pay off.** Companies with a strong brand can benefit tremendously from it. A vibrant brand and its implicit promise of quality can provide businesses with the power to command a premium price among customers and a premium stock price among investors; it can boost their earnings and cushion cyclical downturns.

- The most important brand functions in B2B are **increased information efficiency, risk reduction and value added/image benefit creation**.

Notes

[1] David A. Aaker and Erich Joachimsthaler, *Brand Leadership,* 2000, p. 22; Mia Pandey, "Is Branding Relevant to B2B?," *brandchannel.com* (27 January 2003).

[2] As quoted in Gerry Khermouch, Stanley Holmes and Moon Ihlwan, "The Best Global Brands," *Business Week* (6 August 2001).

[3] Gerry Khermouch, Stanley Holmes and Moon Ihlwan, "The Best Global Brands," *Business Week* (6 August 2001).

[4] Web site of *The Boeing Company*, Chicago, IL, cited August 2005.

[5] Paul Hague and Peter Jackson, *The Power of Industrial Brands*, 1994.

[6] Peter de Legge, "The Brand Version 2.0: Business-to-Business Brands in the Internet Age," *Marketing Today*, 2002.

[7] Scott Bedbury, *A New Brand World*, 2002, p. 14.

[8] James C. Anderson and James A. Narus, *Business Market Management: Understanding, Creating, and Delivering Value,* p. 136.

[9] Dan Morrison, "The Six Biggest Pitfalls in B-to-B Branding," *Business2Business Marketer* (July/August, 2001): p. 1.

[10] Tom Blackett, *Trademarks,* 1998.

[11] Jim Collins, *Good to Great. Why Some Companies Make the Leap and Others Don't,* 2001.

[12] Gerry Khermouch, Stanley Holmes and Moon Ihlwan, "The Best Global Brands," *Business Week* (6 August 2001).

[13] Mia Pandey, "Is Branding Relevant to B2B?," *brandchannel.com* (27 January 2003).

[14] Michael Dunn, Scott M. Davis, "Creating the Brand-Driven Business: It's the CEO Who Must Lead the Way," in *Handbook of Business Strategy* (Vol. 5 No. 1, 2004), pp. 241-245; Duane E. Knapp, *The Brand Mindset,* 2000, p. 7.

[15] David A. Aaker and Erich Joachimsthaler, *Brand Leadership,* 2000, p. 8.

[16] Scott Bedbury, *A New Brand World,* 2002, p. Intro.

[17] David A. Aaker and Erich Joachimsthaler, *Brand Leadership,* 2000, p. 9.

[18] Source: *BBDO Consulting Analysis* 2005 – reprinted with permission.

[19] Gerry Khermouch, Stanley Holmes and Moon Ihlwan, "The Best Global Brands," *Business Week* (6 August 2001).

[20] Rita Clifton and John Simmons, *Brands and Branding,* 2003, p. 5.

[21] Mirko Caspar, Achim Hecker, and Tatjana Sabel, "Markenrelevanz in der Unternehmensfuehrung – Messung, Erklaerung und empirische Befunde fuer B2B-Maerkte," 2002, p. 13.

[22] Ibid.

[23] We understand the Guiding Principle as the leading idea and guiding help to follow our thinking and the structure of the chapters.

CHAPTER 2

To Brand or Not to Brand

Destiny is not a matter of chance, it is a matter of choice; it is not a thing to be waited for, it is a thing to be achieved.

William Jennings Bryan, former presidential candidate (1860-1925)

Millions of words, thousands of articles and hundreds of books have already been written on the subject of branding. How many of them have you read? Not too many, we suppose, since almost all of them are dedicated only to consumer products and markets. So when it comes to the decision of "to brand or not to brand" in a business-to-business environment, many marketers push forward the fundamental differences between industrial and consumer markets as justification for neglecting the relevance of brands and branding. But as William Jennings Bryan said, destiny is only a matter of choice. In this case we argue for the positive **B2B branding decision**.

If you take a look at the guiding principle graph (Fig. 3) it becomes quite clear what we mean. As indicated by the black arrows in the middle of the transition point, most B2B companies share a modest growth rate throughout their whole lifetime. Now, you might be thinking, "Well, that's probably just the way it is." Our theory is that by implementing a **holistic brand approach,** companies can accelerate and increase their overall success. Numerous, very successful B2B brands are the "smoking gun" for this theory. While some of them tapped into branding rather by accident, the majority made a conscious decision for B2B branding. They identified the great potentials that a well-managed B2B brand can offer them at an early stage.

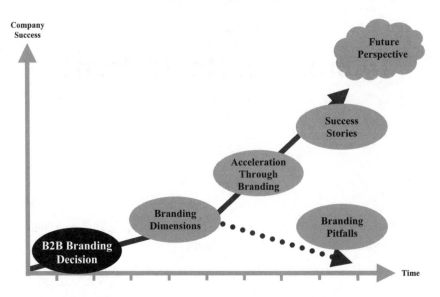

Fig. 3. Guiding principle B2B branding decision

Holistic Branding

If you are wondering what is meant by the holistic approach that we are advocating in this book, the answer to your question is as follows. Holistic means that everything from the development, design, to the implementation of marketing programs, processes, and activities is recognized as intersecting and interdependent. The days when each was handled separately are gone for good. Holistic marketing, just as holistic brand management recognizes that "everything matters". It is necessary to have a broad, integrated perspective to assure consistency of the comprehensive approaches. Relationship marketing, integrated marketing, internal marketing, and social responsibility marketing are components of a holistic marketing concept. It is thus an approach to marketing that is characterized by the strong alignment of all marketing activities to their overall scope and complexity.

Caterpillar

Let us take a look at *Caterpillar*. For eighty years now, the earth-moving equipment of *Caterpillar Inc.* has boldly shaped the world's landscape and infrastructure. It is one of the few high-profile brands that are prominent and successful in two very different fields: heavy machinery and clothing. In the B2B area, the stylish yellow-tabbed CAT logo is best-known as the symbol of the leading global manufacturer of construction and mining equipment, diesel and natural gas engines and industrial gas turbines.

The history of *Caterpillar* dates back to the late 19th century, when Daniel Best and Benjamin Holt were experimenting with ways to fulfill the promise that steam tractors made for farming. The Best and Holt families collectively had pioneered track-type tractors and the gasoline-powered tractor engine. In 1925 the Holt Manufacturing Company and the C.L. Best Tractor Company merged to form the *Caterpillar Tractor Corporation*.

In 2004, the company gained sales and revenues of US$30.25 billion and a profit of US$2.03 billion. Today, CAT is a truly global brand. Approximately half of all sales are targeting customers outside the United States. The products and components of the global supplier and leading U.S. exporter are manufactured in 49 U.S. facilities and 59 other locations in 22 countries around the globe.

As a technology leader, the construction-equipment giant is represented worldwide by a global dealer network that serves customers in more than 200 countries. The mostly independent and locally owned dealerships provide CAT with a key competitive edge since customers deal with people they know and trust while benefiting from the international knowledge and resources of the company.

The company sets a strong focus on testing and quality processes that aim to secure its **reputation for reliability, durability and high quality.** Although *Caterpillar* products are highly priced, they are said to be more effective and money-saving in the long-term because their systems are proven to work harder and longer than their competitors'. Faced with the threat of potential brand erosion and customer confusion due to decentralized divisions the company decided to develop a program to secure and foster the integrity of their corporate image. The result was the *One Voice* campaign that put a strong focus on the corporate brand strategy.

The strength of this iconic American brand moreover was extended very successfully to the B2C area in 1994. To most consumers the brand is more familiar on a range of expensive heavy duty boots and associated apparel. The strength and extraordinary appeal of the *Caterpillar* brand in B2C lies in its brand heritage for rugged durability. CAT footwear, for instance, combines the rugged durability of work shoes with the easy comfort of casual footwear.[1]

MTU AERO

Here is another interesting example. *MTU Aero Engines* is a highly regarded brand in the global aircraft engine business. Headquartered in Munich, Germany, it develops, manufactures and provides service support for commercial and military aircraft and helicopter engines. Revenue wise, it is one of the largest aircraft engine module and component manufacturers delivering large parts for the new airplane titan *Airbus A380*. Technological leadership, excellent product quality as well as their highly regarded brands are the cornerstones of their **strong market position**. According to Hans-Peter Kleitsch, Vice President HR, *MTU Aero Engines* is continuously expanding its leading-edge position through cooperative efforts and joint ventures. Among its major partners are *Pratt & Whitney*, *General Electric*, and *Rolls-Royce*.

The company was founded in 1969, when the engine activities of *Daimler-Benz* were merged with those of *MAN*. Back then, the *MTU Group* (which stands for *Motor & Turbine Union*) included the *MTU Munich* as well as *MTU Friedrichshafen*. It is striking that the company stuck to its branding efforts although it had to go through various changes. In 1985, *MAN* sold its stake in the company to its partner, making it a wholly-owned *Daimler-Benz* affiliate. Only four years later the group became part of the just founded *Deutsche Aerospace (DASA)*. With the foundation of the *European Aeronautic Defense and Space Company (EADS)* in year 2000, there was another reshuffle. Again, it became a directly managed *DaimlerChrysler* affiliate, involving a comprehensive change in its corporate identity. This change included the renaming of *MTU Munich* into *MTU Aero Engines*.

The peak was reached when *DaimlerChrysler* sold its subsidiary to the private-equity investor Kohlberg Kravis Roberts (KKR) in 2004. Regardless of the split of the *MTU group* and its sale, *MTU Aero Engines* **never questioned its branding efforts**.[2] By 2010, *MTU* expects to be the most eligible subsystem supplier to system integrators, and consolidate its position as the world's largest provider of independent engine services. With its recent successful IPO it secured its financial future. *MTU Friedrichshafen*, the much smaller manufacturer of large diesel engines, went also through a branding exercise, and outperformed its competitors dramatically. Today when you want to order a stand-by unit for hospitals or a diesel for fast racing boats, there are only a few choices: one is *MTU Aero Engines*.

Accenture

Another successful company that never questioned the power of a B2B brand is *Accenture*. When *Andersen Consulting* had to change its name because of the split from its affiliate *Arthur Andersen*, it was never put into question whether **to brand or not**. After nearly three years in a courtroom squabble, they had less than five months left to come up with a new name and brand strategy that would fit their business strategy. What followed is considered one of the most ambitious re-branding efforts ever undertaken in the professional services industry.

Its main aspiration was to remain one of the world's leading consultancies. In the course of these changes the company intended not only to change its name but also to reposition itself in the marketplace to better reflect its new vision and strategy. By executing a new business strategy and refocusing its capabilities, *Accenture* wanted to become a market maker, architect and builder of the new economy. Six WPP agencies were assigned to assist in the **re-branding process**, among them *Landor Associates* and *Young & Rubicam Advertising*. The intensive three-month research and analysis process was definitely worthwhile. *Accenture*, the word that won the race was coined by an employee in Norway in an effort to denote the company's strategy of putting an *accent on the future*. Nowadays *Accenture* is a very successful global management consulting, technology services and outsourcing company, with net revenues of US$13.67 billion in 2004.[3]

The advertising for the re-branding effort required high investments. Created by *Y&R* New York, they were part of a US$70 million global brand positioning campaign by *Accenture* that ran in 31 countries. "I am your idea" was seen in leading business and news television programs, leading business newspapers and magazines and also appeared in airport posters and outdoor advertising. In addition to the *Accenture Match Play Championship*, the company leveraged sponsorship opportunities with institutions such as the Louvre, Spain's Info Forum, and the British Film Institute. A web cast featured various elements of the campaign was broadcasted to *Accenture's* more than 75,000 employees worldwide. Stephan Scholtissek, *Accenture's* Country Managing Director Germany is convinced that this was a viable investment.

2.1   B2B ≠ B2C

We must emphasize that there are many differences that have to be taken into consideration when thinking about building a brand in B2B. Before deciding whether to establish a branding strategy for a product, service or business you need to be well aware of differences relative to B2C markets. In the following section we will therefore address the most important distinctions of B2B and B2C markets.[4]

B2B Markets

Businesses that operate in industrial markets acquire goods and services to use in the production of other products or services which are sold, rented or supplied to other businesses. Even most manufacturers of consumer products have to sell their products to other businesses (retailers or wholesalers) first. In one way or another, almost all companies are engaged in business markets. Therefore,

fore, B2B sales far outstrip those of B2C. The main differences of business markets compared to consumer markets are found in the nature and complexity of industrial products and services, the nature and diversity of industrial demand, the significantly fewer number of customers, larger volumes per customer, and last but not least, closer and longer-lasting supplier-customer-relationships.[5]

The Complexity of Industrial Products

Ranging from pencils you use in the office up to turnkey operations for power plants – the variety of industrial products and services is so huge and complex that it is almost impossible to make universally valid statements about them. Researchers around the world have developed different typologies to reduce this immense complexity. In general, business markets can be broken down into these markets:

- materials and parts
  e.g. raw materials, manufactured materials, and parts

- capital items
  e.g. buildings/equipment used in buyer's production/operations

- supplies and services
  e.g. operating supplies, repair/maintenance item.[6]

These kinds of typologies are quite useful if you want to simplify a complex issue and still encompass the lot. This book is mainly written for practitioners and marketers in B2B; as such you are undoubtedly well-informed about the business you are in. *Jack Welch* from *GE* may have liked it, because he followed the B2B branding principle instinctively to lead his complex organizations with thousands of complex products. Many managers struggle daily to lead and motivate mere handfuls of people. Many CEOs wrestle to squeeze just average performance from companies a fraction of *GE*'s size.

As a result of this enormous complexity of industrial products is that the process of purchasing quite often requires qualified experts on both sides. In contrast, the purchase of consumer products can usually be accomplished with little or even no expertise. Unlike the often standardized consumer products, industrial products tend to be individual solutions that require high levels of fine-tuning. In many cases they even have to be integrated into larger systems which again imposes very specific requirements for certain product specifications. These factors have a great impact on the way industrial products have to be marketed.[7]

Derived Demand

Do you have a demand for silicon dioxide? Assuming you do not happen to be in the purchasing department of a computer chip manufacturer, we suppose you don't. Silicon is one of earth's basic inexhaustible chemical elements and it's quite unlikely that we will run out of this resource anytime soon. This is good news for us since it is in high demand for all kinds of high-tech products, for instance the omnipresent microprocessors.[8] These in turn are in demand for the production of PCs, cars, cellular phones, electric razors, and scores of other products.

Despite this apparent simplicity in the demand for silicon dioxide, the value chain of **industrial businesses causes enormous complexity**. Generally, the demand of B2B companies is derived demand pulled through the chain as a result of demand for the final end product. The demand for silicon dioxide only exists because of the demand for PCs and related products. Everything starts and ends with consumer demand.[9]

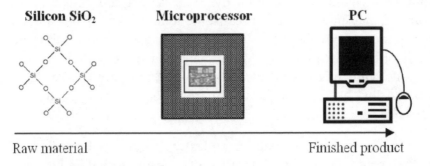

| Silicon SiO$_2$ | Microprocessor | PC |

Raw material   Finished product

Fig. 4. Derived demand

Since most industrial businesses only produce a limited number of goods and services, changes at the end of the value chain can have serious repercussions on all the suppliers concerned. Industrial demand therefore tends to be **more volatile than consumer demand**.[10] This leveraged impact can cause wide swings in demand, sometimes referred to as the "bullwhip effect".[11]

Just imagine what would happen if a company discovered an even better material for the production of chips than silicon. At the end of the value chain there would probably be only a few changes – a microprocessor will still be a microprocessor, no matter what material the chips are made of. On the other end though, it looks somewhat different. Chip manufacturers just cannot convert their billion-dollar factories overnight. The implications there would be truly tremendous.[12] Moreover, **derived demand** is by nature far more inelastic than consumer demand. For a business it makes little sense to buy more of a needed resource, just because the price is temporarily low.[13]

Internationality

Because business markets are predominantly concerned about functionality and performance, industrial products and services are similar across the world. This stands in sharp contrast to the B2C markets, where **national differences in culture, taste, and values** can have tremendous implications on the way certain products or services are perceived and valued. Market offerings for business markets require much less adaptation in order to sell them across borders. In general, customers from all over the world – the United States, Asia, or Europe – are seeking essentially the same functionality and performance from industrial products and services. The ongoing worldwide globalization, liberalization of trade, innovation in logistics and transportation, as well as advances in communication and information technologies continue to erode the barrier of geographical distance between B2B companies in different countries. This implies that B2B companies should always pursue **global branding** in their market offerings.[14]

Organizational Buying

B2B companies usually have fewer customers than B2C companies. Most B2B companies have a customer distribution where a very small number of buyers is providing the vast majority of the turnover and sales volume. While businesses selling consumer products quite often have thousands or even millions of customers, it is not unusual for B2B companies to only have a hundred or fewer valuable customers. Customers for industrial goods can generally be classified into three groups: users, original-equipment manufacturers (OEM), and middlemen:[15]

- As the name implies, the **user** makes use of the purchased goods in their businesses. A manufacturer who buys a machine to produce parts for his finished goods, for instance, belongs to this group.

- **OEM**s on the other hand incorporate the purchased goods into their final products. In the automotive industry, for example, many parts of a car – sometimes even the whole assembly – are out-sourced by the car-manufacturers.

- The last groups of industrial **middlemen** are essentially composed of distributors and wholesalers who distribute industrial goods from the manufacturers to users, to OEM's, and to other middlemen.

How do organizations actually "buy"? As mentioned in the beginning, most people would respond that the industrial buyer would make the most rational, lowest-cost, most-profitable decision, based on price, features/functionality and service. We are not implying that this is not true; it is, but only up to a certain point. Any industrial buying decision is a complex process. Questions such as why buying occurs, when it occurs, how it is processed, how suppliers are chosen, who takes part in the buying process and why one product or a service is chosen over another, need to be considered.

Due to this **huge complexity**, an organizational purchase usually involves inputs from many different departments in the organization. People from different disciplines at many levels contribute their expertise to assure the selection of the best solution for the organization.[16]

Buying Situation

A business buyer has to face many decisions when it comes to making a purchase. The amount and complexity of these decisions depend on the respective buying situation. For almost four decades, marketing literature has persistently broken them down into three types of recurring buying situations: the straight re-buy, modified re-buy, and new task.[17]

- The **straight re-buy** is the most common buying situation and usually involves the least risk. Does your purchasing department compare the terms of all relevant suppliers of pencils every time you need new ones? Probably not. Ordinary, low-cost items like most office supplies are bought on a routine basis. Most companies have some kind of "approved list" that specifies adequate and preferred suppliers.

- The **modified re-buy** is a situation in which a company aims to satisfy an existing need in a modified way. Motivations for the reevaluation of alternatives can be, for instance, to simply reduce costs or to improve performance but also compulsory changes due to new regulations fall in this category.

- In a **new task** purchase situation, a company is confronted with a new requirement for a product or service. When you are about to buy something for the first time the lack of experience generally increases the level of uncertainty and risk involved in such a buying situation. The greater the cost and risk of a new task, the more people are involved in the buying decision and the longer it takes until they come to a decision. Ideally all information available is gathered, checked and evaluated to ultimately choose the best solution. Branding can speed up this process, which is especially important when under time pressure.

Buying Center

Depending on the respective buying situation, there are several participants involved in the purchasing decision, forming the so-called **buying center**.[18] Contrary to what the name implies, a buying center is neither a formal nor structured center. Its size and composition varies greatly depending on the complexity of the respective need that has to be satisfied.[19] In a straight re-buy situation, for instance, it is most likely only one individual – probably a purchasing agent, whereas the buying center for a new task can include up to 20 representatives from different levels and departments (finance, production, purchasing, engineering, etc.) within an organization.[20]

In alignment with the role each individual of the buying center can play, marketing literature generally distinguishes between initiators, users, influencers, deciders, approvers, buyers, and gatekeepers:[21]

- **Initiators** are generally those who detect that there is a need for something and subsequently request a product purchase. They may be front line employees or high level managers.

- No matter how complex the product or service to be bought is, in most cases there will be a **user** who – big surprise – will have to use it in the end. The influence of the user on the buying decision depends on the sector of activity and the corporate culture. Usually, the higher qualified the users, the more weight is given to their opinion.

- **Influencers** are people who have the power to guide the buying decision by defining specifications or providing further information for the evaluation of alternatives.

- The final decision of the purchase is made by the **decider**.

- Before the final decision translates into proposed action there are **approvers** who have the authority to approve or disapprove it.

- **Buyers** are the ones who are formally authorized to select the supplier and arrange the purchase terms.

- **Gatekeepers** are all people who have the power to control the information flow to the members of the buying center (purchasing agents, receptionists and telephone operators, etc.).

To get away from this rather theoretical explanation, let's have a look at an example. Take the case of the new super jumbo *Airbus A380* – already months before its virgin flight in April 2005, *Airbus*, based in Toulouse, France and a unit of *European Aeronautic Defense and Space Co. (EADS)*, had taken orders for more than 150 of the *A380s*. As the largest commercial passenger jet ever built, the *A380* can accommodate up to 555 passengers in a standard, three-class configuration – easily eclipsing its main competitor, *Boeing's 747*. What would a buying center for such a purchase look like?

Most probably the **initiators**, **approvers** and/or **deciders** in this case were high level managers of airlines who undoubtedly had their reputation as high-end service providers in mind. As proof are the orders of *Emirates Airlines* (45 planes), *Singapore Airlines* (10 on firm order with an option for 15 more), *Lufthansa Airlines* (seven planes), and *Atlantic Airways* (six planes).[22] To really provide high-end service, *Singapore Airlines* (SIA), for instance, will even have less than 500 seats in a three-class configuration. This way, *SIA* wants to ensure the highest quality flying experience for its customers.[23]

Cost efficiency, most probably also played a major role in the buying decision for **influencers**, notably the finance people of these airlines. The average costs per airplane are about 15-20% below *Boeing 747*. Moreover, since *Airbus* is using the latest state-of-the-art technologies, the *A380* has lower fuel burn and emissions.[24] The pilots, as the ultimate **users** of the airplanes, no doubt, were involved in the decision as well.

Another institution that also has the power to guide the buying decision is the scheduling department. With the increased number of seats, the *Airbus A380* is especially valuable for "thick" routes, which encompass both strong leisure and business markets.[25] The scheduling department is responsible for finding possible routes

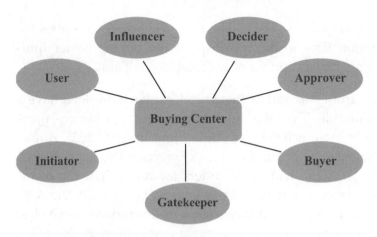

Fig. 5. Roles of the buying center roles

and therefore has major input as **influencers** on the total number of planes to be bought. Undoubtedly, there are many more buying center members in such a complex purchasing decision, but we think we have made our a point.

As shown above, buying decisions in an industrial context are substantially more complex than B2C buying decisions: More people, more money, and more technical and economic considerations, more risk. Due to this complexity, it became necessary to break down the organizational buying process into several stages. One of the most a common and accepted concept is the phase model of Robinson, Faris and Wind (1967) who distinguish between eight buying stages:[26]

Stage 1: Problem recognition: The first stage of the organizational buying process starts with the anticipation and recognition of a certain need. These needs can range from a trivial re-buy situation for office supplies up to the acquisition of a new machine, just about everything that is necessary to keep the business going. Customer needs, internal goals and/or objectives, and external environmental factors can be driving forces for the determination of a need.

Stage 2: **General need description**: After having the information of a new need, the next step is to outline the estimated quantity and timeframe for the procurement of the required products and services.

Stage 3: **Product specification**: In this stage, detailed specifications for the final products or services are defined. Contrary to the previous stage, it not only involves technical but also commercial terms clarifying payment, maintenance and after-sales service conditions.

Stage 4: **Search for and evaluation of potential suppliers**: The best case scenario for this stage is that the buyer uses various media to search for really all potential suppliers and then evaluate whether they are able to fulfill the expressed need.

Stage 5: **Proposal solicitation and analysis**: Besides obtaining proposals from qualified potential suppliers, it is also about defining important criteria for the latter evaluation and selection.

Stage 6: **Supplier evaluation and selection**: Which company will it be in the end? It is now time to weigh the different criteria established in the previous stage.

Stage 7: **Order-routine specification**: Depending on how the production of a company is organized the selection of an order-routine can vary greatly.

Stage 8: **Performance review**: Consequently, the organizational buying process is finished after the product or service has been received and checked by the company.

Human Factors in Business Decisions

Quite frequently, B2B transactions are described as being primarily technical selling. Logical benefits of a product or service are presented, and, provided that they are better than the competitive offering, a selection is made. This simplistic concept works in theory.

However, reality is actually far more complex in the majority of cases. Since business buying decisions are still made by human beings and not by unfeeling machines, they are subject to human factors which eliminate the probability of an entirely objective decision.

Individuals engaged in the buying center can be very different from one another. Every person is an individual who reacts to situations with a certain belief system – the **professional buyer**, though specifically trained, is no different. Individual and interpersonal factors can shape the decision making in different ways. Personality types and individual preferences, for instance, can have tremendous influence on the buying decision. Differences in authority, status, and interests are inevitable in a buying center. That people react to such differences may not be "rational" but perfectly human. Personal motivations, perceptions, and preferences of the buyer's are generally strongly influenced by their job position, age, income, education, personality, attitudes toward risk, and culture.

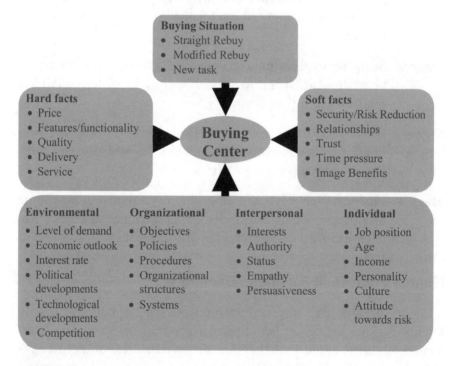

Fig. 6. Influential dimensions on the buying center

To understand aspects and implications of different social styles and human relationships can significantly contribute to the persuasiveness of a marketer's position. Therefore it is important for **business marketers** to search for any information available about individual, interpersonal, as well as organizational factors in relation to buying center members. As the following diagram shows, influential dimensions on the buying center are rather complex and intersecting. Depending on the buying situation the importance and influence of other factors vary greatly.

Airbus

Let's look again at the formerly mentioned example of the *Airbus A380*. In this case, **political influence** was especially strong since *Airbus* receives controversial start-up loans from the governments of France, Germany, Britain and Spain whenever it builds a new plane. Its main competitor Chicago-based *Boeing* has criticized the government loans to *Airbus* as being anti-competitive.[27] In May 2005 the situation grew even more acute when EU member nations made preparations to commit US$1.7 billion to *Airbus* for developing a new airplane, the *A350*. In the market for midsize, long-distance jets, this model would be a direct competitor to *Boeing's* new *787 Dreamliner*. After failed negotiations, the Bush administration decided to take the EU to a legal panel at the WTO. Instantly, the European Union filed a counter-complaint at the WTO saying that *Boeing* also receives illegal government aid.[28] By the way – no U.S. passenger airline has so far ordered the A380.[29]

The desire to get the most advanced state-of-the-art technologies, to have the world's largest airplane in its fleet, can also be traced back to certain image benefits. In 2006, SIA will be the first airline in the world to commercially operate the *Airbus A380*. To benefit from this event it even created a special logo with the taglines *First to Fly – the Singapore Airlines A380* and *Experience the Difference in 2006*.[30]

By being the first carrier to fly an *Airbus A380*, *SIA* underlines its commitment to remain the most innovative and service-oriented company in the air travel industry.

Fig. 7. *SIA's Airbus* logo, source: www.singaporeair.com

Now try to imagine what would happen if there was a big disaster involving the *Airbus A380*. Such an event would certainly weaken the brand image as in the case of the Air France jetliner that burst into flames after skidding off the runway in Toronto's Pearson International Airport. Although this was actually the first A340 plane to crash since *Airbus* introduced this series more than a decade ago and the cause was due to natural weather conditions, the accident definitely gave a negative image to the brand. This example shows how hard-earned image can be destroyed by things entirely out of the company's control.

To bring up another example, let's turn to the common lubricants that go in the sump of any kind of machine. Can buyers of these materials really be influenced by a brand? Usually, when asked in a typical market research survey why they choose a certain supplier, company employees tend to rationalize their decision with all the usual hard or tangible facts like the performance of the product, the price, the quality, the availability, etc. But if this were really true, why do most buyers of lubrication oils stick to the brand they use for years and years? Of course it could be habit, keeping it the way it is because it actually isn't worth the effort to change. The money spent on lubricants does not have a high enough impact in the context of all other purchases. But what does this say about the initial justification of the buyers?

Klueber Lubrication

A strongly branded company in this special area is *Klueber*. It is one of the world's leading lubricant suppliers, backed by more than seventy five years of research and development experience. *Klueber* offers a comprehensive range of specialty lubricants for all kinds of machines and components in various branches of industry. The range of highly cost-effective lubricants includes such well-known and universally trusted brands as *Barrierta, Isoflex, Hotemp* and *Staburags*. Today, *Klueber Lubrication* has become synonymous with competence and experience in all matters regarding lubrication and turbo-engineering.[31]

Is it possible after all that the brand of the product may be something beyond the hard facts? Could it have a much greater influence than is initially acknowledged? The truth is that the brand encompasses everything, conscious or unconscious. Fig.6 illustrates that the brand is present in every influential dimension affecting the buying center.

Soft facts like security, risk reduction and trust are the most susceptible to brand and brand message. Brands reduce risk; if a buyer

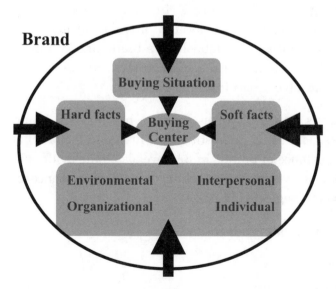

Fig. 8. Brand influence on buying decision

chooses a well-known brand he thinks he is on the safe side. Best example: "Nobody ever got fired for buying an *IBM*". Brand influence doesn't stop there, unconsciously, it can also heavily impact the way a person perceives hard facts like price, quality or service as in the case of *IBM* – *IBM* products are generally not cheap, nevertheless, quite often; a higher price is regarded as acceptable because people automatically associate high quality and service with it. What do you expect – it's an *IBM*!

2.2   B2B Brand Relevance

Many B2B marketers consider the development of a brand only as a variable marketing expense with a high risk of failure. Whether to brand an industrial product, service or business quite often doesn't even come into question for many companies. But do they really have a choice? Hasn't branding in the B2B context become just as important as it is in B2C? The industrial marketing environment is changing so rapidly that businesses, failing to adapt to these new circumstances will inevitably drop out of the race. Industry consolidation, a **tepid global economy and exchangeable market offerings** are driving competitive forces. In such an increasingly competitive environment, it is not enough anymore to just offer great products and services. By establishing a brand and gaining a favorable competitive position in the marketplace, businesses can successfully set themselves apart from the pack.

There are numerous powerful forces that are making B2B brand building a crucial factor. It is interesting that the main factors that leveraged the importance of brands in B2C are also quite evident in B2B, which makes it even more puzzling that the importance of branding is still being neglected in B2B:[32]

- Proliferation of similar products and services

- Increasing complexity

- Incredible price pressure.

- Before we delve deeply into these three main factors, we would like to first walk you through the general market trends, developments and changes that have generated and facilitated them in the first place.

Globalization

Driven by the ongoing globalization in sales and procurement markets, global **transportation and logistic networks** are constantly improving their performance. Whether it is about the distribution of a tiny part or a huge machine – through the ever faster and even more effective transportation and logistic networks, it is becoming possible to send anything to almost any place in the world at even decreasing costs.[33] Especially, the so-called containerization of cargo and inter-modal transportation, along with further innovation in logistics and transportation, enable companies to reach foreign markets more efficiently and cheaply.[34]

Another result of the globalization trend is the **worldwide assimilation of technical norms and standards** which is especially important in the B2B context. The ongoing reduction and elimination of these and other trade barriers as well as tariffs are pushed particularly by the World Trade Organization (WTO). The further liberalization of trade also backed by the worldwide expansion of free trade areas results in decreasing restraints of competition. This literally opens the door for small and midsize companies to sell their products worldwide thereby increasing competition.[35]

In recent years the number of **mergers & acquisitions** (M&A) as well as **strategic alliances** increased considerably in almost all industry sectors. The above mentioned liberalization of trade is driving consolidation in many industries. It also enabled businesses at a progressive rate to break into new markets. Nowadays, national differences in labor costs and resources are of major importance, especially when it comes to the choice of new production or development locations.[36] It is not surprising, that much of this merger and acquisition activity has involved brand-owning businesses.

Because of their durability, quality of earning power, and their widespread appeal, brands have become highly desirable properties.

While globalization trends mainly concern product-based businesses, some service companies are also strongly affected. Take the international shipping industry as an example. They are not only facilitating and expediting the globalization processes and the implications involved, they are also affected by it themselves. With the increasing importance of container transportation grew accordingly the number of competitors as well as the M&As. The industry as a whole had to find solutions to meet the increasingly complex transportation needs of customers while continuing to flow their cargo efficiently.

Neptune Orient Lines Limited

One of the world's largest container shipping lines was created with the merger of the container transportation division of the Singapore state enterprise *Neptune Orient Lines Limited (NOL)* and *APL Ltd.* of the U.S. (formerly American President Lines). The new entity continued to operate under the *APL* brand name. With the *APL* buyout, *NOL* obtained a strong logistics brand and presence, and used this opportunity to refocus its business strategy to become an **integrated logistics service provider** that covers all parts of the supply chain spectrum. Moreover, through strong brand management the company wanted to differentiate itself as a provider of high quality and value-added transportation and logistics services.[37]

A great brand always starts with great products and services. Consequently, the next step is to constantly innovate and improve your offerings in order to keep your brand where it is. *APL*'s strong customer focus and commitment to provide innovative solutions has led to several industry firsts. In 1995 it was the first container shipping company to launch a Web site, and four years later it introduced the first customizable online portal for customers.[38] Due to its commitment and continuous investment in new technologies, *APL* enjoys a strong reputation for quality customer support and service innovation in the industry. Their efforts are regularly recognized with industry and technology awards. Today, *APL* is one of the global top-10 container transportation businesses.

The container shipping industry saw phenomenal growth in 2004, strengthened especially by the continued growth of the Chinese economy. Actual developments and the severe cyclicality of the industry are now further pushing industry consolidation since this would bring greater stability to the liner trades. *A.P. Møller-Mærsk A/S*, the parent company of the world's biggest container line, *Mærsk Sealand*, unveiled a €2.3 billion bid for Dutch rival *P&O Nedlloyd* in May 2005. Should the merger go through, it would increase the market share of *Mærsk* from 12% to 17 or 18% and create a fleet that would be more than twice as large as its nearest competitor.[39]

Hypercompetition

The ongoing globalization is the driving force of another factor that increases the importance of B2B brands: hypercompetition. Hypercompetitive marketplaces are characterized by **intense and rapid competitive moves**. Competitors have to move very quickly, constantly trying to erode any competitive advantages of their rivals in order to stay ahead of them.[40] Beside globalization trends, the phenomenon of hypercompetition can be attributed to appealing substitute products, more educated and fragmented customer tastes, deregulation, and the invention of new business models. Hypercompetition generally leads to structural disequilibrium, falling entry barriers, and sometimes even to the dethronement of industry leaders.[41]

In such a dynamic competitive environment, ever faster business and production processes together with the continuous development of new technologies lead to ever **shorter product life cycles** (PLC). In many industries, especially high-tech industries, the time period from the development of a new product up to its market saturation spans sometimes only three to six months. An important implication of this trend is that the increasing costs for research and development have to be amortized in ever shorter time periods.

This makes it also even more difficult to differentiate products or services based only on features or functionality.

Intel vs. AMD

The best example for this kind of development can be found in the computer components industry: microprocessors. The life expectancy of personal computers (PC) computer hardware is generally quite short, since technology is changing and improving rapidly. The two major players in this field are *Intel* and *AMD* and they both are introducing "new" processors every 2-4 months. The market structure of the industry requires Central Processing Units (CPU) manufacturers to obsolete their own products in a relatively short period to maintain profits. As newer CPUs are introduced for the desktop market, production of the current chips is discontinued in short order.

Although the change in one product generation to the next is rather minor or evolutionary (e.g. changes in chip speed, or memory size), major technological changes or innovations take more time to develop, and therefore involve larger time intervals between the introductions of products with these changes.[42] The new dual core chips for desktop PC's as well as servers released in April/May 2005 are more or less representative of such a major technological change.[43] It is beyond question that *Intel* and *AMD* are trying constantly to stay ahead of each other. While the *Intel* brand is one of the top ten known-brands in the world, *AMD* is still rather unknown to the majority of PC users.

An obvious source that has, without question, dramatically increased the amount of choices for industrial buyers is the **Internet**. This global marketplace cuts the costs for searching and comparing product and service offerings to near zero. The Internet and further developments in the information technology made all kinds of information easily accessible. Just like their opposites in consumer markets, buyers in B2B markets are faced with a continuously increasing number of potential suppliers for covering all different kinds of needs. The more potential suppliers, the higher the costs for information gathering and the longer the time needed for evaluation. When **marketplace choices** increase, buyers undoubtedly have an increased preference for companies and brands they already know because it saves research time and limits their exposure to risk.[44]

This is the right time to throw in another catch phrase: **time pressure**. Businesses generally face time pressures in two main directions – competition and innovation. Actually, they are not really completely separate from each other but rather intersecting. Competition is especially fierce in respect to newest technology, cooperation, channels of distribution and the acquisition of **best talent**. *IBM*, for instance, created strong pressure on themselves. To increase their service levels they engaged in various alliances in this area. Later on, when the cooperation stopped, they had to buy into these segments in order to be able to continuously meet the new and self-imposed service requirements.

Nowadays, businesses, especially in the high tech sector, have to be one step ahead of competitors. One way to accomplish this is to innovate constantly products and services, assuring their relevance and up-to-date-ness. If a company fails to respond respectively to these kinds of time pressures it may have to face severe consequences. A great example in this respect is *Siemens AG* with its segment mobile communications which encompassed both business and consumer applications. The company failed to respond to certain pressures and literally overslept important trends in the fast moving mobile market. This considerably weakened their position even before the disastrous software-related defect in the summer of 2004.

The newly released 65 product series had an acoustic issue which could arise when a telephone call was automatically cut off because the battery had run down. If the mobile phone was held up directly to the ear while the disconnection melody started to play loudly, the volume was loud enough to lead to hearing damage. The launch of the highly innovative *Siemens SK65*, a high performance business phone that incorporates BlackBerry Built-In™ technology (the first handset to offer complete e-mail management), also came far too late to save the business segment.[45] In June 2005 *Siemens* finally announced a hand over of their ailing mobile communications division to the Taiwanese technology group *BenQ*.[46]

Another aspect in this matter is **individual time pressure**. Let's be realistic – quite often, B2B buyers just don't have the time or even resources to thoroughly check and evaluate all potential suppliers. The companies that end up on their short list of potential sources will undoubtedly encompass many well-known businesses and brands. So, how can you break through the clutter, become heard and at least get on their short list? Right, by establishing a strong brand!

Now you might be thinking "**Globalization**, better transportation and logistic networks, shortening product life cycles, hypercompetition, etc., are they anything new?" Well, they may not be new discoveries, but these developments are the results of still ongoing and very current processes that change the market environment of all businesses every day. They may not be surprising novelties but they also definitely are not diminishing in importance. In the following section, we will delve more deeply into the three main factors that leverage the importance of brands in B2B.

Proliferation of Similar Products and Services

An overabundance of choices is not only prevalent in B2C. It is nowadays also more than true for B2B markets. The proliferation of similar products and services leads to **increasingly interchangeable offerings** across industries. Merely innovating products and services won't necessarily achieve a long-term, sustainable competitive advantage since these functional advantages are usually quickly imitated and therefore rare and short lived. Technical superiority is no longer the only crucial factor to success. In markets where products and services are becoming more and more conformed to each

other, almost identical, a strong brand may be the single character-
istic that differentiates a product or service from competitive offerings. *IBM* is a special kind of best-practice in this case. Although
many *IBM* products don't provide a distinct functional advantage,
professional buyers may select *IBM* over lesser-known competitors
merely because it is a "trust" brand. *IBM* has managed to offer additional value beside technical performance.

Increasing Complexity

Today, almost all businesses are confronted with a strong tendency
towards complex solution-based market offerings. Companies have
stopped selling a single product or service, they sell solutions.
These solutions can encompass a whole bunch of different products
and services and due to their complexity; they tend to be quite the
opposite of self-explanatory. Given this, brands can be a very helpful tool in reducing the complexity involved and for communicating pivotal and relevant information.

SAP

Who can think of a more complex product than *SAP*? The huge
complexity of this enterprise resource system and related software
solutions such as supply chain management (SCM), customer relationship management (CRM), product life-cycle management and
supplier relationship management is bundled in one single word.

Founded in 1972, *SAP* is the world's largest inter-enterprise software company. Its solutions meet the challenge of aligning the
unique business processes of more than 25 distinct industries, including high tech, retail, public sector and financial services. The
variety of solutions offered by *SAP* ranges from individual solutions that address the needs of small and mid-size businesses up to
enterprise-scale solutions for global organizations. Today, more
than 26,000 customers in over 120 countries run more than 91,500
installations of *SAP*® software. This sheer enormity clearly demonstrates the huge complexity involved in such a product.[47]

An important implication of the increasingly complex market offerings is the **information overload** B2B buyers are confronted with. To communicate their solution-based market offerings, industrial businesses tend to inundate customers with loads of information. Whether that may be through brochures, specifications sheets, catalogs, websites, etc., the buyer gets confronted with information about technical specifications or features, whether they asked for it or not. In such a complex world, B2B marketers have to recognize the need to simplify their offerings to customers. Not all information available about a complex offering automatically concerns all members of a buying center to the same degree. This could be helped by bundling all relevant information in the brand.

Magna International

Not only have suppliers' market offerings increased in complexity, the **suppliers themselves have become more and more complex**. *Magna International* for instance, the most diversified automotive supplier in the world has a decentralized multilayer operating structure. The huge complexity is due to this breadth of capability. Its automotive divisions are arranged along seven global automotive systems groups that provide full service systems integration with more than 250 different products and services on offer. Each division is focused on a specific vehicle area.

Magna Steyr, for one, provides complete vehicle engineering and concept development and is the world's leading supplier of OEM contract vehicle assembling. Exterior and interior mirrors, as well as engineered glass systems for instance, are the sectors of Magna Donnelly. Cross-division coordination of all seven groups guarantees an optimization of meeting customer needs. Hence, it is not surprising that you can find all the major original equipment manufacturers (OEM's) of cars and trucks in the world among *Magna Steyr's* main customers: *DaimlerChrysler, General Motors, BMW* and *Ford*. In 2004 it had record sales of US$20.7 billion, an increase of 35% over the previous year.[48]

High Price Pressures

In a hotly contested environment, businesses are also confronted with enormous price pressures. Businesses cannot realize higher prices for their products by merely offering special functional advantages. Brands can provide an additional value for customers, for they incorporate and communicate both tangible and intangible factors. *Mercedes-Benz* trucks, for instance, are generally sold at a much higher price than *Volvo* trucks. Their resale value is about 20% higher than for a comparable *Volvo* truck. The market position of *Mercedes-Benz* trucks in Europe corresponds approximately to the one of Freightliner in the States.

B2B marketers need to start thinking outside the box. Brands have to be recognized for the great potential they can offer them. They differentiate market offerings, reduce the associated complexity and offer an additional value by communicating tangible as well as intangible factors. Now you might be thinking "Okay, the market environment changes, competition increases, but why should I get on the branding bus? Aren't other marketing tools like CRM much more important in B2B than building a brand?" Of course they are important – but incorporated into a **holistic branding** strategy, they can be even more effective. The brand should be the thread and marketing the subject that surrounds it. Why should you get on the branding bus? Simply because branding is probably one of the best solutions to counter the above mentioned market changes and increased competition.

Recent research studies conducted by *McKinsey* and *MCM* demonstrate and underline the importance and relevance of brands in various B2B markets. They examined the inherent brand functions with respect to their importance and relevance in a B2B environment. They revealed that the most important brand functions are:[49]

- **Increase Information Efficiency**. Branded products make it easier for the customers to gather and process information about a product. Bundling information about the manufacturer and origin of a product in the form of a brand helps them to find their way in a new or confusing product environment. Moreover branded products have recognition value: customers can repeatedly find trusted brands quickly and easily.

- **Risk Reduction**. Choosing a branded product reduces the customer's risk of making the wrong purchasing decision. Brands create trust in the expected performance of the product, and provide continuity in the predictability of the product benefits. Especially in B2B, brands can help to ensure and legitimate buying decisions, since B2B buyers have a real penchant for avoiding risk.

- **Value Added/Image Benefit Creation.** For consumers, the value added/image benefit usually lies in the self-expressive value that brands can provide them. In a B2B environment the additional value provided by brands is usually not anchored in purely self-expressive values. Nonetheless, it can be very important. Through a brand you do not only present your employees to the world but also the whole corporation.

Placed against the three main factors that leveraged the importance of brands in the B2B environment it becomes strikingly obvious that brands are among the best solutions for businesses to counter them.

Brands are an **effective and compelling** means to differentiate your offerings from competitors. They help businesses to counter the increasing proliferation of similar products and services. While products or services can be easily imitated a brand cannot. Sometimes a brand can be the only true differentiator in a highly complex environment. The brand is the one thing that can break through the clutter and get companies to be recognized and heard by prospective customers. The higher risk involved in today's increasingly complex world can be countered by building a strong and trustworthy brand. Brands reduce risk because they convey a certain picture of what the product, service or company is about. Of course, this is only true if the company succeeds in continuously delivering on its brand promise.

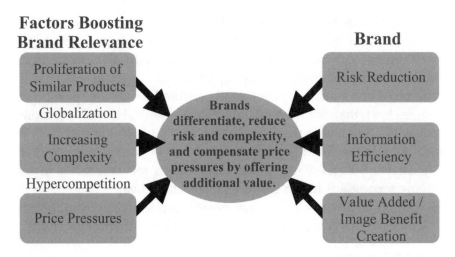

Fig. 9. Brand relevance and brand functions in a B2B environment

The penchant of buyers to reduce risk wherever possible makes them even more susceptible to brands. After all factors have been considered and two or three equivalent market offerings have made it to the last short list, buyers will most probably choose the branded one because it provides them with the feeling that they can be sure of what they get. Obviously, this hypothetical talk really proves nothing in the end, but just take one moment and look around you in your office. How many branded products do you use? How many brands do you incorporate in your operations?

Take the above mentioned example of *SAP*. Do you use one of their installations or did you choose to employ a less well-known equivalent software for your ERP, CRM and SCM?[50] From the view of your employees, *SAP* is a huge and complex system that needs a lot of training. The employer's perspective is not really different but *SAP* is nonetheless seen as a valuable means to get all relevant and important information in your business systematically consolidated. Anybody who ever used a no-name business software knows that they are not less complex or easier to handle. The real point of interest here is your expectations of them – the no-name or the brand.

The importance of brands generally depends on one main circum-stance: Do they generate a positive and quantifiable profit contribu-tion? Businesses don't run their operations in the dark. Since implementing a holistic brand approach does require a certain amount of investment, it is absolutely justified to ask for appropriate results. Isn't that what companies usually are all about – making money? To guarantee that your brand does pay off you first have to find out whether brands do actually matter in your respective mar-ket. This is the case if the brand represents a relevant factor in the buying process – it has to generate an additional value of some kind. Since buying processes can vary greatly across different industries and product markets it is indispensable to discuss them separately.[51]

Based on an empirical survey of more than 750 deciders and apply-ing a comprehensive valuation system, *McKinsey* and *MCM* have determined the relevance of brands in 18 representative business markets. Although the overall survey was conducted in the German market, the approach and its general implications can be applied on an international level. They examined the inherent brand functions and the discussed brand functions formed the basis for the valua-tion system.[52]

One of the major findings of the study is that **Risk Reduction** is by far the most important brand function in the B2B area with 45 per-cent, closely followed by information efficiency (41 percent). Value added/image benefit creation (14 percent) is less distinctive in B2B. It is interesting that these results are just the opposite of those in consumer markets where Value Added/Image Benefit Creation captures clearly the leading position (40 percent).[53] These results provide valuable information about where the brand relevance ac-tually originates from:

- To reduce risks involved in the buying process is especially important when buying complex high-profile products.

- Information Efficiency is of particular importance for the pur-chase of very complex and capital-intense items and systems.

- The importance of Value Added is highest for publicly visible products and services.

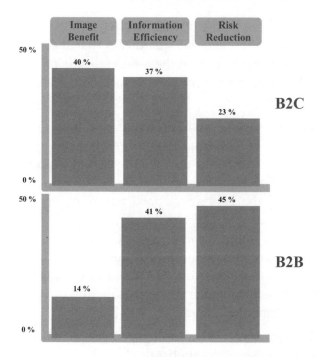

Fig. 10. Importance of brand functions in B2C vs. B2B

Along with *MCM, McKinsey & Company* developed a method that allows us to make profound statements about brand relevance. Through this method it is possible to determine the brand relevance of any kind of B2B market. The evaluation is based on certain context factors:

- Supplier structure in the market
- Number of competitors
- Complexity of the buying process
- Size of the buying center
- "Public" visibility of the brand

These criterias are crucial in the determination of the relevance of brands in different markets. Altogether they provide information about whether or not investments in branding efforts are "making sense" or not. Of course these are only general rules and implications, acting as a guide and not as the one and only truth. It is important to recognize them as the general statements that they are and to accept that exceptions can occur. In the following, we are going to exemplify the effectiveness of these context factors in relation to brand relevance.

- The more fragmented a supplier market, the more difficult it is for one brand to stand out. The situation of the European market for specialty tools for car repair only a few years ago can be used as an example. The highly fragmented market was less competitive because of the very specialized nature of the required tools for car makers like *DaimlerChrysler*, *BMW* and *VW*. *Star Equipment* was supplying *DaimlerChrysler*, *CarTool* to *BMW*, *Matra* to *VW*, and so on. Hence the brand relevance of each supplier was quite low. But when the *SPX Corporation* entered the game by M&A they turned everything upside down. Their actions literally de-fragmented the market step by step.

  ➜ **Highest brand relevance in monolithic markets with a low or medium number of competitors.**

- In a very complex buying process the final decision usually is the result of many preceding partial decisions. That radically reduces the possible impact of the supplier brand. An example would be the product markets of automotive parts and supplies like screws, batteries, and similar items. The buying process is relatively simple compared to those of systems and modules. The brand relevance therefore is quite high, which is the case for highly branded products like *Varta*, *Bosch* or *Wuerth*, to name a few.

  ➜ **Highest brand relevance in product markets with simple buying processes.**

- The more people are involved in the buying process, the higher the importance of brands. Large buying centers are usually involved in purchasing decisions of products with a very long life expectancy, fast changing technologies and when selling to commercial and government institutions.

  ➜ **Highest brand relevance in purchase decisions involving a large buying center.**

- If a product or service and its inherent brand are clearly visible to the user, other stakeholders and the general public, brand relevance increases significantly. This is probably self-explaining – branding can only be effective if it really reaches the customers and stakeholders.

→ **Highest brand relevance in product markets where the brand is clearly visible.**

Of course these results are not linear and mathematical solutions that cannot be applied without making any amendments or adjustments. Just take the first one – a completely monolithic market with a low number of competitors has the highest brand relevance. Mathematically, the lowest number would be one, and it makes absolutely no sense to speak of high brand relevance for a monopoly. If people don't have another choice than buying from you or leaving it out, your brand is probably not very important to them. So it is important to regard these results as general guideposts that aim to point into the right direction but nevertheless can differ tremendously when analyzing certain industrial markets directly. The following graph summarizes the findings.

The relevance of a brand in B2B **buying decisions** also varies greatly depending on the different buying situations that a company

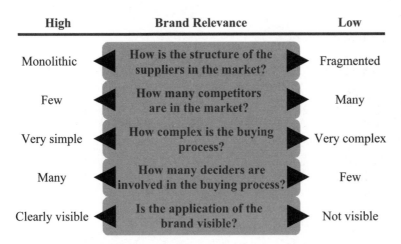

Fig. 11. Brand relevance according to context factors

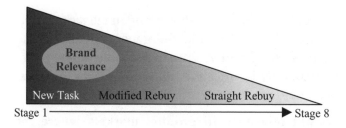

Fig. 12. Brand relevance in relation to the buying situation and the stages in the organizational buying process

faces. It is quite obvious that the brand of a new potential supplier is not very important in the case of a straight re-buy, whereas the brand relevance is at the highest for new task purchasing decisions. In relation to the stages of the organizational buying process it is vice versa. In the beginning of the purchasing process the brand relevance is very high and decreases from stage to stage.[54]

2.3 Power of the Business Brand

Though still neglected as irrelevant and unimportant by many B2B marketers, establishing brands for B2B companies and products is not really a new invention. Many industrial brands actually have a long history:[55]

Table 1. B2B Brand history

Saint-Gobain (1665),	Daimler (1901),
Siemens (1847),	General Motors (1908),
Bosch (1886),	UPS (1913),
General Electric (1892),	IBM (1924),
Ernst&Young (1894),	Caterpillar (1925),
Goodyear (1898),	Hewlett-Packard (1939),
	Tetra Pak (1951),
	FedEx (1973),
	Microsoft (1975)

These companies and their corporate brands have been around for decades. However, age alone doesn't make a brand successful. Shooting stars like *Grainger.com*, *Intel* along with its *Pentium*, *Tyco* in the United States, or *Wuerth* in Germany have shown that it is also possible to create strong brands in a short period of time. They are also living proof of the increasing use of branding in industrial markets. However, it is crucial to understand that these rocket-like successes are not easy if not impossible to imitate. Even in the hyper-speed online world we live in today, brands cannot be built overnight.

While products or services can become outdated or easily get imitated by competitors, a successful brand is timeless and unique. It not only simplifies the **decision-making process**, it also affords the opportunity for premium prices. Why has branding been overlooked by many suppliers? One reason may be that their executives are often engineers who have spent almost their entire careers in B2B.

The power of a business brand, measured in brand equity, lies in the fact that it can be one of the most important assets a company owns. It is a huge mistake to consider the **development of a brand**, or rather a positive perceived image of a brand, only as a variable marketing expense. Building strong brands is an investment, aimed at creating long-term intangible assets thereby ensuring the future success of the company. Capitalizing on strong brands facilitates a business to achieve its long-term growth objectives not only more quickly, but also in a more profitable way. Brands are not only what a company sells, they represent what a company does and, more significantly, what a company is. Actually, most brands are the reason why a business exists, and not the other way around.[56]

Enduring brands can give businesses more leverage than any other asset, serving as an emotional shortcut between a company and its customers. A differentiated "ownable" brand image can build an emotional and rational bridge from customers to a company, product or service. A **brand's personality and reputation for performance** can distinguish it from the competition, engendering customer loyalty and growth. Truly successful brands most often occupy unique positions in the consumer's mind. A strong and motivating identity that customers know and trust can be elevated above price and feature competition.

Yet, there are still only a few successful B2B brands that already prove the potential in that area. In many industries there are still no brands at all, leaving a gap with huge **unrealized brand potential**. Not only could companies profit from a tremendous first mover advantage by deciding to jump onto the brand wagon, future oriented companies may even be able to set the business standard with their brands. The role of brands in B2B can be summarized as follows:

Fig. 13. The role of B2B brands

- **Differentiate** – Brands are an effective and compelling means to "decommoditize" product categories that are highly undifferentiated. Examples include *Intel*, *IBM*, and *General Electric*.

- **Secure Future Business** – Quite often it is important to establish brands for your products or services in order to prepare for the future. There are many business areas where only those companies survived that chose to brand their products from the beginning. Take for instance the well-known brands *Caterpillar* and *Komatsu*. Some years ago there were many companies in this business segment especially in Japan – today these two are more or less the only ones that have survived. With a strong brand it is much easier to withstand any kind of crisis and the brand is moreover appealing to financial and investor markets.

- **Create Brand Loyalty** – Brands assist companies in transitioning from a transaction-based selling model to one that is relationship-based. The customer always comes first. Brand loyalty is created when the business manages to consistently deliver on what its brand promises. *HSBC* with its campaign, "The Worlds Local Bank," is one of the big winners according to *Interbrand*. As one of the companies with the biggest increase in brand value in the 2005 ranking they are benefiting from higher brand loyalty.

- **Differentiate Marketing Efforts** – Businesses with strong brands can benefit from increased communications effectiveness. Marketing efforts will be more readily accepted than those of complete no-name products and services.

- **Create Preferences** – Brand preferences at its best lead to the rejection of competitive brands. Though this may sound a little too B2C it also does happen in B2B markets. A strong brand will act as a barrier to people switching to competitors products. *Shimano*, the world-leading Japanese bike component manufacturer, managed to create strong preferences for its hub gears among bikers.

- **Command Price Premium** – A business with well-known brands can command premium prices for their products and services. It makes it automatically less susceptible to competitive forces. That B2B brands are valuable resources is also reflected in the acquisition prices. Brands can balloon these prices tremendously.

- **Create Brand Image** – Brands enable companies' value propositions to be more emotive and compelling. Above all a positive brand image also appeals to all other stakeholders – it makes it even easier to recruit and retain talent.

- **Increase Sales** – The main goal of most businesses is naturally to make money. Companies with strong brands can benefit not only from higher margins but also from higher sales volumes.

Not only are there considerable benefits for industrial companies in building strong brands, there are serious penalties for those who do not. The alternative is to rely on price cutting, discounts and cost reduction programs.

Creating Trust, Confidence and Comfort Through Branding

As trust builds, the relationship between the buyer and supplier moves into a partnership which recognizes that the goals of both organizations can best be met by working together. In many industrial markets, buyers are inundated by suppliers trying to get a foot in the door. It is not unusual for a buyer of bearings to receive five calls per week from suppliers who are full of promises about how they can offer better service, cheaper prices and a bigger range of products. Each of the would-be suppliers is presenting its best case in an attempt to win a customer and yet the buyer knows that much of what he hears cannot be true. The chances are that the company is not much better than the suppliers already used, after all, the **competitive influences of the market place** cause his existing suppliers to stay in line with the competition.

A new supplier may make an extra effort to begin with, perhaps a gesture on price or a special endeavor when it comes to service, but will they sustain it? There will be five more people knocking on his door next week saying that they can do better but he has neither the time nor the inclination to constantly be reviewing his suppliers. A strong brand provides companies with far more credibility compared with those which are unknown. In a **critical investment decision** chances are high that businesses may choose a better known brand. Brands act as a short-cut of attributes, benefits, beliefs and values. They incorporate literally everything a company and its products or services stand for.

The **branding triangle illustrates** visually the marketing-related connections between a company, its collaborators and its customers. Collaborators refer not only to employees but also to wholesalers, dealers, ad agencies etc. (Collaborators) It aims to act as a principle of the intersecting market participants. It is essential to provide a consistent picture of the company and its brands across all different media and to all stakeholders. Only then is it possible to guide their perception throughout the huge flow of different information. Nowadays brand management – especially in B2B – is not only related to one product, service or market offering but rather to the whole company itself. Therefore it is important to recognize the value that a comprehensive brand portfolio together with a corporate brand can provide. In this respect it is important to find the right combination of presenting your company geared to the respective target groups and stakeholders while keeping the necessary consistency outside as well as inside the company.

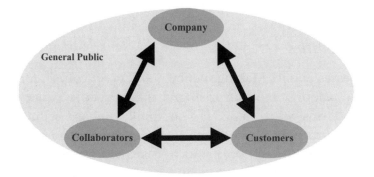

Fig. 14. The branding triangle

The company stands for everything, the tangible and intangible, whether it is service or product, it incorporates the history as well as the prospective future. The image of the company, from its foundation to the present, is usually mainly formed by **external marketing communications**. Few customers or other stakeholders deliberately make efforts to find out everything there is to know about a company. They usually only know what the company "tells them". Not less important of course is the performance of the employees and other related co-operators. What picture are they drawing in the customer's minds? If they internalized the message of the brand they are representing, guided by **effective internal marketing communication**, that necessary consistency is assured. So you see the brand is the one thing that connects everything across all touch points.

At the same time, brands are opalescent but fragile figures. It is much easier to dilute or even to ruin a brand than to build one. Yet, many business decisions on a daily basis are based on opinions that do not precisely reflect the real situation of the brand. In times where marketplaces change so rapidly it is absolutely crucial to base every important decision on accurate, current, relevant and objective information in order to protect the brand. To ensure consistent performance, some kind of **brand checklist** can be very helpful. If you are about to make extensive decisions in which the life of a brand is at stake you should rigorously stick to that checklist.

Branding Commodities

What are businesses about? Making money – except, of course, for non-profit organizations. Not surprisingly, many people equate price/monetary terms with value. If you think you are selling commodities you probably also assume that your **customers perceive value** to mean lowest price. Such a marketing position though, is usually the most difficult to sustain. And they are right; the only distinct point of differentiation of commodities is price. The solution for such a dilemma is: stop thinking of your products and services as commodities! A strong brand that customers know and trust can be elevated above price and feature competition. Just about every brand in existence today could be reduced to commodity status if it does not successfully evolve its products, services, and marketing communications.[57] Put it the other way around – commodities can be branded successfully – just don't let anybody know that you are selling one!

Acme Brick

Acme Brick of Fort Worth, Texas, is a perfect example for how to brand a commodity. What else could be perceived more as a commodity than a plain brick? Nonetheless, *Acme* has managed to brand its bricks very successfully, targeting homeowners as well as architects. Through their brand they are able to charge a premium price of 10 percent and enjoy the largest market share in several of their main markets.

They are not only producing high-quality bricks, they also provide a 100-year guarantee while the norm is five years. In addition, the company shows a strong commitment to the communities it is active in. For instance, every time a house is built with *Acme* bricks, the company contributes to the Troy Aikman Foundation for Children. Furthermore, local and regional Acme offices support charities such as Habitat for Humanity, Ronald McDonald Children's Charities, American Cancer Society, American Red Cross, National Multiple Sclerosis Society, and many others. That branding efforts are really paying off can also be highlighted by the results of a telephone survey in four major *Acme* markets that revealed an 84 percent preference for *Acme* bricks, leaving all of its competitors far behind.[58]

Tata Steel

Another pure commodity that seems to be impossible to brand is steel, but contrary to this assumption, *Tata Steel* is highly branded. Facing an industry trend towards over-supply, the management acknowledged that the only solution was to move away from selling commodities into marketing brands. *Tata Steel* started to brand their products in 2000. Meanwhile it introduced various brands like the product brands *Tata Steelium* (the world's first branded Cold Rolled Steel), *Tata Shaktee* (Galvanized Corrugated Sheets), *Tata Tiscon* (re-bars), as well as the family brands *Tata Pipes, Tata Bearings, Tata Agrico* (hand tools and implements) and *Tata Wiron* (galvanized wire products).[59] You will find a more detailed presentation of *Tata Steel* in chapter 5.8.

The Role of Emotions in B2B Branding

Forget about the entirely rational and perfect "business" person. They no longer exist if they ever did at all. We are all human beings with emotions and feelings and this makes us automatically susceptible to branding whether we are at home or at work. If your neighbor tells you about his experiences with a certain brand, you won't forget that conversation as soon as you get to the office. We are all subject to a **great deal of information** across a range of social strata, embedded in multitudinous emotional contexts. This literally opens the door for branding in B2B markets.

The most emotional decision in a CEO's life will probably be the decision of what kind of corporate jet to buy. He has the choice between *Lear Jet*, *Falcon*, *Bombardier*, etc. **Rational factors** are usually used only to legitimate their decisions. The main reasons for deciding on what corporate jet to buy are generally to be found in the CEO's ego. Of course we cannot deny that there really is a justifiable business purpose for corporate jets, but there are quite a few companies that probably wouldn't have bought their own aircraft in the first place if it wasn't for the CEO's ego and the desirable toy factor.[60]

Emotions are not only triggers that can make us laugh or cry. They are also vital to our decision making. Countless studies have proven that if the emotion centers of our brain are damaged[61], we are not only unable to laugh or cry anymore, we also lose the ability to make any kind of decisions. While reason does lead us to conclusions, emotions are the ones that lead to action. This should ring the alarm bell for every business.

A few years ago, when Waldemar Pfoertsch was working for *IBM*, he participated in a study that sought to determine the ideal brand attributes that would tip the scales in favor of one middleware vendor over another. They were surprised by the results. Conservative IT B2B decision makers consistently **identified emotional brand attributes** as determining factors. Of course, the products needed to be reliable and secure. But for those vendors that met the rational criteria, the emotional connections were pivotal.

This probably doesn't come as a surprise. After all, we *are* human. And even the most rational person (whether he or she admits it or not) **is influenced by emotion**. In his book, Kevin Roberts, CEO of Saatchi and Saatchi, argued even more strongly for the connection between emotion and the success of certain brands. He illustrated how some brands command **greater loyalty**. He calls them "Lovemarks" and describes them as brands that inspire loyalty beyond reason. Interestingly, out of his list of 200 Lovemarks several industrial brands such as *AMD*, *Caterpillar*, *Cessna*, *IBM* and *Zeiss* are mentioned, too.[62]

Caterpillar, for instance, is a great industrial and yet **very emotional brand**. There are only few brands that evoke the pride of ownership quite like *Caterpillar*. The strong emotional appeal and passionate loyalty fostered by the CAT brand addresses both the employees who design, build, sell and support CAT machines, and those who own or aspire to own CAT machines.[63]

Summary

- **Establishing brands in a B2B environment is different** from branding to the general public. The role and the mechanism of an industrial brand strategy have to be more focused than those pursued and implemented in consumer markets.

- The main difference between B2B and B2C markets can be found in the **nature and complexity of industrial products and services**, the nature and diversity of industrial demand, fewer customers, larger volumes per customer, and last but not least, closer and longer-lasting supplier-customer-relationships.

- A **holistic branding approach** is required, that everything from the development, design, to the implementation of marketing programs, processes, and activities is recognized as intersecting and interdependent.

- The **buying situations of B2B companies** can be broken down into three recurring types: the straight re-buy, modified re-buy, and new task.

- The **members of the buying center** can be classified according to their role in the buying decision: the user, buyer, decider, and influencer. They all have to act considering the complex influential dimensions on and in the buying center.

- An **organizational buying process** can encompass the following stages: problem recognition, general need description, product specification, search for and evaluation of potential suppliers, proposal solicitation and analysis, supplier evaluation and selection, order-routine specification, performance review.

- **Interpersonal and individual factor** of the buying center members are human factors in business decisions.

- **Establishing B2B brands** encompasses creating trust, confidence and comfort for all partners in the buying process

- **Even commodities can be branded** as our examples of *Acme Brick* or *Tata Steel* show.

- **Emotions in B2B Branding** play a major role in business decisions, even if they are easily recognizable.

Notes

[1]   Web site of *Caterpillar Inc.*, Peoria, IL, cited August 2005.

[2]   Web site of *MTU Aero Engines GmbH*, Germany, cited June 2005.

[3]   Web site of *Accenture*, New York, cited June 2005.

[4]   If you desire more detailed information on this subject we recommend reading Philip Kotler's book *Marketing Management* or *Business Market Management* by Anderson and Narus.

[5]   Philip Kotler and Kevin L. Keller, *Marketing Management*, 2006, pp. 210-211; Philippe Malaval, *Strategy and Management of Industrial Brands: Business to Business Products and Services*, 2001, p. 16.

[6]   Robert P. Vitale and Joseph J. Giglierano, *Business to Business Marketing: Analysis and Practice in a Dynamic Environmen*, 2002, pp. 37-38.

[7]   Paul Hague, Nick Hague, and Matt Harrison, *Business to Business Marketing*, White Paper, B2B International Ltd.

8   Jim Turley, "Silicon 101," *Embedded Systems Programming* (27 January 2004).

9   Paul Hague and Peter Jackson, *The Power of Industrial Brands*, 1994.

10 Philip Kotler and Kevin L. Keller, *Marketing Management*, 2006, p. 211.

11 Robert P. Vitale and Joseph J. Giglierano, *Business to Business Marketing: Analysis and Practice in a Dynamic Environmen*, 2002, p. 11.

12 Jim Turley, "Silicon 101," *Embedded Systems Programming* (27 January 2004).

13 Philip Kotler and Kevin L. Keller, *Marketing Management*, 2006, p. 211.

14 James C. Anderson and James A. Narus, *Business Market Management: Understanding, Creating, and Delivering Value*, pp. 15 and 213.

15 Waldemar Pfoertsch and Michael Schmid, M., *B2B-Markenmanagement: Konzepte – Methoden – Fallbeispiele*, 2005, pp. 9-15.

16 Robert P. Vitale and Joseph J. Giglierano, *Business to Business Marketing: Analysis and Practice in a Dynamic Environmen*, 2002, p. 61.

17 Patrick J. Robinson, Charles W. Faris, and Yoram Wind, *Industrial Buying and Creative Marketing*, 1967; Philippe Malaval, *Strategy and Management of Industrial Brands: Business to Business Products and Services*, 2001, pp. 26-28.

18 Frederick E. Webster and Yoram Wind, *Organizational Buying Behavior*, 1972, pp. 33-37.

19 Philippe Malaval, *Strategy and Management of Industrial Brands: Business to Business Products and Services*, 2001, p. 23.

20 Robert P. Vitale and Joseph J. Giglierano, *Business to Business Marketing: Analysis and Practice in a Dynamic Environment*, 2002, p. 62.

21 Frederick E. Webster and Yoram Wind, *Organizational Buying Behavior*, 1972, pp. 78-80; Philippe Malaval, *Strategy and Management of Industrial Brands: Business to Business Products and Services*, 2001, pp. 24-26; Philip Kotler and Kevin L. Keller, *Marketing Management*, 2006, pp. 214-215.

22 David Armstrong, "A Whole New Magic Carpet Ride: SFO up and Ready for 2006 Arrival of Airbus A380," *San Fransisco Chronicle* (27 January 2005).

23 Web site of *Singapore Airlines Ltd.*, cited June 2005.

24 „Flugzeug mit Doppelbett und Schoenheitsfarm," *Frankfurter Allgemeine Zeitung* (19 January 2005, No. 15), p. 14.

25 David Armstrong, "A Whole New Magic Carpet Ride: SFO up and Ready for 2006 Arrival of Airbus A380," *San Fransisco Chronicle* (27 January 2005).

26 Philippe Malaval, *Strategy and Management of Industrial Brands: Business to Business Products and Services*, 2001, pp. 18-21; Robert P. Vitale and Joseph J. Giglierano, *Business to Business Marketing: Analysis and Practice in a Dynamic Environmen*, 2002, p. 62.

27 David Armstrong, "A Whole New Magic Carpet Ride: SFO up and Ready for 2006 Arrival of Airbus A380," *San Fransisco Chronicle* (27 January 2005).

28 "EU, U.S. Duel over Plane Subsidies," *USA Today* (30 May 2005).

29 David Armstrong, "A Whole New Magic Carpet Ride: SFO up and Ready for 2006 Arrival of Airbus A380," *San Fransisco Chronicle* (27 January 2005).

30 "SIA Reveals The 'First To Fly' Logo For Its A380," *Singapore Airlines Ltd.*, News release (5 January 2005).

31 Web site of *Klueber Germany*, cited June 2005.

32 Mirko Caspar, Achim Hecker, and Tatjana Sabel, "Markenrelevanz in der Unternehmensfuehrung – Messung, Erklaerung und empirische Befunde fuer B2B-Maerkte", 2002, p. 7; David A. Aaker and Erich Joachimsthaler, *Brand Leadership*, 2000, p. ix.

33 Waldemar Pfoertsch and Michael Schmid, M., *B2B-Markenmanagement: Konzepte – Methoden – Fallbeispiele*, 2005, pp. 12-13.

34 James C. Anderson and James A. Narus, *Business Market Management: Understanding, Creating, and Delivering Value*, p. 15.

35 Waldemar Pfoertsch and Michael Schmid, M., *B2B-Markenmanagement: Konzepte – Methoden – Fallbeispiele*, 2005, pp. 12–13.

36 Ibid.

37 Herman R. Hochstadt, „Chairman's Letter," *NOL Review 1998*.

38 "APL Web Site Makes Hot 100 For Fourth Year Running," *APL Ltd.* Press release (18 September 2003).

39 Unni Einemo, "AP Møller-Maersk and P&O Nedlloyd in Merger Talks," *Bunkerworld.com* (10 May 2005).

40 Richard A. D'Aveni, *Hypercompetition*, 1994, pp. 217-218.

41 Shona L. Brown and Kathleen M. Eisenhardt, *Competing on the Edge,* 1998; Richard A. D'Aveni, *Hypercompetition,* 1994, pp. 217-220; Gary Hamel, *Leading the Revolution,* 2000.

42 "Technology Product Life Cycle," White Paper, *Myxa Corporation.*

43 Web site of *Advanced Micro Devices, Inc.,* Sunnyvale, CA, cited June 2005; Web site of *Intel Corporation,* Santa Clara, CA, cited June 2005.

44 Peter de Legge, "The Brand Version 2.0: Business-to-Business Brands in the Internet Age," *Marketing Today,* 2002.

45 Axel Hoepner, „Siemens hat bei Handys den Anschluss an die Welt-spitze verloren," *heise mobil* (6 June 2005); „Siemens warnt vor Hoer-schaeden durch Handy-Ausschaltmelodie," *heise mobil* (26 August 2004).

46 Georgina Prodhan and Baker Li, "BenQ to Take over *Siemens'* Mobile Unit," *Reuters.com* (7 June 2005).

47 Web site of *SAP AG,* Walldorf, Germany, cited June 2005.

48 Web site of *Magna International Inc.,* Canada, cited June 2005.

49 Mirko Caspar, Achim Hecker, and Tatjana Sabel, "Markenrelevanz in der Unternehmensfuehrung – Messung, Erklaerung und empirische Befunde fuer B2B-Maerkte," 2002, pp. 23-26.

50 ERP, CRM and SCM stands for Enterprise Resource Planning System, Customer Relationship Management, and Supply Chain Management Systems.

51 Mirko Caspar, Achim Hecker, and Tatjana Sabel, "Markenrelevanz in der Unternehmensfuehrung – Messung, Erklaerung und empirische Befunde fuer B2B-Maerkte," 2002, pp. 4.

52 Ibid., pp. 38-43.

53 Ibid., pp. 38-43.

54 Philippe Malaval, *Strategy and Management of Industrial Brands: Business to Business Products and Services,* 2001, pp. 18 -28.

55 Ibid., p. 5-6.

56 Scott M. Davis, "The power of the brand," *Strategy & Leadership* (28 April 2000, Vol. 28, No. 4), pp. 4-9.

57 Scott Bedbury, *A New Brand World,* 2002, p. 5.

58 Bob Lamons, "Brick Brand's Mighty – Yours Can Be, Too," *Marketing News* (22 November 1999), p. 16; Web site of *Acme Brick Company,* Fort Worth, TX, cited June 2005.

[59] Web site of *Tata Steel Ltd.*, Fort, Mumbai, India, cited October 2005.

[60] Gary Strauss, "The corporate jet: Necessity or ultimate executive toy?," *USA Today* (25 April 2005).

[61] D.J, Buller, *Adapting Minds. Evolutionary Psychology and the Persistent Quest for Human Nature*, Cambridge MA: MIT Press 2005.

[62] Some strong brands such as Intel are not mentioned, which could have happened because they are not on the client list of Saatchi and Saatchi. Nevertheless, Intel should be mentioned because many software and electrical component engineers love to work with Intel chips.

[63] Web site of *Caterpillar Inc.*, Peoria, IL, cited August 2005.

CHAPTER 3

B2B Branding Dimensions

If one does not know to which port one is sailing, no wind is favorable.

Lucius Annaeus Seneca

Marketing Management in an industrial context became widely accepted years ago – leading to the establishment of several B2B marketing professorships of B2B marketing in the United States. This was in response to competitive pressures and a fast-changing environment that forced businesses to become more customer-focused. Many B2B organizations recognized that by adapting the concepts and practices of consumer companies to the B2B setting, they could benefit in the same way as their B2C counterparts.

Unfortunately, the subject of branding was overlooked in most cases. In recent years a large number of books dedicated to business marketing have appeared. A very profound and valuable book in this area is *Business Market Management* by Andersen and Narus. In their second edition, they added new sections devoted to brands and brand building, thereby acknowledging that these are concepts of growing interest in business markets.[1] We are willing to go even further: Branding should be the thread running through the subject of marketing.

To regard brand management merely as naming, design or advertising seems to be too superficial and tends to shorten the brand's life expectancy. If a company wants to take full advantage of its brands as strategic devices, it needs to be prepared to carry out a considerable amount of marketing analysis and brand planning. However, many businesses are too busy with tactical issues and thus fail to generate the best possible results for their brands. It requires understanding of the role of marketing as being different in the short versus the long-terms, with strategic marketing and operational marketing being two distinct activities. Although branding is as much art as science, it goes far beyond cute logos and sharp package designs. It is a discipline that has the power to lead and influence; a discipline that belongs to the long-term strategy of an organization. **Brand management** therefore is the organizational framework that systematically manages the planning, development, implementation, and evaluation of the brand strategy. This chapter addresses all fundamental branding basics and concepts that are relevant in B2B markets.

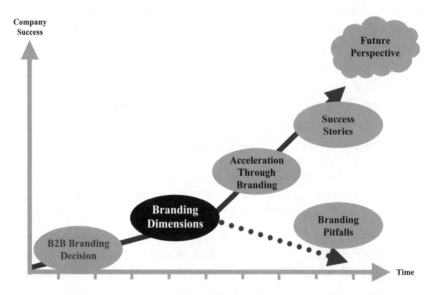

Fig. 15. Guiding principle branding dimensions

The development of a holistic brand strategy has to involve all levels of marketing management. The active involvement of all other relevant internal departments and external agencies is also necessary to create a better chance of success.[2] Such a holistic perspective can moreover provide valuable insight into the process of capturing customer value. For long-term success of a business it is indispensable to continuously identify new **value opportunities** (**value exploration**), realize them in new and promising value offerings (**value creation**), and last but not least to use capabilities and infrastructure to deliver those new value offerings efficiently (**value delivery**).

Integrating the value exploration, value creation, and value delivery activities within a holistic marketing concept is an effective way of building the basis for **competitive advantage and long-term profitability**. These value-based activities have to be put in the context of all relevant actors in the **branding triangle** (customers, company, and cooperators). By shifting the view from a fractional focus to an overall picture, a company can gain a superior value chain that delivers high level of product quality, service, and speed. The objective is to generate profitable growth by increasing customer share, building customer loyalty, and capturing customer lifetime value. To take advantage of customer value more effectively also translates into mutually satisfying business relationships and co-prosperity among key stakeholders.[3]

Holistic marketers achieve profitable growth by expanding customer share, building customer loyalty, and capturing customer between relevant actors (customers, company, and collaborators) and value-based actives. In order to create and maintain the sustainable competitive advantage offered by the brand, companies need to concentrate their resources, structure and financial accountability around this most important asset.

An efficient branding strategy for a company consequently identifies which brand elements are useful in bringing your brand message to the aimed target group. But before you can slam your foot on the branding accelerator it is important to create a proposition that your product or service delivers on, time and time again.

How Brands Create Value in B2B

A strong brand is about building and maintaining strong perceptions in the minds of customers. In order to attach a certain value to a brand, you need to know at first what values are already seen in that brand. The brand name and its associations are a shorthand for everything that is being offered. The product quality, the reliability of delivery, the value for money, are all wrapped up in people's perceptions of that brand. Working out what people associate with a brand is only one part of the equation. It is necessary to go a step further and put a monetary figure on those brand values.[4] Even the **best advertising cannot create something that is not there**. If a company lacks soul or heart, if it doesn't understand the concept of "brand", or if it is disconnected from the world around it, there is little chance that its marketing will resonate deeply with anyone.[5]

It is also about understanding how consumers perceive every aspect of what the organization does. Branding must be consistent and clear in order to really be meaningful. Wordy corporate objectives alone with some logo-twiddling definitely do not make a brand. Moreover, brands are not static but rather always evolving. They can change according **to stakeholder expectations** and **market conditions** whether you see it coming or not. It is important to manage that evolution, unexpected or expected, rather than to simply let it happen to you.

In order to establish an effective branding approach, it is necessary to track and measure the strength of the current brand and the entire brand portfolio. To grasp the business landscape in more depth, it is essential to do some research that can later serve as **the foundation of the future brand strategy.** Modern research tools are easy to employ and at the same time very sophisticated but if a company wants to get a market and customer driven perspective of its brand portfolio it cannot get around this. All the information has to be evaluated carefully and all factors taken into consideration.[6]

Take three brands of computers – *Dell*, *Sony* and *IBM* – basically doing the same thing. However, prospective buyers may see one standing for flexibility, another for innovation and yet another for quality. All of them possess all three values but the high ground for each value is occupied by just one of the companies. This provides them with the opportunity for gaining a **competitive advantage**. Although this may be self evident, too few industrial companies have strategic plans for managing their company brand to reach this level.

Very few companies have a brand essence that is reflected in every thing they do. This is not always easy. Inside the company some people will suggest values or a position that is future oriented while others will want something that is more reflective of the here and now. Some will want a complicated essence while others will try to find simplicity. Some will be happy to run with internal opinion while others will insist on an independent external view. A company that gets this wrong will lose its single most important differentiating opportunity.[7]

In a world where everything increasingly looks the same, brands are one of the few opportunities for **making a difference**. So what is brand equity? The concept of brand equity generally is meant to capture the value of a brand. According to Anderson and Narus it can be reflected in various preferential action or responses of customers:[8]

- Greater willingness to try a product or service

- Less time needed to close the sale of an offering

- Greater likelihood that the product or service is purchased

- Willingness to award a larger share of purchase requirement

- Willingness to pay a price premium

- Less sensitive in regard to price increases

- Less inducement to try a competitive offering

Different definitions of brand equity also exist. Duane E. Knapp for instance defines I^t as "the totality of the brand's perception, including the **relative quality of products** and **services, financial performance, customer loyalty, satisfaction**, and **overall esteem** toward the brand."[9] According to Aaker, brand equity refers to "the assets (or liabilities) linked to a brand's name and symbol that add to (or sub-tract from) a product or service."[10]

Whether you define it in common terms or use a technical or even mathematical approach in defining brand equity, they will both end up meaning the same. Drivers of brand equity can be summarized as follows:

- Perceived quality

- Name awareness

- Brand associations

- Brand loyalty

Of course it is unquestioned that the perceived quality of a product is an essential value driver. Name awareness is quite important, too, but shouldn't be over-estimated as we will show in chapter six. **Brand associations** are generally everything that connects the cus-tomer to the brand, including user imagery, product attributes, use situations, brand personality, and symbols. The most important driver of brand equity though is brand loyalty.[11]

In order to create a holistic brand strategy you must also strive for complete alignment between what you're promising outside and the reality of what you're delivering within the organization. The **brand strategy** has to match the **corporate strategy**. If there are any misalignments or chinks, it will soon be spotted, first by employees, then by consumers.

One thing of crucial importance if not even the most significant thing in B2B brand management is: **consistency**. Let's have a look at the example of digital imaging: Publishers, advertisers, corpora-tions. They all have valuable digital assets that are part and parcel to their business. An image originally used in print can, technically, be used equally well on TV, the Web, or a DVD. Unfortunately however, many corporate publishers are forced to reinvent the graphics wheel every time they move a brand to a new medium.

Make a Consistent Impression

As noted earlier, brands are a set of expectations and associations evoked from experience with a company, or product or service – how customers think and feel about what the business or offer does for them. To that end, brands are built from the customer's entire experience with a company, its products and services, word of mouth, interactions with company personnel, online or telephone experiences, and payment transactions, not just marketing efforts. Therefore it is entirely natural that **brand building concerns** every single touch point. In order to leverage a brand it is indispensable to know all of the brand's touch points with the customer, ranging from call centers to the direct sales people.[12]

Whether you call it touch points, points of interaction or brand contacts, they can be summarized as any **information-bearing experience** a customer or prospective customer has with a brand.[13] This also underscores how a brand's influence extends well beyond the marketing department and into all corners of the organization. The brand must be embraced as key strategic business asset that needs to be protected, nurtured and built over time. To internalize the concept of "brand" as a promise to your customers means that you have to consistently deliver on that promise on and on again, across every point of touch. An **effective brand promise** needs to be clearly defined, relevant and meaningful, not to be mistaken with exaggerated marketing promises. You have to continuously deliver on your brand promise and provide a consistent impression across every point of touch. Or as Kevin Roberts, author of the book "Lovemarks" puts it:[14]

> **"Perform, perform, perform.**
> **Respect grows only out of performance.**
> **Performance at each and every point of interaction."**

To assure a consistent impression, a holistic branding approach needs to be implemented and executed at every single point of touch. This means that you have to know them all. This is especially important in the service sector where the companies tend to have more direct contact to customers than in other business sectors. Thousands of employees need to behave in **accordance with the brand and its promise**. To control every single point of interaction a stakeholder may have with the brand is quite a challenging task. Yet, there are many businesses that prove by their excellent branding strategies and implementation that it is possible to provide that consistent impression. *FedEx*, for instance is doing a great job in this respect. So, what is meant by "everything" touch? Figure 16 shows the brand customer relationship from the pre-selection phase to ongoing relationship.

Fig. 16. The brand customer relationship

The control of all possible **touchpoints** of the brand customer relationship does not imply that these touchpoints should be kept as clear and concise as possible. To work closely with your customers, pushing forward the customer supplier relationship towards a strategic partnership is recommendable in almost any business. *Caterpillar* provides an excellent example of a company that extends its **relationships with customers** to produce maximum benefits for both parties. CAT engineers work closely with OEM, providing them with the information on all factory-applied coatings of all types of the construction equipment. This reduces development time, tooling and production costs. At the same time, it increases the performance of CAT products. The result is a successful combination of iron and electronics in machine produced by CAT produced machines that make them powerful and productive.

3.1   Brand Distinction

Brand Architecture

A brand strategy can be generally defined as the choice of common and distinctive brand elements a company applies across the various products and services it sells and the company itself. It reflects the number and nature of new and existing brand elements while at the same time guiding decisions on how to brand new products.[15] To put it in other words, the brand strategy lays out a future image for the company to aim for, providing a plan of action and criteria against which to judge it. It is based on certain future goals. Among others the most common goals related to the customers are to **increase brand awareness**, create a positive brand image, and to establish brand preferences and brand loyalty. The brand strategy also aims at increasing the appeal and attraction of the company in the eyes of the stakeholders, who underpin the management of the company, and to give the employees criteria with which to judge the value of their own actions.

The strategic branding options in B2B markets are generally the same as those in their consumer markets. The branding strategy in general can be defined as the choice of common and **distinctive brand elements** a company applies across its various products and services it sells and the company itself. It reflects the number and nature of new and existing brand elements, guiding decisions on how to brand new products. To structure and manage their portfolio of brands is one of the biggest challenges businesses face nowadays.

To develop a company-owned brand architecture is essential since it defines the relationship between brands, the corporate entity, and products and services. For B2B companies, defining the brand hierarchy to pursue is the most important aspect of their branding strategy. The brand hierarchy can be described as a means of summarizing the branding strategy by displaying the explicit ordering of all common and distinctive brand elements. It reveals the number and nature of all brand elements across the companies' products and services.[16] The spectrum of **possible relationships** between brands that businesses can employ nowadays is almost unlimited.

The following chart provides an overview of the brand relationship spectrum developed by Aaker and Joachimsthaler.[17] The range of **possible brand architectures** reaches from a branded house to a house of brands. In-between one finds lots of hybrid forms, generally cut into subbrands and endorsed brands.

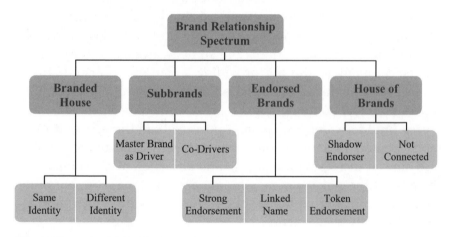

Fig. 17. Brand relationship spectrum

In order to keep it simple, we will illustrate the view of brand strategies available to companies from the German business point of view. It is a simple but comprehensive overview. Traditionally, the strategic branding options are comprised of three major tiers:

- Individual brands
- Family brands
- Corporate brands

The three options mentioned above can also be seen as some kind of basic underlying principle of the strategies at hand. In reality you will rarely find any of them in their pure theoretical form.[18] There are mostly intersecting hybrid forms of these generic brand strategies. If you compare them to the **brand relationship spectrum** you will see that they are not really that different. The branded house refers to a corporate (master, parent, umbrella, or range), while the house of brands is comprised of an individual (product) brand strategy. The main difference is that Aaker's model incorporates many more variations and **hybrid forms**. It also displays the whole brand portfolio of a company at once rather than looking at the possible brand strategies separately.

Each form comes with its own advantages and disadvantages. Generally it depends strongly on the type and nature of business, the industry it operates in, the social and economic environment, and customer perceptions when choosing and developing proper branding strategies for your business.[19] **Brand strategy decisions** generally come up when a company is about to develop or buy a new product or service that should be branded or if already established brand portfolios are being restructured.

In the last 10 to 20 years, many multi brand B2B companies emerged mainly through mergers and acquisitions. One example from the automotive world; *Ford Motor Company's* acquisition of *Aston Martin* (UK), *Jaguar* (UK), *Land Rover* (UK), *Volvo* (Sweden), and a controlling stake in *Mazda* (Japan). They are all part of a *Ford Motor Company's* family of primary brands, together with *Ford* (US/Global), *Lincoln* (US), *Mercury* (US), and soon, *Ka* (Europe). As cars are becoming more and more of a commodity, the Michigan-based carmaker is evolving toward traditional brand management, with a lot of (invisible) parts-sharing under the hood.

Morgan Stanley

Morgan Stanley's 1997 acquisition of *Discover Dean Witter* clearly exemplifies an acquisition where a sound transition strategy was incorporated and the consistency of the brand assured. *Morgan Stanley* understood that *Discover Dean Witter* brand carried **considerable equity** which could be benefited from. The first step was to transfer the name of the combined organizations to *Morgan Stanley Dean Witter Discover and Co.* Then almost a year later the *Discover* was removed from the corporate name. In 2002 the transition was completed with the elimination of the *Dean Witter* name. *Morgan Stanley* was reconstituted, but the brand had absorbed new equity from *Discover* and *Dean Witter*. They had entered the credit card business and other new markets, for example in UK and other countries.

MBtech

Similar developments can occur when corporations agree to the emancipation of certain divisions. An impressive success story of that kind is provided by the former engineering division from *Mercedes-Benz* (today *DaimlerChrysler*). The spin-off could expand its services into outside business. Today the company name is *MBtech*. Founded in 1995, it takes an active role in the **future-oriented globally competitive market**. It is operating worldwide via its international companies, subsidiaries, and strategic alliances. The company's major business focus lies on opening up and developing business segments that promise to be viable into the future. This overall objective translates into the goal to offer customers an attractive portfolio of engineering and consulting services.

Coordinated around five business segments, the *MBtech* group provides customers with technologically innovative, market-oriented and professional automotive engineering. They develop and test components and systems for vehicles and other drive units. Customers can profit from the continuous technology and innovation transfer offered by the bundled know-how of the company. **Knowledge transfer** ensures utmost quality, short lead times and maximum profitability – from the particulars to the complete solution. In the meantime they have acquired a brand portfolio of more than 10 sub brands, which are consistent with all the aspects of the *Mercedes-Benz* engineering quality.

The following graph shows the generic strategies along with the strategic branding dimensions width, depth, and length.

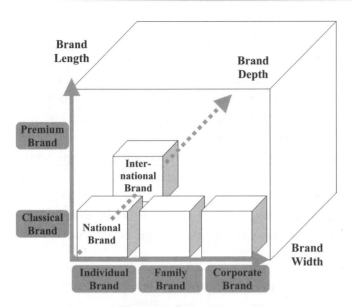

Fig. 18. Generic brand strategies[20]

Brand width, depth and length distinguish the strategic branding options as follows:[21]

- **Brand Width** – Number of products/services sold under one brand

- **Brand Depth** – Geographical range of the brands

- **Brand Length** – Basic positioning of the brands

They are brought together in one context since these are essential factors in every brand. A brand lacking any dimension is simply impossible. Just as in Aaker's brand relationship spectrum, the possible variations in this model are almost unlimited. There are national, classic, corporate brands (*Acme, Covad*) – **international, classic, corporate brands** (*IBM, Intel, HP, Dell, SAP*) – international, classic, individual brands (*Barrierta, Isoflex*) – international, premium, corporate brands (*ERCO, Swarovski, Festool*), etc. Therefore the generic brand strategies should be seen as what they are: **options**. How you combine them depends on the overall brand strategy.

IBM

An example to illustrate and clarify the potential levels of a **brand hierarchy**, from highest to lowest, is *IBM* with its *ThinkPad X30*. *IBM* is undoubtedly the corporate brand, followed by *ThinkPad* as the family brand for all notebook computers. The *X* series refers to the individual brand referring to extra-light, extra-small, and ultra-portable notebooks. The 30 is a so-called modifier that refers to the models with Ethernet connection. While some marketers include the latter in the branding hierarchy, we would define it as distinguishing name or part of the product name. It is absolutely comprehensible to speak of the X series as a brand but a number can rarely be one.

IBM learned this lesson already years ago when they started to brand their server line *eServers*. One important aspect of branding is that it simplifies the buying experience for customers. Before the re-branding they used simple alpha numeric product naming which had the effect of confusing customers. Millions of marketing dollars were wasted on similar products. The re-branding effort was used to streamline the market offerings in this area. It also made it easier for **customers to understand the differences**. By linking the new brand clearly to its *eSolutions* brand of IT consulting, *IBM* even improved their cross-selling opportunities. Although the re-branding effort cost US$75 million, it is considered a huge success. Not only did *IBM* outpace *Sun Microsystems* by a 32% margin, becoming no. 1 in worldwide server revenues in that year, but it also bypassed *Hewlett-Packard* for the first time in the UNIX server market share.

Because of the intersecting nature of the branding options there are many divergent models that businesses can apply to **create and manage their own brand portfolio**. Beforehand, we will walk you through each of them in isolation, and pointing out the respective strengths and weaknesses.

Corporate Brands

Corporate or master brands usually embrace all products or services of a business. The brand hereby represents the total offerings of the company. A corporate brand is strongly related to the parent organization, benefiting from positive associations with it. Visually spoken the corporate brand serves as some kind of **umbrella** and encapsulates the corporate vision, values, personality, positioning, and image among many other dimensions. It helps to establish brand equity for a range of individual or sub brands. A wider organizational contexts and richer history facilitates the generation of strong relationships with its key stakeholders (employees, customers, financial and investor communities, etc.) A **strong corporate branding strategy can add significant value** to any corporation since it facilitates the implementation of the long-term vision and provides a unique position in the marketplace. It helps a company to further leverage on its tangible and non-tangible assets leading to branding excellence throughout the corporation. There are many very successful corporate brands. Famous examples are *Intel*, *IBM*, *Microsoft*, *SAP*, *Siemens*, *Singapore Airlines*, and *General Electric*.

If the corporate brand is named after the founder of the company, as is the case for *Peugeot*, *Ford*, *Bosch*, *Dell*, *Hewlett-Packard* and *Siemens*, it is also called a **patronymic brand**. These big multinationals though are more exceptions, since patronymic brands are most common in small and medium sized companies.

Corporate brand strategy is said to be the most common brand strategy in the B2B environment. The industrial marketing environment is changing so rapidly and erratically that corporate brands are a great possibility for B2B companies to **create something constant and lasting**. In an ever-changing environment it usually doesn't make sense to establish many individual or family brands. PLCs are getting shorter and shorter for many industries and products. Especially in hypercompetitive markets where product innovations and competitive advantages are eroded very quickly, it is much too expensive to focus on a product branding strategy that becomes out-dated quickly. In addition, strong corporate brands make it easier to introduce new products in various markets within a short period of time. In this case, corporate branding helps a company to significantly shorten the payback period of an investment.

The nature of most B2B companies also further drives the importance of corporate brands. Most of them have market offerings that are characterized by a broad spectrum of distinctive, complex and moreover individual solutions. The **corporation standing behind** certain market offerings moreover tends to be much more important in industrial buying decisions as compared to B2C markets. Another important aspect that speaks for the usage of corporate brands in the B2B area is the global reach of this strategy. As mentioned before, industrial companies should pursue a global strategy because of an intense global competition. Individual brands are difficult to establish on an international level since they are usually restricted by language barriers and cultural differences.

Successful corporate brand management is based in **a company's corporate identity** (CI) and explicitly geared to the different needs of its stakeholders a company has, yet still always based on its own corporate identity. While product brands are mainly focused on B2B customers, the broad alignment is an essential feature of corporate brands.

> **Strong corporate brands are characterized by the precise, distinctive and self-contained image they hold in the minds of stakeholders.**[22]

One of the central goals of corporate brand management therefore is to provide a clear, consistent and unique picture of the company and its corporate brand across all target groups. The importance of a clear brand image can be underlined by its **positive correlation to stockholder's** disposition to buy stocks. With the increased clarity of the brand image, stockholder's acceptance rises.

In order to leverage a corporate brand careful thinking is required since it can have a significant impact on enhancing business results.

The most critical factor is to find **synergies between the corporate, business and brand strategy**. Understanding, comparing and in some cases challenging these business strategies will provide the foundation for a corporate branding decision. The variety of options available to leverage a corporate brand ranges from the dominant to the invisible, with a lot of interesting considerations in between. The range of possibilities is shown in the brand relationship spectrum above.

HSBC/Citibank

Corporate brands facilitate the general goal of growth generation. The two global financial powerhouses *HSBC* and *Citibank*, for instance, have tremendously profited in this respect. Both acquired a vast number of companies across the globe in recent years and successfully integrated them entirely under their international corporate brands within a short timeframe. A strong brand is mainly based on strong perceptions customers have of it. Usually this takes quite a lot of time and resources to establish, but in the case of *HSBC* and *Citibank* hardly anybody remembers what the once local and independent banks used to be called. Through their strong corporate brands both banks have managed to **transfer the brand equity** from the acquired brands into their own corporate brand equity.[23]

A corporate brand strongly reduces the risk involved in a complex buying process since it adds a sense of continuity. The positive image and good reputation associated with a corporate brand also reduces product complexity which is especially important for experience goods that can only be checked thoroughly after their purchase. B2B companies can tremendously profit from the **entrepreneurial competence and business capability** a strong corporate brand radiates on all aspects of the business. In addition, they are more strongly related to the future of the business since they reflect the whole corporation, whereas individual brands can come and go in a certain period of time. If a corporate brand disappears, the company is most probably ruined, too. The corporate name of a business is not automatically a corporate brand. Only if the market offerings of the company are continually marketed and sold under the corporate umbrella, does the name transform gradually into a brand. Furthermore, it is essential to clearly define the **corporate values** as well as **future aspirations** and **expectations** and incorporate them in the brand.

There are several benefits for employing a corporate brand strategy compared to other branding options. The positive image of a strong corporate brand can extend to and boost the credibility of everything it has on offer under this brand. It is the face of the corporate business strategy, portraying what the company reflects and stands for in the market place. It is by far easier to go global with a corporate brand than with a portfolio of specialized individual brands. As the cases of *HSBC* and *Citibank* have shown, it is less complex to implement a stringent corporate branding strategy throughout the globe. *HSBC* furthermore employs one single marketing strategy based on the slogan "The world's local bank" worldwide. If planned and implemented carefully, a corporate branding platform enables businesses to build bridges between many cultural differences.

New products and services can especially benefit from well-established master brands, since they can rely on the values associated with them. But it is not only new products that can **profit from synergy effects**, but also the complete marketing communications aligned around this strategy. Brand investments, time and resources are used most effectively, saving money on brand creation, advertising, and diffusion. These cost efficiencies can often be sizable, especially in comparison to a large multi-brand strategy. Even a combined corporate and product branding strategy can lead to **reduced marketing and advertising costs**, enabling a company to exploit synergies from a new and more focused brand architecture. The continued use of one and the same brand drives furthermore awareness, **facilitating the spread** of its offerings across different target groups.

Ironically, the strongest point of a company brand is also its weakest link. If a company relies on its corporate brand, it can lead to unfortunate bad-will transfer should any product or service fail to satisfy customer needs or worse. Minor problems can cause wide-spread damage across sub brands, even if only a single product is involved. *Siemens* for instance tests new innovative solutions and business areas initially under unrelated names. Only if they prove valuable and have the potential to position themselves in a leading market position, the company starts selling them under the *Siemens* corporate brand. This way the brand is effectively protected from any damage to its reputation. On the other side of the spectrum, individual brands can stay virtually unscathed when their corporate parents stumble upon mishaps.[24] Another disadvantage of this strategy is the more or less generic brand profile. A corporate brand strategy cannot target all market segments as comprehensively and precisely as is possible with a product brand strategy.

Family Brands

A family brand strategy involves using the same brand for two or more related or similar products in one product line or group. Usually there is no relation to the company that sells them. The main difference from a corporate brand strategy is that a business using this option can have several family brands in its portfolio while the corporate brand is the only umbrella brand used to cover all products and services the company sells. An important prerequisite for successful family branding is **the adequate similarity and coherence** of all products and services of one line. This means an equivalent standard of quality, a similar field of application and a matching marketing strategy (pricing, positioning, etc.)

A rare example of an industrial family brand is STYROFOAM®. Today, the brand includes a variety of building materials (including insulated sheathing and house wrap), and pipe insulation as well as floral and craft products. It was invented by the *Dow Chemical* company more than 50 years ago and was identified worldwide by a distinctive blue color which has become a trademark of the brand. It is the most widely recognized brand in insulation today.[25]

Nowadays, many family brands **tend to transcend the boundaries** of closely defined product lines. Therefore, it makes sense to divide the classic family brand strategy into a line brand strategy and a range brand strategy. As the name indicates, the latter comprises a wider range of products and services, not grouped together in one line. Family brands are quite common in the B2C area. For instance, *Uncle Ben's* by *Mars* sells rice, sauces, and curries under its family brand. Another classic example of family branding is the *Nivea* product line.

Most family brands were not launched as family brands but were converted over time by **brand extensions**. In today's highly competitive marketplace, well-established brands are constantly under fire. As the intensity of competition grows and the costs of introducing new products and services escalate, competitors are tempted to emulate established brands and identities in order to derive the benefit of a successful brand's reputation and gain quick acceptance in the marketplace.

It is much easier to introduce new products or services under an already well-established and recognized brand than to build an individual brand from scratch. Another advantage is the cost-efficient distribution of the brand investments over several products. All products of the product line can benefit from positive synergy effects related to the brand. Of course, similar to the corporate brand strategy, the same effects can be very negative in case of the failure of one product or service. The **damaged reputation** of a product sold under a family brand can have serious negative spill-over effects on all other products sold under this brand name. Such negative effects are also possible if not all products and services grouped under one family brand fit with each other in terms of quality or price.

The possibilities of positioning each product are quite limited. Therefore, family brands are generally only applicable in less complex and diversified businesses. It is for this reason that they are rarely found in B2B companies. Compared to the other branding options it is less valuable and practical. A corporate brand better reflects a value like reliability, quality, capability and competence than it is the case for a family brand. Customers of industrial businesses moreover tend to relate personal experiences to the whole organization/corporate brand rather than to a special group of products. Compared to an individual brand strategy family brands lack the product-specific and precisely targeted presentation of all products sold under one brand.

Individual Brands

To follow an individual brand strategy means to sell every single product or service under its own distinctive brand name. There is no relation to the company that owns or manages it. Examples are *Barrierta, Isoflex, Hotemp* and *Staburags* by *Klueber Lubrication* or *Flygt, Bell & Gossett, Gilfillan* and *Goulds Pumps* by *ITT Industries*.

The individual brand strategy aims to create clear, unique, and distinctive brand identities, specifically aligned to the product or service it represents. A product-specific profile facilitates the **capitalization of brands** since it is effectively targeted at customers. This way, every product gets its own highly focused brand name which is one key advantage compared to the other brand strategies. Another huge advantage of individual brands is that they can stay virtually unscathed when their corporate parents are in any kind of trouble. Any kind of bad-will transfer can more or less be avoided. This enables companies to create diverse growth platforms on the basis of their brands.

Since establishing brands requires huge investments, it is not the most cost-efficient way to manage a portfolio of individual brands. The high brand expenditures for a single product can usually only be amortized if it has a relatively long PLC. Therefore it needs to be checked and evaluated carefully whether to create individual brands for industrial goods that typically have short PLCs. Of course, it is easy to generalize and to say that in most circumstances there are few real opportunities for product brands in an industrial context. The small and specialized nature of most industrial markets makes it even more difficult for B2B companies to support the cost and attention required for a large number of such brands. Every brand promoted by a company needs strong promotional support and expenses. A high brand variety also weakens the receptiveness of customers faced with an information-overload concerning all brands. Companies applying this strategy are more vulnerable in times of crisis.

The most **recommendable brand strategy** for B2B companies is a corporate strategy combined with a few individual brands. New and highly innovative products or services that dispose of a unique selling proposition (USP) are the best potential basis of a successful individual brand. Every company should be careful with the number of product brands it has since a proliferation of brands ends up either doing nothing useful or sucking the blood from the corporate brand. In most cases, the corporate brand should be the only one that really matters, supported by product brands, not the other way around.

Premium Brands

Premium brands are generally characterized by high-quality materials, exclusive design, first class processing, and are sold at a high price (achieving a price premium). Such a **high-profile and high quality positioning** is quite expensive to implement, since all communication and distribution channels have to meet these requirements. The use of premium brands in the B2B context is quite restricted because goods and services are purchased for use in the production of other products or services. Premium brands can mainly be found in the business-to-consumer segment. Gucci, Rolls-Royce and Rolex are examples of elusive luxury items sold under premium brands. But they do also exist in an industrial context.

ERCO

ERCO is a notable example for a premium brand. The company sells luminaires for all areas of architectural lighting. *ERCO* actually sell light and not luminaires which is absolutely comprehensible if you look at their works. Their product program comprises indoor luminaires, outdoor luminaires and controls systems. The company cooperates with internationally renowned designers, lighting engineers, and architects in order to assure the quality of its premium brand. Founded in 1934, the family business today operates over 60 subsidiaries, branches and agencies all around the world.[26]

Porsche Consulting

Another example of an industrial premium brand, if we go right to the top, is *Porsche Consulting*. "The name *Porsche* is associated with countless success stories. However, the latest one has got nothing to do with automotive dreams, but is concerned with the hard facts of economic necessities", as Eberhard Weiblen, managing director of *Porsche Consulting* points out. In the last 10 years, *Porsche Consulting* has improved the profitability of the *Porsche* manifold and has helped other companies to enhance the efficiency of their processes at all points of the value chain. The list of clients is endless and contains the Crème de la Crème: Automotive OEMs like *DaimlerChrysler, VW, BMW, Smart, EvoBus, Steyr,* and *DucatiMotor;* suppliers like *Marquardt, Recaro, GF Georg Fischer, Miba, Fischer Automotive Systems, Bosch, Pierburg, ZF,* and many more.[27]

Classic Brands

A classic brand is a core product or service with certain additional characteristics attached to it that differentiate it from similar offers. They are generally what we all understand to be a brand. They are an effective and compelling means to communicate the benefits and value of a product or service.[28] They **facilitate the identification of products**, services and businesses and differentiate them from competition.[29] Classic brands do approach a much larger target group than premium brands and can become trust marks for customers. In order to be successful, they need to be coherent, consistent, and relevant to the respective target group.

National Brands

Only a few years ago most B2B sectors were characterized by many small national companies, offering their products and services only in their home market. The obvious branding strategy used, if any, was a national brand. As the name indicates, a national brand is specially aligned to match the local conditions. Consequently, there is no **language or cultural problem** involved. Increased competitive pressures, driven by businesses all over the world make mere national brands difficult to maintain. To use a single brand only on a restricted **geographical area** only can be moreover quite expensive. If the company intends to internationalize and sell its products and services it can be very difficult or impossible to adapt the national brand to the new requirements.

International Brands

B2B companies continually had to face new and demanding challenges in the last decades. One of these challenges has been the development of hypercompetitive markets **transcending geographic and cultural barriers**. If a company wants to survive, it is no longer sufficient to solely compete in the domestic market.

As indicated earlier, business markets are predominantly concerned with functionality and performance. Therefore, the local differences of industrial products and services are mostly insignificant if there are any at all. Market offerings for business markets require much fewer adaptations in order to sell them across borders. This facilitates the generation of international or even global brands. The ongoing changes and trends in the B2B market environment continue to **erode barriers of geographical distance**. It has become almost imperative for B2B companies to pursue international branding in their market offerings. Global branding is quite beneficial for companies, since it can decrease marketing costs, realize greater economies of scale in production, and provide a long-term source of growth. But everything that sounds too good usually has a hitch in it. If not designed and implemented properly, it has the power to backfire.

Every brand that is sold in at least two different countries can be called an international brand. Unfortunately, it doesn't stay that simple. For businesses that want to internationalize and are looking for a proper branding strategy to pursue on an international level, there are several possibilities:[30]

- **International Brand Strategy** – Businesses that operate in international markets without extensively customizing its market offerings, brands or marketing efforts to match different local conditions pursue an international brand strategy. Such a strategy is suitable for companies whose brands and products are truly unique and do not meet any serious competition in the foreign markets as is the case for *Microsoft*. They possess a valuable core competence which is hard to imitate. The internationalization, therefore, has less to do with cost pressures and economies of scale, which are the main drivers of the global brand strategy.

- **Global Brand Strategy** – A global branding strategy is characterized by the strong focus on increasing profitability by reaping the cost reductions that come from standardization, experience curve effects and location economies. Companies that pursue a global strategy don't adapt their branding concept to possible national differences and use the same brand name, logo, and slogan worldwide, as *Intel* did in the early days. The market offering, brand positioning, and communications are also identical across all markets. The standardized brand performance leads to significant economies of scale with respect to brand investments. Most B2B companies comply with the requirements for a global brand strategy and it is therefore often pursue it in practice.

- **Transnational Brand Strategy** – Businesses that pursue a transnational brand strategy develop individual branding concepts for all foreign markets they operate in. Not only the brand but also the whole market offering and the marketing efforts are specifically customized to match different local conditions. Yet, the corporate concept of the brand is still visible and acts as an overall framework guiding the local adaptations within its scope. The company can still position its brand differently and pursue adapted price and product policies. An example of a transnational advertising campaign would be generally standardized advertising with national celebrities. The transnational strategy is designed to best satisfy national needs. Negative in this respect are the high investments that are necessary to comply with this requirement as well as the lack of standardization advantages.

- **Multidomestic Brand Strategy** – The multi-domestic brand strategy is characterized an extensive and complete customization of brands, market offerings and marketing efforts. It is geared to the different domestic markets – nations or regions. Business can sometimes be forced to apply the multi-domestic brand strategy due to market regulations and external circumstances. In certain markets, it is inevitable to completely adapt to local conditions. Legal services, for instance, can be promoted by communication instruments in some countries while this is prohibited in others. The multi-domestic brand strategy makes most sense when a company faces high pressure for local responsiveness.

None of these strategies mentioned above are easy to implement. Fluctuating conditions and market developments need constant adaptation. The three basic brand strategies – corporate, family, and product brand – are hardly seen in their pure form as well. They may be possible theoretically but in reality there is a huge variety of many variations and hybrid forms. Nevertheless, they are a good starting point and help to characterize the overall direction of the brand strategy at hand.

The branding strategy with the highest potential for B2B companies is a strong corporate brand in relation with few product brands.

Combined strategically, corporate and product brands can benefit from each other and generate even greater results. Because of the dominance of the corporate brand strategy in B2B and the greater potential of it we will take it as the basic underlying strategy when talking of brands in the following chapters. To assist your decision we summarized all the advantages and drawbacks each strategic option entails in the following table.

Table 2. Comparison of the Generic Branding Options[31]

Brand Strategy		Pro	Contra
Brand Width	Corporate Brand	• Widest and most efficient use of time, resources and brand investments • Highest stability, less complexity. • Reinforces comprehensive solutions. • Maximum market impact.	• Generic brand profile. • Possible bad-will transfer on all products.
	Family Brand	• Brand investment covers a product line. • Positive image and brand transfer on all products (synergy effect). • Use of brand-related interconnections.	• Possible brand dilution. • Limitations for product positioning.
	Product Brand	• Product-specific brand profile. • No bad-will transfer. • Creates diverse growth platforms.	• Expensive product-specific brand creation. • High brand variety weakens the perception of single brands.
Brand Length	Premium Brand	• High-profile, high quality positioning. • High price premium.	• Expensive brand creation. • Difficult to approach with a family brand.
	Classic Brand	• Applicable in mass markets. • Creates high brand reliance.	• Requires ubiquity. • High level of brand awareness needed (cost intensive).
Brand Depth	National Brand	• No language problems. • Adapted to national requirements.	• Can become useless with later internationalization. • Can be too expensive (less standardization).
	International Brand	• Potential standardization. • Cost effective (economies of scale). • Use of international media.	• Necessary to comply with different legal requirements. • Possible image dilution. • Language/cultural problems.

Brand Elements

Now that we have covered the potential strategic options that companies can apply in an industrial context it is time to move on to the more concrete brand elements. Brand elements are the **visual** and **sometimes even physical devices** that serve to identify and differentiate a company product or service. The adequate choice and coordination of them is crucial when it comes to brand equity. When building a strong brand the following brand elements are key:

- Name

- Logo

- Tagline (or Slogan)

- Brand Story

The formal brand elements like name, logotype, and slogan taken together form the **visual identity** of a brand or company. They should reflect the brand essence, brand personality, and corporate culture of the business. The visual identity has to be designed with a long-term perspective. In order to assure the consistency of the brand performance it is also very helpful to define branding guidelines that exactly specify the use of each brand element. Such a guideline is called **visual identity code**. This visual identity code for the brand elements should follow a set of choice criteria in order to reduce the risk of diluting or weakening the brand:[32]

- **Available** – They should be available and usable across all markets. Today it is also very important to check the availability of the Internet domain for possible brand names.

- **Meaningful** – Ideally the brand elements should capture the essence of the brand and communicate something about the nature of the business.

- **Memorable** – Good brand elements are distinctive and should be easy to remember. Brand names should be moreover easy to read and spell.

- **Protectable** – It is essential that the brand elements, especially the brand name can be legally protected in all countries in which the brand will be marketed.

- **Future-Oriented** – Well-chosen brand elements can position companies for growth, change, and success. To be future-oriented also means to check the adaptability and updatability of the brand elements.

- **Positive** – Effective brand elements can evoke positive associations in the markets served.

- **Transferable** – Is it possible to use the brand element to introduce new products in the same or different market.

The first four criteria can be characterized as "brand-building" since they are concerned with major implications when choosing and creating the brand elements in the first place. The latter three are more defensive. They are important for the general value and brand equity creation. In making a business brand, marketers have many choices of brand elements to identify with their product and services.

Before we walk you through each and every brand element separately, it is important to cover certain aspects that are very important in relation to choosing brand elements.

Brands and Image

As a basis to start on, one must understand that image is a perception and need, not necessarily a fact. Buyers cannot know in a factual sense all there is to know about a company. What they do not know they may assume or expect with or without any objective evidence. The so-formed perceptions are influential to the buyer, just as real factors based on harder evidence are, and may well **determine the purchasing decision**.[33]

Usually a company has several different identities: the communicated, actual, conceived, desired, and ideal identity.[34]

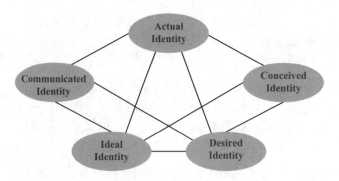

Fig. 19. Five brand identities

According to Aaker, the brand identity consists of a **unique set of brand associations** that represents what the brand stands for and promises to customers.[35] At first, you need to know where you actually are (actual identity) in order to find a way to your **desired brand identity**. Ideally the desired identity is also the ideal identity. However, what you're communicating and how people conceive it can be two very different things. Now you may wonder what the difference is between **brand identity** and **brand image.** Well, the latter is more a tactical asset that can change from time to time while brand identity a long-lasting strategic asset that represents the timeless values of the brand.

As we've already mentioned before, there can be no great brand without great products or services. To specify this in marketing terms: You should have a USP. It is simply a special feature that **provides additional value** to your customers and cannot be easily copied or imitated by competitors. A USP does not necessarily need to lie in the product or service itself; it can be a special production or delivery process, extraordinary services, or industrial design.

A company may not be picked as a supplier because of a negative (and in an objective sense, erroneous) image. It is often not understood that **potential customers** who have never had any contact with a supplier may nevertheless hold a strong image of that company. Far away from being determined by a purchasing experience, image may decide whether a supplier is used at all. Many B2B companies falsely construe that they know exactly what's on their prospects' minds. Since this "knowledge" is quite often based only on the reports of sales people it simply does not reflect the truth in most cases. In order to really get to know where a company and its brands are **perceived in customers minds** they have to do thorough research.

One of the most important things in B2B brand management is to **reduce complexity**. This means "less is more". Nobody and no company can be all things to all people. It is essential to reflect upon what's essentially important.

Brand Name

The name of a brand is the first and probably the greatest expression or "the face" of a product. The huge complexity of names and their associations has led to a new profession of naming companies, products, or services. All names usually have some kind of **associated image**, whether it is cultural, linguistic or personal. Brand names should be chosen very carefully since they convey important information to stakeholders. This is especially true for brands that intend to cross geographic and cultural boundaries; it is a very challenging task to find the right name for different audiences.

The **extraordinary power of a name** can be exemplified by the following case. In 1969 Sir Roger Penrose, a Cambridge physicist, announced his discovery of what he called a "gravitationally totally collapsed object" while speaking at a small scientific conference. The response to it was quite unspectacular, but when he changed his description to call it the "black hole" months later, the news of his discovery raced around the world. Today, the term "black hole" is a part of every day language.

A **well-chosen name** for a company, product, or service can be a valuable asset, just like the brand itself. The name directly affects the perception of the brand. We hear and read various brand names many times every day, in emails, business cards, brochures, websites, and product packages. The brand name will be used in every form of communication between a company and its prospective customers. An ineffective brand name can hinder marketing efforts, because it can lead to miscommunication if people can't pronounce it or remember it. Ultimately, the brand name is the expression that conveys all the values and promises of a company. In order to build a brand it is essential to continually keep the name present.

Especially in B2B, it is unfortunately quite common to **use ineffective stereotypical names**. There are thousands of companies that use the following name elements such as: "Net", "Sys", "Tech", "Tel" and "Pharm". It is quite obvious in what they are meant to reflect but if such elements are used too often and become stereotypes, they lose their distinctiveness and fail to differentiate. This **lack of distinctiveness** makes it very difficult to effectively position a brand since the names is not very memorable but easily confused with other brands of competitors. Although it's quite alluring for many companies especially in B2B to resort to such stereotype names, they should be avoided! The more complex a company is in terms of divisions and operating companies, the harder it gets to find the right mix of related or unrelated brand names. There is nothing worse than a confusing "mish mash" of brand names that may or may not be related to the parent company brand. There are several types of names companies can use for brands:[36]

- **Name of Founders** – Many great companies and brands simply have been named after their founders like William E. Boeing, John Deere, Paul Julius Reuter, Werner von Siemens, and John Pierpont Morgan.

- **Descriptive Names** – Another option is to use descriptive names that accurately convey the nature of the business, such as *British Airways, Airbus, Caterpillar, Deutsche Telekom, International Business Machines,* and *General Electric*. Descriptive names are the easiest to come up with and clearly communicate the intent of the company. Unfortunately they also tend to be quite constraining when it comes to future aspirations.

- **Acronyms** – Initials can also serve as names. As we all know International Business Machines resorted to its initials *IBM* when they extended beyond their core business. Their legal entity though still remains the same. This has become common practice today for companies that have evolved and left behind their initial brands. Many industrial companies are using such acronyms for naming their brands. Beside *IBM* there are *BASF, BBDO, DHL, HP, HSBC, LEK, SAP,* and *UPS,* just to name a few. A huge disadvantage of such names is their low reminder value. People are confronted with a constantly increasing number of acronymic names which makes it more and more difficult to learn and distinguish them. In the case of *EADS* (European Aeronautic Defense and Space) for instance, many people don't know what the letters stand for and therefore falsely relate it to all kinds of different industries. Because of the unrelated nature of these names they require substantial investment in advertising and educating its market of who they are. This is also true with the next type of name.

- **Fabricated Names** – Such neologisms are completely made up. *Accenture, Agilent, Exxon, Lanxess* and *Xerox,* are examples of fabricated brand names. Such abstract names are of course highly distinctive, can easily be differentiated, and legally protected. Unusual names also tend to be more memorable than more mundane ones.

- **Metaphors** – Based on things, places, animals, processes, mythological names, or foreign words, metaphors are used to allude to a certain quality or feature of a company, product, or service. *Oracle* is a B2B company that successfully uses a metaphoric brand name. Metaphors are especially good in terms of differentiating you from the competition. In the beginning of the 1980's, when the computer industry was dominated by companies that had names like *IBM, NEC,* and *DEC,* a new competitor wanted to differentiate and distance itself from the cold, unapproachable, complicated imagery conveyed by the others. Guess what name was chosen? Right, *Apple.* The metaphor of "Byte into an Apple" served the company very well. It is possible to combine certain forms and use different approaches at the same time. *GE,* started by Thomas Edison in 1890, for instance uses both the acronym and the written descriptive form in its brand names.

To find a name that is suitable globally is quite a **challenging task**. Even today, with various helpful tools and access to international brand libraries, mishaps do happen. For example, when the two American gas producers *Inter North* of Omaha and *Houston Natural Gas* merged, they came up with the name *Enteron* for the new group. As intended, the name attracted a lot of attention but unfortunately for the wrong reasons: the Greek origin of the word enteron means male anus. This led to the company changing its name immediately to *Enron*.

A widely quoted example of marketing blunder is the *Chevy Nova* fiasco, the car that wouldn't go since "no va" means "it doesn't go" in Spanish. However, this is an urban legend that never really happened. Actually, *Chevrolet* did reasonably well with the *Nova* in Latin America. Customers didn't confuse *Nova* with "no va" since they don't really sound alike, just as "carpet" and "car pet" in English. No English speaker can imagine that the two could be confused in English.[37]

Beside unexpected meanings in other languages, the pronunciation of international brand names can be quite problematic. Some companies even launched extensive communication campaigns to educate their customers how to pronounce their brand names, as the Korean company *Daewoo* (pronounced De-Ou) and the German company *Hoechst* (just say Herkst) did.[38]

Logo

The logo is the "graphic look" of the brand name or company. Too often, small and medium-sized companies use a logo which is clearly the work of a member of the family or a friend who is considered to have some artistic talent. Frugality in general may be a virtue but skimping on your companies brand design is definitely not worth the effort. If a logo fails to communicate and express what the company represents, it is a wasted opportunity.

A good logo fulfills both graphic and functional imperatives. In order to do so, brand architects have to keep the big picture in mind.

Corporate values and characteristics need to be reflected in the logo and the brand, should be safely incorporated in the overall marketing strategy. It can be said that this is true for every aspect of a corporation's visual identity.

By creating a **powerful visual image** for a company, it will achieve not just a name display, but a long-lasting image that connects customers with your brand. But the power of symbols should not be underestimated, since human beings tend to be more receptive to images and symbols than anything else. The old adage "one picture is worth a thousand words", holds quite a lot of scientific truth in it. A strong logo can provide cohesion and structure to the brand identity, facilitating recognition and recall. It is easier to communicate an attribute or value by using a symbol than to use factual information, especially in the B2B area where complex functional benefits need to be explained in a vivid and memorable way.[39]

UPS

Sometimes even long-lasting and unique symbols become outdated and need a change. A very successful logo change has been conducted by *UPS*. In 2004 it was dubbed the "World's Most Admired" company in a Fortune magazine survey and ranked among the world's best known service brands, yet mostly acknowledged for their ground shipping business. But *UPS* has far more to offer. The company also comprises supply chain management, multi-modal transportation, and financial services. In March 2003, being perceived as "package delivery experts", the company began repositioning its brand in order to draw customer attention to their broader scope of business dealings. The mission was to let the world know that it delivers in more ways than only one. The brand overhaul was initiated to unify the identity of all of its entities. One step in this repositioning process was the change of the company's 40-year old shield logo. In 1961, when the third *UPS* logo was adopted, the company did not even provide service to all 50 US states. Today, *UPS* has over 360,000 employees serving more than 200 countries and territories.

The first logo appeared in 1919 in the design of a shield which has not been changed in the course of the repositioning and not very surprising since this special design stands for **integrity and reliability**, not only of the company itself but also of all the people standing behind it. The change of the logo was considered necessary since it failed to reflect the new capabilities of *UPS*. Nonetheless the company tried not to step away from the company's established expertise but to communicate a positive evolution in the new logo.[40]

Fig. 20. Development of the *UPS* logo

The new, redesigned logo retained the approved shield design, maintaining the positive attributes of the old logo. By removing the package with the bow above the shield, replacing it by a larger sleeker emblem in a three-dimensional appearance it better reflects all business areas covered by *UPS*. This provides it with an energized look and gives it a stronger visual presence.[41] In regard to the color brown, *UPS* found out by extensive research that it was instantly identified and positively correlated with *UPS* and therefore shouldn't be changed. Not only the color, also the term "brown" was associated with the company. The underlying meaning in the color stands for trust and reliability, fostering customer loyalty. It ultimately even led to the introduction of *UPS*'s "What Can Brown Do for You? " advertising campaign.[42]

Color is of major importance and should not be underestimated when it comes to the design of a brand logo. In the 1999 Fortune 500 issue, *IBM* was called a "big blue dinosaur" relating to their blue *IBM* logo. Today, there are still many people that refer to *IBM* as "Big Blue" instead of naming the company *IBM*. This illustrates that colors are especially important when it comes to terms of brand recognition. What would *Caterpillar* or *Kodak* be without their personalized color yellow? The spectrum of different colors, the related connotations and meanings, can provide companies with great opportunities to fill their brands with purpose, meaning and life. A well chosen combination of all visual elements can increase the level of brand recognition tremendously.

Tagline (or Slogan)

The brand slogan or tagline plays a unique and distinct role in creating a harmonious brand identity. It is an easily **recognizable and memorable phrase** which often accompanies a brand name in marketing communications programs. The main purpose of a slogan is to support the brand image projected by the brand name and logo. These three brand elements together provide the core of the brand.

Some marketers falsely construe that the whole brand identity should be captured in the slogan. This is a common brand management mistake, viewing the brand too narrowly. Even the brand mission statement, though representing the core of the brand, cannot capture it all. A brand is more complex than a simple phrase can represent. It stands for much more. Another problem is the fixation on product-attributes, that only accounts for the functional values a product or service can provide. Especially in the high-tech and B2B area, companies tend to focus too narrowly on factual information.[43] A slogan though should represent both functional and emotional values at the same time.

Let us go to another aspect that is very important in this area: the brand mantra. It is the basis for the brand slogan. The slogan represents the **translation of the mantra in customer-friendly language** that is used in advertising and other forms of communication. Examples of slogans for industrial brands which reflect underlying brand mantras are *Agilent Technologies'* "Dreams Made Real", *Emerson's* "Consider It Solved", *GE's* "Imagination at Work", *Hewlett-Packard's* "Invent", *Novell's* "The Power to Change", *United Technologies'* "Next Things First", and *Xerox's* "The Document Company".[44]

A good slogan captures a company's brand essence, personality, and positioning. It also helps to differentiate it from competition. Many taglines of B2C companies have managed to become a part of our popular culture. There are probably very few people that don't know the brands related to "Just do it," "Think different," or "Got milk?" In B2B, it is still not common to **create a slogan**, despite their obvious benefits. Consistent and well-known B2B examples are *HSBC* "The world's local bank", *HP* "Invent", and *Singapore Airlines* "A Great Way to Fly" brand.

Philips

Taglines can sometimes backfire as the case of *Philips*, the large Dutch electronics company, shows. A few years ago they introduced the slogan "From Sand to Chips" in an **effort to communicate** that it produced light bulbs and silicon chips, both from the same raw material – sand. Unfortunately, people not only did not understand this, but the slogan was moreover irrelevant to customers. This is a common mistake that we are also addressing in chapter 6. Although the slogan may have been important to employees, customers didn't care about it. The following tagline "Philips Invents for You" was much better in terms of customer-focus and relevance, yet it was still too product-oriented and conveyed a misleading and unfavourable attitude (Who asked you?). Their next slogan "Let's Make Things Better" finally hit the bull's eye and was used for nine years. Today, the company uses "Sense and Simplicity" as a tagline.

Slogans or taglines can be either **descriptive or abstract**. In both cases they should be phrased very carefully and exactly in order to be highly memorable. The most important thing when choosing a slogan is not to lose sight of the brand essence and values. The brand slogan moreover can contribute significantly to the clear and successful positioning of the brand. If a tagline fails to be directly linked to the brand and the company that sells it, it is simply worthless. Usually, slogans have a shorter life span than the brand name and logo since they are more susceptible to marketplace and lifestyle changes.[45]

What's Your Brand Story?

Storytelling has become more and more important in corporate life, even in B2B markets. As a concept, it even has won a decisive foothold in the debate on how brands of the future will be shaped. Many marketers though still think of **storytelling** as a wishy-washy device reserved for PR and advertising executives. The insight that storytelling can really make a difference, in an industrial context, is still lacking conspicuously.[46] If you want your brand to be really special you need to have a story, some **kind of legend** about how you got started, for instance. In the case of *FedEx*, it is about a young, ambitious student whose idea for a specialized overnight delivery business did not at all impress his professor at Yale. He actually got only a "C" on his term paper, which outlined this concept. An important aspect of storytelling hence can be to celebrate the history of a business if there is something interesting and relevant.

Hewlett-Packard celebrates the work of its founders, Bill Hewlett and Dave Packard, who started in a small garage to develop their innovative instruments. In that garage they initiated the innovative spirit of *HP*. The corporate communication uses this story about the garage today to demonstrate the spirit of innovation within the whole corporation.

Michelin

Another way to get the emotional aspect of a brand story transferred is the use of symbols in form of mascots. The most famous story is probably the story of the *Michelin Man*. In 1898, André Michelin commissioned the creation of this jolly, rotund figure after his brother, Édouard, observed that a column of tires piled high resembled a human form. The sketches of a bloated man made of tires by the illustrator O'Galop was exactly what the brothers had in mind.

One ad, in particular, that pictures the character lifting a beer glass and shouting, "Nunc est bibendum! (It's time to drink!)" seemed to fit extraordinarily well. A clever association between this Latin verse from the poet Horace, the cartoon character and the piles of tires

Fig. 21. The *Michelin Man*[47]

gives rise to the new slogan *"Michelin* tires drink obstacles" and the *Michelin Man* with a goblet of nails and glass in his hand replacing the beer bottle. This ingenious and witty combination embodied everything the company stood for at that time and still stands for today.

Today, the *Michelin Man* is one of the world's oldest and most recognized trademarks. It represents *Michelin* in over 150 countries and the story is told in many truck stops around the world. This example clearly shows that a brand story should not be about lofty, business talk describing what a company is all about. It is rather about **telling something essential** about it in a way that all stakeholders (from employees to shareholders) can really relate to. This means that it also could be a story about how a business handled a certain crisis, even if there is actually no 'Hollywood Happy End' to it.[48]

Penske

In a similar way, the brand of *Penske Corporation* is loaded with the spirit and the stories of Roger Penske. *Penske Corp.* is a closely held transportation services company that encompasses retail automotive sales and services, truck leasing, supply chain logistics management, transportation components manufacturing, and high-performance racing. "Racing is about intensity, decisiveness, organization and execution," says Roger S. Penske, Chairman and company founder of *Penske Corporation* and *Penske Racing, Inc.* "These metrics have been the baseline for *Penske Corporation* and its subsidiaries, and are the reason that racing is the common thread throughout our organization. *Quicken Loans* products and services can improve the home owning environment for our employees and fans."[49]

Domino's Pizza

There is an interesting story about a *Domino's Pizza* outlet that was in danger of running out of pizza dough due to an unusually busy afternoon. The local manager alarmed the national Vice President of Distribution for the United States, explaining the situation. With the imminent public embarrassment in mind that would assail on them if one of *Domino's* outlets failed to deliver as promised, the vice president jumped into action. He arranged everything in his power to avoid a mishap: A private jet, full of *Domino's* special deep pan dough was dispatched immediately. Unfortunately, all their efforts were in vain. Even the private jet did not get there on time, and many hungry customers were sent home hungry and disappointed on that night at *Domino's Pizza*. During the following month all employees went to work wearing black mourning bands.[50]

As mentioned above, **happy endings** are not necessarily required. What is important in this story is the significance the company places on its ability to deliver on what it is promising its customers. After all, their brand is built on their huge commitment to this promise. This story gives employees a very clear idea of what their brand values are, resonating strongly throughout the organization. Customers on the other hand can see what promise lies at the heart of the *Domino's* brand.

A **brand story can be extremely powerful** because it is a big part of the brand itself. A brand does do not only offer inspiration and optimism, it also preserves and enhances its heritage thereby motivating customers, employees, and everyone else related to the brand.[51] The true power of a good brand story lies in the depth, credibility and punchy message that it provides to all stakeholders. The story makes it easier for everyone related to believe in the corporate vision and mission. Therefore, the brand story needs to give a clear and relevant picture of what the business is about.[52]

3.2   Brand Communication

Never promise more than you can perform.

Publilius Syrus, first century Roman author

Because of its targeted nature, it is usually much less costly to implement a branding strategy for B2B companies than for businesses in the B2C market. The content of B2B brand communications is also different compared to B2C. The primary purpose of B2C content is to create awareness and and an emotional experience that leads to brand preference, while B2B content serves important practical and pragmatic functions. Communicating too many complex details about the company though should be avoided, as this would leave the reader with information indigestion. The communication tools should ideally focus on the advantages of a product or service as well as the explicit needs that are being met by the offer. These needs can include reducing costs, time, overheads, improving productivity and/or quality, for instance, increasing flexibility and expandability.[53]

Assuming that your customers and prospects as well as the press are as interested in and as knowledgeable about your product, or even your product category, as you are, can lead to misguided communication efforts. Customers are not interested in the product itself, they usually are interested in a **solution of their problems**. Before a company can come up with a customized solution that highlights and promotes any kind of specific capabilities the company may have, you have to uncover the explicit needs of the customers. Yet, many companies in the B2B realm still inundate prospective customers with volumes of paper expounding their competencies and capabilities.[54]

In B2B, especially when applying a corporate brand strategy, effective segmentation and targeting is key. Information that is important to your investors is usually not likely to motivate your prospects. A company with a diversified spectrum of products and services has to acknowledge that different target groups often value different benefits. One communication strategy rarely fits all.

Also, participants in a B2B buying centre will vary in their involvement and motivation in the decision-making process. Consequently, it is unlikely that all members of the buying centre will be equally interested in the same brand values. The selling strategies employed by companies in business markets should be underpinned by a clear understanding of the information processing that occurs as B2B purchasers make their decisions. While the nature of many industrial products and markets may call for an emphasis on functional brand values there is a need to recognize that organizational purchasers can still be influenced by emotional considerations such as trust, security, and peace of mind.[55]

An **emotional stimulus** may even be the means through which marketers can gain attention for the presentation of other functional brand values. From a seller's perspective, brand value communication that demonstrates an understanding of the psychological concerns of industrial buyers can be a powerful source of differentiation in markets dominated by a focus on functionality.[56] Brand communication that does not recognize the value attached to intangible brand elements by different buying centre members may undermine the sales process leading to failure. Successful B2B brand communication requires sales strategies that **incorporate brand values** to appeal to the social and psychological as well as the rational concerns of the different organizational buyers involved.

For setting up an appropriate communication strategy it is essential to concisely know who your message is meant for. The solution is to adopt a holistic perspective that takes into consideration that B2B encounters are **complex interactions** affected by multiple players. Such a holistic marketing perspective requires external, internal, and interactive marketing, as shown by the Branding Triangle in Figure 22 below. It clearly illustrates the intersecting relationships of the three most important market participants: company, customer and collaborators (employees, partners). External marketing relates to the regular work of pricing, distributing, and promoting of products and services to customers. Internal marketing describes all actions that train and motivate collaborators to become true brand ambassadors. External and internal communication efforts are directly

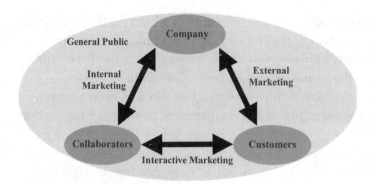

Fig. 22. The branding triangle

affected by the company while interactive marketing is primarily affected by internal marketing activities.

Figure 22 aims at showing the equivalent importance of all three communication approaches. It is no longer enough to merely rely on external marketing efforts if you want to establish a successful brand. Yet, there are still many industrial companies that do not **effectively communicate their brand essence and values internally to their employees**. If no one takes the time to explain the effect of the brand, especially the brand promise, to employees, branding efforts are in most cases doomed to failure. It is essential to realize the internal implications and develop internal brand programs and trainings to educate collaborators on what the brand represents, where the company is going with its brand, and what steps need to be taken to get there.[57] **Holistic marketing** is of utmost importance in the service sector, where customer loyalty and constant service quality depend on a host of variables.

Because B2B encounters are complex interactions affected by multiple elements, adopting a holistic perspective is highly important. Such a holistic marketing perspective requires external, internal, and interactive marketing, as previously shown by the Branding Triangle. Today, it is no longer sufficient to merely rely on external marketing efforts. Nonetheless, there are many industrial companies that do not effectively communicate their brand essence and values

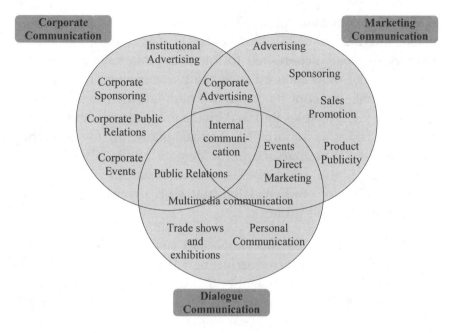

Fig. 23. Tools and interfaces of the corporate, marketing and dialogue communication[58]

internally. The following chapter is dedicated to show and emphasize the importance of motivating and empowering your employees – transforming them into true brand ambassadors.

Another way to classify the brand communication strategy is to set the focus on the general purpose of the respective communication efforts. Accordingly, you can subdivide it into **corporate communication**, **marketing communication**, and **dialogue communication**. Depending on whether this focus lies on the corporation itself, its products or services, or personal contacts communication requires different approaches and instruments. Figure 23 illustrates selected instruments and interfaces of the different communication alternatives.

Many of these instruments can be used for either purpose. Internal marketing for instance is important for all of them. As indicated above in the Branding Triangle it is of major importance to communicate corporate and brand values to your employees. The **success**

of dialogue communication efforts is usually contingent upon effective internal communication. Dialogue communication, on the contrary, is closely connected to interactive Marketing. However, this is not the only connection of the two concepts. If a business wants to make most of its communication efforts, it has to act according to the principles imposed by the branding triangle. Internal marketing is just as important as external marketing for generating effective interactive marketing. The general public is the "world" surrounding it and can never be ignored or considered irrelevant. An efficient brand communication strategy is always based on what the branding triangle imposes.

Consistency is one of the most important aspects of a brand strategy. This should also be respected accordingly when creating a communication strategy. The brand identity that the company wants to communicate has to transverse all marketing materials and communications in order to build brand equity in the intended way.

Brand-Building Tools

Brand building tools are the means of marketing communication by which companies aim to inform, persuade, and remind customers – directly or indirectly – about its products and brands. In a way, they act as the "voice" of the brand and **create a platform to establish a dialog and build relationships** with customers. The brand building tools are not fundamentally different in B2C and B2B areas. The marketing communications program is made up of the same major modes of communication:[59]

- Personal Selling
- Direct Marketing
- Public Relations
- Trade Shows and Exhibitions
- Advertising
- Sales Promotion

However, priorities typically vary significantly. In B2B markets, the focus is typically set on the first one – personal selling. But understanding the concept of "brand" as **holistic experience** also conveys that "everything matters". Therefore, all elements in the marketing communications mix are potential tools for building brand equity. They contribute to brand equity in manifold ways: by creating awareness of the brand; linking the desired associations to the brand image; eliciting positive brand judgments or emotions, and/or facilitating a stronger customer-brand relationship.[60]

Personal Selling

Face-to-face interaction with one or more prospective customers for the main purpose of obtaining orders is generally called personal selling. In business markets it is by far more common to serve business customers directly than in consumer markets. Due to the rather restricted number of customers and prospects in B2B markets, personal selling is the norm. It is individualized communications tailored and adapted to the particular needs of the customers. At the same time, it is the primary driver in building effective long-term business relationships, based on close personal interactions and a profound product and market knowledge of the sales representatives. It is the most expensive communications method.[61]

To fully realize the potential of B2B brands, effective communication of brand values is essential. In most B2B markets, the primary form of brand communication is through a company's own sales force. As the direct link between the buying and selling organization, the communication skills and abilities of the sales staff play a key role in determining the way in which brand values are experienced by customers.[62]

In addition to restricted number of customers, business customers tend to buy larger quantities and require technical support. Altogether, these factors represent a powerful economic incentive for businesses to market their offerings directly to customers. Direct channels therefore are both practical and cost effective, facilitated by popular direct marketing tools like catalogs, e-mail ordering systems, and e-business. *Cisco Systems*, for instance, has built its entire business around its Global Networked Business (GNB) model – a direct Internet-based channel.

Personal selling is an important brand building tool because everything involved in it actually affects how the brand is perceived by customers. The appearance and manner of the salesperson is just as important as their factual knowledge about the products and services. Every brand contact communicates something to customers and thereby delivers a certain impression about the brand and/or the company that can be either positive or negative.[63]

Direct Marketing

Direct marketing tools include the use of direct mail, telemarketing, fax, e-mail, newsletter, catalog, internet, and others to **communicate directly** with specific customers and prospects. Other definitions of direct marketing already include personal selling as tool which we discussed separately. Direct marketing tools provide companies with several attractive ways of conveying customized messages to individuals. They usually contain up-to-date information because preparation time can be neglected. While being instantly applicable, they need to be integrated into the long-term corporate brand message.

The use of direct marketing tools has been constantly growing over the last two decades. This is partly due to **technological advances** of new and improved direct marketing channels but has also to do with the decline in effectiveness of the conventional marketing tools such as advertising. Direct marketing is a tool which allows marketers to reduce wasteful communication to non-target customers or customer groups.[64]

A direct marketing tool that has experienced a major take-off in the last decade is **electronic shopping**. In the B2B context dot-com sites such as *Grainger.com* or auction portals such as *COVISINT* or *SupplyOn* are becoming more and more important. Interactive messaging via CD-ROMs or mini-CDs – sometimes even linked to online portals or web sites – have become increasingly affordable and effective means to market directly.

Among the benefits of direct marketing tools are the special possibilities to adapt and personalize the messages conveyed. They facilitate the establishment of **continuous customer relationships**.
They are moreover among the most cost-effective tools because
marketers can measure success according to customer response for
each campaign.

For direct marketing tools it is also very important to achieve consistency of the **brand appearance**. Brand building through direct
marketing is only achieved if customers' expectations are met by
the brand performance. Therefore, listening and responding to customer feedback regarding positive and negative experiences is important.

Public Relations

Public relations (PR) are about generating coverage in the media
that reaches various stakeholder groups. It involves a variety of
programs designed to promote or protect the image of your brand.
Well-thought out programs coordinated with the other communications elements can be extremely effective. Their appeal lies mainly
in the higher credibility of news stories and features, especially
compared to advertising. Because of their **authenticity** they are
more credible to readers. PR can moreover reach potential customers that tend to avoid salespeople and advertisements.[65]

Many B2B marketers tend to under use PR or even misuse it by
splashing the budget of their PR program on the walls of editors'
offices with news releases. Most publications still receive too many
news releases from various companies every day. You can probably
count on one hand how many of them are used at the end of the
day. If they do make coverage by the media however, brands can
gain significant attention from **well-placed newspapers** and
magazine stories.

Effective public relations have to be managed carefully by continuously monitoring the attitudes of customers and all other groups
that have an actual or potential interest in your company. Without

having to pay for the space or time obtained in the media, PR can affect brand awareness at only a fraction of the cost of other communications elements. An interesting story, picked up by the media can be worth millions of dollars in equivalent advertising.[66]

In their 2002 book *The Fall of Advertising & the Rise of PR*, Al and Laura Ries attribute the principal success of the high-tech industry to successful public relations. They point out that PR is most effective at building brands while advertising is particularly adept for maintaining already-built brands. **High-tech companies** like *Microsoft*, *Intel*, *SAP*, *Cisco*, and Oracle are illustrations of companies that built their initial identities via PR before spending big bucks on ad campaigns.[67]

The reason PR is so effective in brand building is because it delivers credibility. With limited resources, PR delivers the most bang for the buck while also delivering the highest level of credibility. PR builds brands by building positive, pervasive word of mouth. PR is one of the most effective ways to get people talking about your brand and it gets them moreover believing. PR therefore is most effective at building and sustaining your business.

Trade Shows and Exhibitions

Trade shows and exhibitions are of major importance in the B2B environment. They represent a great opportunity for businesses to build brand awareness, knowledge, and interest at one place at a time. They also provide customers with access to many **potential suppliers** and **customers** in a short period time at relatively low costs compared to regular information gathering methods. Customers can easily compare competitive offerings at one place. In Europe and Japan, trade shows and exhibitions can attract up to tens of thousands of active and informed business marketers from all functions. Germany, for instance, provides four of the ten largest exhibition locations in the world. There are trade fair grounds (Messe) in over 20 German cities. In a year, over 130 international and national trade fairs take place in Germany. More than 140,000 exhibitors come to display their products. About 45% exhibitors are from foreign countries. Asian exhibitors form about 15% of total foreign exhibitors. The German trade fairs attract about 9 million visitors, of which over 1.5 million come from outside Germany.

Amphenol-Tuchel Electronics

A common mistake that B2B companies make is to create tradeshow booths without a demonstrable message to show and without integration of their branding efforts. *Amphenol-Tuchel Electronics*, for instance, did not leave anything to chance when preparing for the Electronica 2004 in Munich. Electronica is one of the most **important international trade shows** of the electronic industry covering the sectors electrical engineering, electronics, trade (distributors), telecommunications, engineering, service-providers, software technology, and data processing. The company *Amphenol-Tuchel Electronics* is an independent company within *Amphenol Corporation*. It is one of the leading companies engaged in the development, production, and marketing of a variety of electrical and electronic connectors (see Figure 24 for a current *Amphenol* campaign).

Fig. 24. *Fly Higher* campaign of *Amphenol*

In order to provide a unique picture of their company *Amphenol* assigned an agency to assist with the trade show and communications concept including slogan, newsletter and customer invitations. The result was the successful *Fly Higher* campaign. As mentioned above – nothing was left to chance – from the determination of target figures, multi-layer invitation concept, special training of the trade booth personnel, consistent planning of trade show program, up to the completely integrated pre- and post processing of all related actions and processes with final ROI-examination. The success of the detailed marketing concept was doubtless confirmed by the huge success of the company's trade show participation and consequent increases in sales.

Lapp Cable

Another example of B2B branding, also from the electronic industry, is provided by the *Lapp Cable* company. *Lapp* is a family-run business with headquarters in Stuttgart-Vaihingen. The *Lapp Cable* company is part of the *Lapp* group with more than 50 companies, around 60 agencies and approx. 2,600 employees. As one of the leading suppliers worldwide for wires and cables, cable accessories, industrial connectors, and communication technology they presented themselves at the *Hannover Fair* 2004. Their trade show slogan was to "Get in Contact" which was quite intriguingly depicted in a short slow-motion movie. The quite emotional short film showed different scenes of contact being made, with the aim to create a metaphorical connection to the actual products of the company (as can be seen in Figure 25).[68]

Fig. 25. Sample pictures of the *Lapp* trade show movie

Sponsoring

Sponsorships of public events such as world-famous bicycle and car races are quite common for B2B brands. Corporate goals for sponsorship can be: increase revenue, create a platform for developing relationships, and provide an opportunity to entertain customers in a unique environment as well as to generate benefits for employees. *FedEx* is a company that uses sponsoring quite intensely. While many companies merely try to increase brand awareness by sponsoring famous events, *FedEx* sponsorships are focused on driving business, not awareness. It even integrates the sponsorships throughout the marketing mix, not the other way round. Certain events are used as content useable in media, promotions, employee incentives, and online. Examples include National Football League (NFL)-themed promotions, Orange Bowl-flavored retail incentives, and Professional Golf Association (PGA)-related TV spots.[69]

Master Yachting

Another example of B2B sponsoring is provided by Master Yachting. In August 2005 the charter company of first class yachts started sponsoring the *Eichin Racing Teams* at the German *Porsche Carrera Cup*. The yacht charter agency from Wuerzburg, Germany, is pioneering in this respect because this is the first time that a German yacht agency has become involved in motor sports. The overall goal of the sponsorship is to arouse interest in the direct environment of the *Porsche* team and of companies who have a stake in motor sports. This kind of B2B Marketing is quite successful since more **and more companies are discovering the appeal of yachting** as a customer drawing event for their own promotion. The feedback of Master Yachting's sponsorship thus soon exceeded their own expectations. For the future they are even considering a Formula One sponsorship.[70]

Bearing Point

BearingPoint, one of the world's largest business consulting and systems integration firms, announced in 2005 that reigning Masters

Champion Phil Mickelson has signed a three-year contract with the company and will continue to wear the *BearingPoint* brand on the front of his headwear during tournament play and other promotions. Mickelson will also continue to speak on behalf of Bearing-Point at various promotional and client events.

UBS

Another example is *UBS*. The Swiss bank was pleased to renew its partnership with the Ravinia Festival in Chicago as lead sponsor, apparently looking forward to another summer of beautiful music under the leadership of Ravinia's new Music Director James Conlon. The list of innovative sponsorships could go on and on; municipalities like the City of Chicago investing in advertisement airtime with CNN or, a tour of the Chicago blues nightlife for visiting business persons. In all these cases it is necessary to measure the effort, the purpose and success to justify any B2B promotion.

Advertising

For many people it seems that the majority of today's advertising has lost its sense of purpose. In order to grab attention or to get noticed, many TV commercials and print advertisements tend to emphasize the fun and entertaining part, thus the exerpiential side of their products and services.[71] Sometimes it seems to be the only purpose of the message. In these cases very little awareness of a corporation or brand is being raised. Many marketers criticize that this trend is misleading if it remains "on the surface" as a mere advertising approach. We also are of the opinion that every advertisement needs to have a clear message behind it that is clearly connected to the offerings; otherwise it doesn't really make sense to advertise in a way that is not reflected in the product or service.

The best way is to find a compromise between factual information and **emotional appeal**. Advertising is most effective for reinforcing the brand foundation of an already existing brand. The customer needs to be informed, and when this cannot be accomplished

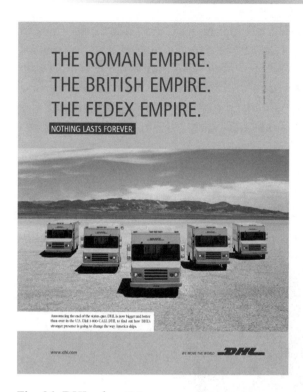

Fig. 26. *DHL* advertising campaign

through your sales people due to their limited reach, the company has to get the message out through mass marketing. But here the dilemma starts: mass marketing is very costly and we know every cent counts. Only a few large corporations can afford to reach the minds of all potential customers through mass marketing in most cases, this is justified by the pull they create from private customers on their own B2B customers, as exemplified by *Deutsche Post* in their attempt to change to the new international brand name *DHL* (see Figure 26).

Fortunately, there is another mean of advertising available that is less costly. **Specialized Press** is a good option to utilize in the B2B area. For the same reasons every industry has trade magazines and journals. PR, product information and advertisement could be combined in them, and most importantly, circulation to a **selected audience** can be controlled. This means maximum and instant results from your investment in the marketing communication budget.

The following ad was designed for the McGraw-Hill Companies in 1958, and is considered one of the most effective and influential works in the genre. The *The Man in the Chair* ad has not lost an inch of its timeliness and relevance and still makes the compelling case in the value of B2B advertising in the sales cycle. In 1999, the ad was recognized as the number one B2B ad of all time by Business Marketing (see Figure 27).

"I don't know who you are.
I don't know your company.
I don't know your company's product.
I don't know what your company stands for.
I don't know your company's customers.
I don't know your company's record.
I don't know your company's reputation.
Now—what was it you wanted to sell me?"

MORAL: Sales start **before** your salesman calls—with business publication advertising.

McGRAW-HILL MAGAZINES
BUSINESS•PROFESSIONAL•TECHNICAL

Fig. 27. *The Man in the Chair* ad[72]

One of the main goals of B2B communication is to provide customers specific, possibly technical information about one's products and services. A great example for a company that started thinking outside the traditional B2B box is the *Covad Communications Group*. Founded in 1996, it is now a leading nationwide provider of broadband voice and data communication for small and medium size businesses as well as a key supplier of high-speed Internet access for competitive voice and Internet services providers. *Covad* owns and operates the only nationwide DSL broadband network in the United States. Already three years after its foundation their network reached more than 40% of U.S. homes and businesses.

A creative and quite **intriguing advertisement** of VoIP (Voice over IP) was launched in early September 2004. Based on a "Who Dunnit?" theme, the initial 30 second ad creates a buzz around a police case, three suspects and *Covad VoIP*. The appeal of *Covad*'s approach of marketing its B2B offering lies in the fact that they do not take themselves too seriously. At first the ad keeps viewers in the dark about its actual content, surprising them at the end with a savvy solution. Endorsed by their own website www.voipthemovie.com the entertaining TV ads can be viewed at any time. The print advertising of *Covad* also combines relevant communication with twists of humor as Figure 28 illustrates.[73]

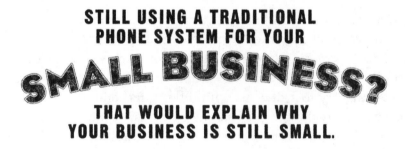

Fig. 28. *Covad* advertising[74]

By the same means *Intel* is **using celebrities** to boost its presence in the mind of their customers. As we know already, for *Intel*, it is not only the limited numbers of members of the buying center of B2B companies that are of interest to them; they would also like to address the mass customer to create pull. In the light of their **ingredient branding concept**, they are now stressing the corporate brand as the key message for potential customers, and using celebrities to spread the news (as shown in Figure 29).

Fig. 29. *Intel* print advertising campaign[75]

Sales Promotion

Sales promotions are incentives of various kinds that are used to increase the value of a **market offering over a specified period of time**. Its usual purpose is to encourage trial or increased usage of a product or service. As consumers we are surrounded by a myriad of products that try to seduce us with little "gifts" and other "add-ons" to have us make the purchase. In B2B this concept usually does not work since buyers of industrial companies only purchase what the company really needs.

In contrast to consumer promotion, trade promotions are targeted at retailers, distributors, and other members of the trade channel. They often come in the form of financial incentives or discounts with the purpose of securing shelf space and distribution for a new brand. Business and sales-force promotion at trade shows, for instance, can be made up by special contests for sales representatives or similar actions.[76]

3.3 Brand Evaluation

The key issue in any marketing investment decision is how much value it provides to the company. Whether it is pricing, distribution, research, or branding, the investment put into operation must pay off. While it is rather easy to **measure success** related to pricing or distribution channels, it is more complicated to measure the success of brands. Nonetheless, a brand is too valuable an asset to manage without the support and guidance of brand metrics.

It is essential to measure brands in a way that is linked to financial performance. In this way, marketers can gain an edge in navigating their brands in the right future-oriented directions. Many companies focus merely on lagging indicators when it comes to measure brand performance. Such a perspective can not only lead to delayed adaptation to certain trends and changes in the markets, it can also harm the brand itself. Brand metrics are critical to provide a quantifiable link to assess possible solutions to new problems and questions.[77]

Although the value of a brand cannot be measured precisely, it is important to **establish estimates** that provide a frame of reference when developing brand building programs and budgets.[78] Some marketers regard brand equity measurement and brand valuation as equal although they need to be distinguished from each other. Over the last two decades a vast number of brand evaluation models have been developed.[79] Most of them fall into the following categories:[80]

- **Research-Based Evaluations** – Brand equity measurement is a behavioral approach that does put a financial value on brands. They measure customer behavior and attitudes that have an impact on the brands. The perceptual brand metrics include awareness (unaided, aided, and top of mind), knowledge, familiarity, relevance, satisfaction and recommendation.

- **Financially-Driven Approaches** – Brand valuation is used to estimate the total financial value of a brand. The estimation of the financial value of a brand is partially based on subjective judgments of knowledgeable people in an organization. It usually involves straightforward logic. First, you have to identify the earnings stream of each major market carrying the brand. Those are then divided according to the following criteria: those attributable to the brand, to the fixed assets, and to other intangibles. After capitalizing the earnings attributable to the brand, you get the estimate value for that brand in the product market. It is especially important for companies that base their growth on acquiring and building diversified brand portfolios. The usual way is to subtract the book value from the market value and attribute the difference to brand equity.

Table 3. *Interbrand* ranking of the world's most valuable B2B brands 2005[81]

Rank	Brand	Rank	Brand
2	Microsoft	33	Morgan Stanley
3	IBM	34	J.P. Morgan
4	General Electric	36	SAP
5	Intel	43	Novartis
6	Nokia	45	Siemens
13	Hewlett-Packard	51	Accenture
27	Oracle	54	Xerox
29	HSBC	70	Caterpillar
32	UPS	74	Reuters

Brand measurement approaches should try to embrace both types of measures.[82] Table 3 displays the world's most valuable B2B brands in 2005 according to *Interbrand*.

3.4   Brand Specialties

So far we covered all basic issues related to B2B brand management, but there are still some aspects that are of special importance that need to be examined separately. This part is dedicated to those aspects that have the power to make your branding efforts even more successful.

In the industrial world, where rational purchasing decisions tend to be the rule, human factors can also play a critical role in **differentiating products and services** from the competition. Even if your company sells so-called "commodities", the human factor is often an unexploited element that could strengthen your competitive position. At the end of the day, all business transactions involve people selling product and service solutions to solve other people's problems.

Living the Brand

What is it that makes a brand successful? Put your brand effectively into operation and become a **brand-driven organization**! More B2B companies are coming to the realization that they need to differentiate themselves, not only through the technical performance of their products, but also through the services they offer (logistics, invoicing, product claims, and other after-sales services) and consequently through the behavior and actions of their own people. In Japan, for example, *Canon* insists on having its repair people wear a white shirt and a tie. The white shirts help reinforce the perception that *Canon's* photocopiers are truly user friendly and easy to service. *Canon's* senior management believes that employees are critical to the B2B customers brand experience and that no one will sound as convincing as sales or repair people who are truly passionate about their products and about what they do.

Employees' attitude (both in the front line and in the back office) plays a critical role in influencing customer trust and corporate reputation. For instance, at *Hitachi Metals*, senior management considers that answering phone calls from customers promptly and nurturing a knowledgeable and courteous staff is as important as turning out flawless products from the steel mills.

Starting from the inside, a strong internal brand delivers very real business returns. There is a strong correlation between employee understanding of brand values and productivity, the advocacy of the organization and the standard of customer service they deliver. It has also been found that companies where staff understands organizational goals enjoy a 24% greater shareholder return[83]. The reasons for this are simple. A strong, clear, and well-defined brand gives focus to employees, motivates them and provides a compass to them. A brand that is understood by all employees helps guide them through most decision processes which they have to go through in their daily work. A strong internal brand is also one of the most important prerequisites to being able to build a strong external brand since it is the employees who make the brand com "alive". They are not just a means to keep your business up and running – **they are the company.** And they represent what your brand is all about.

Caterpillar

Caterpillar is a great example of a company that fosters the brand mentality of its employees and seeks to protect the presentation of their brand in every possible aspect. Because people recognize CAT by the distinctive look of their design, trademarks, logos, and the distinct color, the company sets a strong focus on brand protection. Employees and partners have to stick to a set of usage guidelines and standards that aim to protect the value of the *Caterpillar* brand. Dealers are actively involved in *Caterpillar's* product quality, cost reduction, and manufacturing improvement efforts. Nowadays, *Caterpillar's* division in the US and Canada supports a network of 63 dealers in both countries. The CAT dealers play an important role in providing customers with a wide range of services before and after the sale. These services include advice on the selection and application of a product, financing, insurance, operator training, maintenance, and repair.[84]

Most *Caterpillar* dealers have a very **strong relationship with** the parent company and identify themselves with CAT. They totally live and love the brand. True love for the brand based on mutual respect and trust is demonstrated extraordinarily in the case of *Caterpillar*.

Caterpillar serves its dealers in more than one way by providing them with literally everything they need – from service to technical training and advanced career opportunities. Since the purchasing experience and service provided by *Caterpillar* dealers accounts for the most important part of the CAT brand experience, the company does everything to assure excellence in that area. Considering the longevity of the machines it is selling, maintenance, repair, and service are of major importance.

The "Partners in Quality Program", for instance, links personnel responsible for building a particular machine with selected dealers. These people meet every three months as a team to discuss quality issues. Dealers also audit each *Caterpillar* machine they receive, and if anything is wrong, they feed that information back to the plant immediately so that corrections can be made. As an illustration, a dealer discovered that hoses in a new grader model had been installed incorrectly and immediately notified the factory. *Caterpillar* retrained the assembler, fixed the machines still in the factory, and notified other dealers to repair the machines in their inventories. In another case, *Caterpillar's* dealer in Thailand concluded that a pump in a new line of hydraulic excavators was not durable enough to meet local working conditions. The dealership persuaded *Caterpillar* to use a different pump on the machines until engineers could redesign the one in question.[85]

Find Role Models for Your Brand

There are several ways organizations can empower and motivate their employees. Consider as a B2C example *Wal-Mart's* tactic: Every morning, in every *Wal-Mart* all over the world, employees and managers are shouting the following cheer: "Give me a W! Give me an A! Give me an L! Give me a Squiggly! Give me an M! Give me an A! Give me an R! Give me a T! What's that spell? *Wal-Mart*! Whose *Wal-Mart* is it? My *Wal-Mart*! Who's number one? The Customer! Always!"[86] But we have similar programs seen in successful B2B companies: Among the most notable is *GE's WorkOut* – the initiative pioneered by Jack Welch in the late 1980s. After more than 20 years *WorkOut* still remains ingrained in the *GE* culture[87].

He also dubbed *Six Sigma*, this **total quality initiative** pioneered by *Motorola* in the 80's.

Programs, stories, events, or people that positively represent the brand identity are very important internal role models that can support you in transforming your employees into **true brand ambassadors**. Brand stories can be an effective tool to build a brand. A great story has the power to strengthen a brand both internally and externally. It can communicate the values and identity of a brand, while adding elements of aspiration and emotion. A story can deliver three times more information than a bulleted list. Moreover, a story can be rich and unambiguous, qualities that a bulleted list usually lacks. People can also be powerful role models. A charismatic founder or a strong, visible CEO with a clear brand vision can provide credibility as well as clarity to the brand. The continued use of a visible spokesperson who becomes closely connected to the brand, can also personalize the brand.[88]

Bosch

A very good example of an internal mission statement is provided by *Robert Bosch GmbH*, the largest automotive supplier in the world, and its initiative *BeQIK, BeBetter, BeBosch*. It communicates the core values of the brand to employees. *BeQIK* stands for their commitment to exceed customer expectations in the future. The name comprises the aspects Q for quality, I for innovation and K for customer focus. *BeBetter* is meant to reflect the reliability and stability, while *BeBosch* aims at evoking pride. *Bosch's* corporate statement is aligned to empower, enthuse, and motivate their employees.[89]

Especially in large, multi-national companies it is important to assure that the internal communication and knowledge management are effective and precise. To establish an Intranet where employees can gather specific information **fast** and **trouble-free** has become quite common practice in past years. But whether and to what extent they really use and more importantly find the relevant information is another question. When *Bosch* introduced the new *Bosch* online portal for employees it didn't want to leave anything to chance and assigned an agency to assist in creating an internal communications concept.

In the first place, brand management means **communicating the values** of your brands to your own people; making sure that employees understand these values and thereby leading them to become the best ambassadors of your company and its products. Only then can you expect to **dramatically differentiate** your company from competitors in the eyes of your customers. A strong internal brand is very important since it actually translates into very real business returns. The reasons for this are quite simple. If the brand is clear and well-defined, it provides employees with the necessary focus, motivates them, and provides them with a certain position in regard to the many decisions which they have to make in the workplace (see Figure 30 for details).

Fig. 30. Degree of employee motivation

Branding Inside

Ingredient branding – or short InBranding[90] – is one of the most promising branding strategies for B2B companies. Generally, it is exactly what the name implies: an essential ingredient or component of a product that has its own brand identity.

Ingredient branding is a special form of **co-branding** – the joint presence of at least two or more brands on a single product or service. The scope of possible co-branding approaches can range from a mere joint promotional effort up to the organizational linked development of completely new and innovative products. The regular co-branding approach is mainly used for consumer products and services; application in B2B tends to be quite restricted. An example of industrial co-branding is the joint venture of *Pitney Bowes* and *Royal*

Mail, to offer customized document management and mailroom-related services in the UK as well as the alliance of *Amazon.de* with *DHL* in order to benefit from the positive image of the partner.[91]

Examples of popular **ingredient branding** range from clothing (*Gore-Tex, Lycra*), carpets (*Stainmaster*), diet soft drinks (*NutraSweet*), and cooking utensils (*Teflon*) to bicycle gears (*Shimano*) and sound systems (*Dolby*) as well as gasoline and chemicals (*Techron, Microban*) promoting the inclusion of a value-enhancing, branded ingredient. Of course, we cannot leave out the ultimate, widely quoted best practice example of ingredient branding which we will consider in detail at the end of this chapter: *Intel*. In the following we will provide you with the basic information on how InBranding works and how to position it in the overall marketing concept.[92]

While Ingredient Branding is a form of **multi-stage branding,** most companies only use single-stage marketing approaches. They direct their marketing efforts only to the next stage in the value chain, to their direct customers. Multi-stage or Ingredient Branding is directed at two or more downstream stages of the value channel.

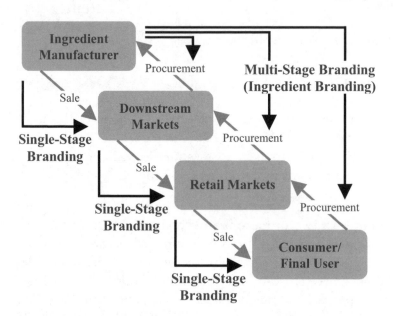

Fig. 31. Multi-stage branding

The basic underlying principle that makes ingredient branding work is the pull principle. According to the pull principle, the manufacturers of the ingredient brand direct their communication efforts directly to the final consumers, thereby bypassing the manufacturers of the finished product. The main idea is to create consumer demand for the ingredient at the retail level, so that they pull the product through the distribution channel, forcing middle stages to use this ingredient. In some very successful cases, the ingredient brand may even become the standard in the product category.

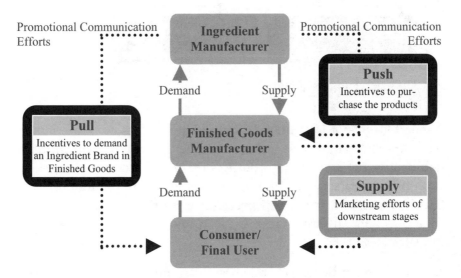

Fig. 32. Push/pull principle

Figure 32 displays the push/pull principle. A **push strategy** means that an ingredient manufacturer concentrates his marketing efforts on promoting his products to the manufacturers of the finished goods. In order to support the branded ingredient effectively, a manufacturer should always use a coordinated push and pull program. The **pull strategy** helps consumers to understand the importance and advantages of the InBrand while the push strategy aims to strive for full support by all channel members. Without the support of the following stages of the value chain, an ingredient branding strategy can rarely be successful.

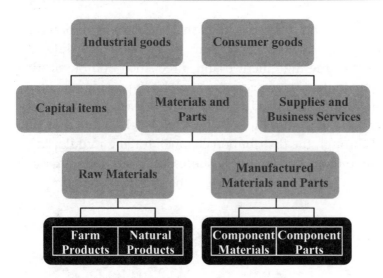

Fig. 33. General targets of ingredient branding

General targets of ingredient branding approaches are materials or parts that enter into final branded products, but lose their individual identity on the way. In order to step out of such an anonymous position, manufacturers attempt to **establish ingredient brands that increase awareness and preference for their products**. Figure 33 shows general targets in relation to the systematic approach of industrial goods.[93]

Not every ingredient can be successfully pushed or pulled. Does anybody really care about what kinds of lubes his favorite car brand uses in its manufacturing process? Not really. So it is obvious that there are certain requirements and restrictions that have to be taken into consideration when thinking about implementing an ingredient branding strategy. The most important aspect is that the "ingredient" should **capture an essential part of the end product**. *Intel* processors, for instance, are regarded as the "heart" of every personal computer. The ingredient should be perceived as important and relevant by consumers and thus, contribute to the performance and success of the end product. The InBrand has to be **clearly marked with a distinctive symbol or logo** on the end product. Consumers need to be aware that the respective product contains this ingredient.[94] Examples of Inbrands include:[95]

- **Farm Products**: *Chiquita, Del Monte, Dole, Sunkist*

- **Natural Products**: *Woolmark, Techron*

- **Component Materials**: *Gore-Tex, Nylon, Lycra, Teflon, Makrolon, NutraSweet*

- **Component Parts**: *Intel, Bosch, Keiper-Recaro, Shimano*

In addition brand alliances provide companies with a large number of potential advantages. By capturing two sources of brand equity, brand alliances can tremendously enhance the value proposition and points of differentiation of all products and services involved. With **equally strong and complementary brand associations** the impact of co-branding can be even greater than expected. Such beneficial synergy effects of combined brand power might also allow greater freedom to stretch.[96]

Quite often companies are confused about the difference of co-branding and ingredient branding. Many marketers even believe that there is no difference at all. The example of *Infineon Technologies* exemplifies this confusion. Until recently they used the term

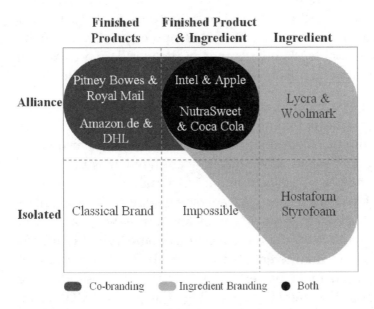

Fig. 34. Comparison of co-branding and inbranding

"co-branding" to ask their business partners "…to put the *Infineon Technologies* trademark onto a product and/or its package and user manuals to signalize that this product contents semiconductor solutions of *Infineon Technologies*."[97]

Such a presentation does leave the impression that co-branding and ingredient branding were identical. Today, you will still find quite different approaches to defining these strategies in the American and European marketing literature. We agree with the straightforward concept of Freter and Baumgarth whose definition of co-branding and ingredient branding is visualized in Figure 34. As shown by the black circle, a combination of both strategies exists.

Intel Inside

The *Intel Corporation* was not the first company that decided to brand the "essential ingredient" of an end product, nonetheless it is the most often quoted best practice example because of its huge and yet unparalleled success. The company is best known and most successful at Branding Inside. Today, the *Intel Inside®* logo is used by some 2700 PC manufacturers around the world, and consumer awareness is about 90 percent.[98] Their story describes the journey from being an anonymous supplier of computer parts to becoming an omnipotent top ten known-brands in the world, in a class with *Coca Cola*, *Disney* and *McDonald's*, according to various rankings.

Prior to the 1990s, before *Intel* started to brand their products, only the most sophisticated computer users knew what kind of micro processing chip their machines contained, let alone who made it. In Europe only 24 percent of PC buyers were familiar with the *Intel* brand. The company has spent hundreds of millions in the past 10 years to achieve their respective leadership positions. Within only a few years, *Intel* went from a completely **unknown component manufacturer** to one of **the most recognized and valuable brands in the world**.[99] In undifferentiated markets the first-mover advantage can be even more powerful for Ingredient Brands than for regular brands. The ingredient branding strategy by *AMD*, for instance, *Intel*'s main competitor met with dramatically less success.[100]

In 1989, *Intel* launched their first program aimed at marketing a microprocessor, the 386SX, to the Information Technology (IT) managers who purchased PCs for business. Although the program was very successful, several challenges quickly emerged, such as legal issues. *Intel* asserted that its 386 and 486 processors were protected trademarks and was fighting in court to protect them so that no other company could use them. Unfortunately, the courts decided otherwise, which opened the door for their competitors to use the well-known numeric at will.

Unimpressed by this set-back, the company immediately started to work on a new, improved and legally protectable branding strategy – a branding campaign that created history. At that time it was clearly an absolute novelty for a semiconductor company to market directly to the end user. As leading strategy the company studied successful consumer marketing techniques and examined tactics used by well-known companies supplying a component or ingredient of a finished product, like *NutraSweet™*, *Teflon™* and *Dolby™*. After a variety of marketing experiments the branded ingredient program in the computer industry slowly took shape. The **successful** *Intel Inside®* program was finally launched in 1991.

Of course, there can be no great brand without a great product. *Intel* clearly demonstrated this by investing billions of dollars in developing their cutting edge technology and billions more in assuring its performance and reliability. The main purpose of the *Intel Inside* program was to gain consumer confidence in *Intel* as a brand and to highlight the value of buying a microprocessor from the industry's leading company. It clearly wanted to differentiate itself from the pack of competitors' products that copied their numeric names for processors but failed to meet their implied performance requirements.[101]

The original tagline for the *Intel Inside* program was *Intel. The computer inside* which was shortened to *Intel Inside* later on. The tagline was aimed at underlining the important role of the microprocessor in the performance of the personal computer, while at the same time pushing desired associations of the *Intel* brand with respect to **"safety"**, **"leading technology"**, and **"reliability."** Besides, one of the main objectives of the campaign was to become the preferred choice, the number one among IT managers. But it also aimed at creating a pull from the consumers to deliberately demand *Intel* when purchasing a PC.[102]

A good communications program though is by far not enough to build a successful ingredient brand. InBranding, more than most other branding strategies, is contingent upon the cooperation of other stages in the value chain, especially the manufacturers of the end products. If they disapprove and counter the initiative, there is only very little chance to succeed. *Intel* was well aware of this and therefore **integrated a cooperative marketing program** in the *Intel Inside* campaign. This was basically an incentive-based cooperative advertising program. The benefits for the OEM's were clear. Not only could they reduce advertising costs for adding the *Intel* logo; it also acted as a sign of quality that their systems were powered by the latest technology.

The program was very successful. By the end of 1991, over 300 OEM's had signed cooperative agreements to support the program by using the promotional materials of the *Intel Inside* program. Approximately one third of these companies also agreed to feature the *Intel Inside* logo in their advertisements. The incentive of covering 50 percent of the advertising costs obviously worked out well. To finance these incentives, *Intel* **created matching funds** up to the maximum of 3 percent of its sales.

The innovative marketing program of *Intel* clearly helped boosting the awareness of the personal computer, thereby fueling consumer demand. By the late 1990s the vast success of the program was widely recognized and *Intel* had captured the place of a world-class player in the public consciousness. Today, the *Intel Inside* program is one of the world's largest co-operative marketing programs, supported by thousands of PC makers who are licensed to use the *Intel Inside* logos.[103]

Between 1990 and 1993, *Intel* invested over US$500 million in advertising and promotional programs designed to build its brand equity. Toward the end of that decade the marketing budget escalated to more than US$700 million annually. As we know, the **investment**

Fig. 35. The first *Intel Inside* ad

did pay off, so let's take a look at some actual numbers: *Intel* in creased its revenues six fold by 2000 (to US$33.7 billion) while its earnings almost doubled that rate of increase (to US$10.5 billion). The launch year of the program is the base year for this account.[104] According to *Interbrand*, *Intel* is ranked number five of the world's most valuable brands in 2005, with an estimated brand value of US$35.6 billion.[105]

The new way of the company is **to target opportunities outside its traditional PC revenue stream**. This means a move from *Intel Inside* to literally *Intel Everywhere* – every type of digital device possible shall be equipped with *Intel* chips. For that reason, *Apple* and its *iMac* computers were added to the list of *Intel* customers recently. Besides computers, *Intel's* target market now encompasses cell phones, flat-panel TVs, portable music and video players, wireless home networks, and even medical diagnostic gear. All in one, the company is targeting ten new product areas for its chips.[106]

Crystallized™ with Swarovski®

Swarovski, established more than 100 years ago, is the world's leading manufacturer and supplier of cut crystal. The company saga began in 1892, when founder Daniel Swarovski invented a **revolutionary machine**, which made it possible to industrially cut crystal jewelry stones to a superior level of perfection and precision than achieved before by traditional manual methods. Three years later, he founded the *Swarovski Company* in Wattens, Austria, which has remained fully independent ever since. The company is currently run by the fourth and fifth generation descendants of founder Daniel Swarovski. In 2004, 16,000 people worldwide contributed to a consolidated group turnover of €1.83 billion.

Swarovski is a globally recognized brand that has made innovation, trend research, creative products and product perfection its hallmarks. These are all perpetuated elements of the philosophy of the company's founder, Daniel Swarovski. His motto "to constantly improve what is good" and vision to "use crystal to bring joy to man" still form the core philosophy that drives the company today. *Swarovski* stands for **exacting workmanship, quality** and **creativity** all over the world.

Their product range comprises almost everything related to cut crystal: Crystal jewelry stones and crystal components as well as crystal objects, crystal jewelry, and crystal accessories. With the brands *Tyrolit* (grinding, cutting, sawing, drilling and dressing tools and machines), *Swareflex* (reflectors for road safety), *Signity* (genuine or synthetic gemstones), and *Swarovski Optik* (High-quality precision optical equipment) the company has also obtained leading market positions in related areas.

Swarovski covers both consumer and business customers with one brand. The corporate division of crystal components is one of the major B2B areas. *Swarovski* supplies crystal components and semi-finished products to the fashion, jewelry, interior design, and lighting industries. With a collection of more than 100,000 stones and a wide range of pre-fabricates, it is a competent partner for businesses that use cut crystal in their products.[107]

In 2004, the company introduced their ingredient branding strategy *A Brilliant Choice* in order to counter the increasing trend of selling anything that glitters and glimmers on clothing and accessories under the name *Swarovski*. This was the first time that the department of crystal components directed any **marketing activity directly at the end user**. The company thus created the label *Crystallized with Swarovski* in response to the demand for a visible proof of quality and origin. The quality label clearly represents a guarantee of the highest quality and perfection in the manufacture of crystalline products.

In the **complex shopping environment** of today consumers are confronted with an explosion of choices where strong brands can provide clear direction of what they stand for. Brands therefore can give consumers the important assurance that they have made the right decision. Since the label *Crystallized with Swarovski* is a symbol of quality and prestige for both *Swarovski's* business partners and for its consumers, it makes *Swarovski* products even more attractive and provides further arguments for the added value. Furthermore, the traditional and approved core competencies of *Swarovski* – innovation and diversity, product and service quality – are emphasized which further differentiates the brand from its competition.

Due to of the limited physical branding possibilities, the company decided to go its own way and designed special tags. Depending on the end product of fashion items, jewelry, accessories, and home décor the label can be a high-class silver metal, a silver-colored paper tag or sticker that testifies the authenticity of the *Swarovski* crystals. The *Crystallized with Swarovski* label is the customer's assurance that only *Swarovski* crystal products have been used in the production of the end product. To officially certify this assurance, each label carries a specific number certified by *Swarovski*.[108]

The ingredient brand was launched with a global advertising campaign at the end of 2004. Print ads in key fashion magazines such as *ELLE, InStyle, MarieClaire, Cosmopolitan, 24Ans,* and *TeenVogue* as well as promotional material, posters, and postcards displayed in stores were used to promote the new InBrand.[109]

Fig. 36. The *Crystallized™ with Swarovski®* label

Branding Online

An excellent example for a B2B website is the business communication platform of the *Swarovski Corporation*. While many companies only make distinctions within product or service categories, *Swarovski* established several websites to serve the respective customer needs properly. Fig. 38 shows the website solely dedicated to business customers.

Fig. 37. *Swarovski* business communication platform

It offers a lot of useful information but for detailed business information you have to request the clearing of a personalized account with user name and password.[110] Buyers who are interested in crystal components for the processing industry (fashion or lighting & interior) can get password protected access to all kinds of information about *Swarovski* products as well as latest news and trends in their respective areas.

In 1995, *Swarovski* celebrated its 100th anniversary. For this occasion the company commissioned the renowned artist André Heller to create Crystal Worlds – a sensual journey through the fascinating world of crystal in an artistic installation adjacent to the company headquarters in Wattens, Austria. With Crystal Worlds, *Swarovski* created a continually evolving exhibition that also hosts special cultural events from time to time. It even has become one of Austria's most popular tourist attractions. So far, it has attracted more than five million visitors. The exhibition is promoted by its own website (www.swarovski.com/kristallwelten). Another online project of *Swarovski* is "thecrystalweb", a virtual crystal museum. It provides comprehensive historical and scientific as well as practical information and resources for everything related to crystal (www.thecrystalweb.org).[111]

As the example of the *Swarovski Corporation* shows, the **possibilities in the online world are almost unlimited**. Innovative companies can always find creative ways to use the internet to attract and inform prospects and to maintain and develop customer relationships. The Internet represents an unparalleled opportunity for all businesses. The amount of time business professionals spend online has dramatically increased in recent years. Yet, almost every B2B website is an underachiever, not fulfilling its potential. In times where the Internet has become one of the most important sources for collecting information and reference material, this is a significant missed opportunity. Business customers tend to scan the web first when buying products and services. It is by far not enough to just keep your product and service information updated on a regular basis.[112]

Some people falsely construe that the only or main purpose of a company website with an online database is to act as some kind of online catalog. Wrong! A website can be a means to communicate your brand. A study conducted by *Accenture* dealing with preferences of online buying decisions in B2B revealed some surprising key findings. According to their report a familiar, reputable brand is the single most important factor to online buyers followed closely by service, price, and variety. Moreover, 80 percent of B2B customers regarded prices as less important.[113]

In the **virtual world,** there is no physical product to touch or feel, no familiar bricks-and-mortar emporium to patronize, and too many comparable sites from competitors to differentiate from. Size may not matter in this respect anymore, since every small or medium sized company can afford to rent space on a server and create a professional website. Online branding efforts therefore need to be different from traditional approaches. Online branding capitalizes on the two mayor advantages that the internet offers for individuals and corporations:

- **Information:**   Instant distribution of the most current information available.

- **Simplicity**:   Possibility of business transactions to take place at any time, in any place.

Seamless business processes and accurate information are the prerequisites for any on-line business. If you want to enhance the brand experience, the various elements of the brand impressions have to function at all times. In principle, we have a one-to-one brand experience opportunity with every on-line interaction. This could be executed in a standardized way and millions of visitors to your website could get the same impression or it could be customized, and it should!

The *Wall Street Journal* does this for its subscribers. The user can choose what he or she wants to see on its entry page. The content and the services can be selected and the feeling of the *Wall Street Journal* brand is part of the client's every day experience.

Similar on-line success can be seen at *eBay*. The majority of internet users knows and probably already has used *eBay*. With its new

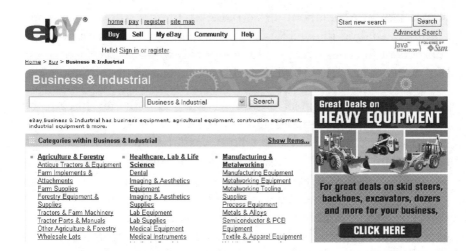

Fig. 38. Business *eBay* Web site

website (business.ebay.com), specially aligned to meet **industrial demands**, *eBay* tries to transfer the well-known feeling and excitement of online auctions into the industrial context. From office supplies to electronic components to heavy equipment, the website offers everything a company may need to buy or want to sell (see Fig. 37 for details).

The online presentation of your brand and your company is relevant to all possible target groups, ranging from small business owners to buyers of large industrial giants. In its research on buying patterns of small business owners, *Hewlett-Packard* found that these **time-strapped decision** makers prefer to buy, or at least research, products and services online. To that end, *HP* has designed a site targeted at small and midsize businesses which pulls business owners to the site through extensive advertising, direct mail, e-mail campaigns, catalogs, and events.

As mentioned before, a true brand has to be perceived as distinctive by its customers. It offers functional as well as emotional benefits. It is a promise you deliver on eagerly, consistently, and at the customer's convenience. **Emotional benefits** can be of major importance when establishing a business website. Human beings tend to lose focus already after about 10 seconds; emotional appeal combined with relevant and interesting content is therefore the most important component in order to capture a visitor to a website. Yet, most of the B2B websites are just as boring as the products they are selling.

Another important aspect of B2B websites is that they have to be found in the first place! Only a few customers are searching deliberately for one company or one brand. It is far more common to look for a certain product, service, or a general solution. Therefore, it is essential to optimize your website in order to appear on the first pages of search engines like *Google* and *Yahoo*.[114] In order to achieve such a search engine optimization, it is usually necessary to consult experts. That's exactly what *Mahler AGS*, a globally operating manufacturer of on-site gas plants for hydrogen generation, oxygen generation, and nitrogen generation did. In order to optimize its online-marketing efforts the company assigned an agency to increase its online hits of prospective customers. The effort soon resulted in increased online inquiries. In addition, online advertising, e.g. *AdWords* at *Google*, should be considered to ensure that your company will be found when certain key words are being searched for.

Social Branding

In recent years an interest in demonstrating ethical and socially responsible marketing appeared. Famous buzz words like "corporate citizenship" and "**Corporate Social Responsibility**" (CSR) are a proof of this.[115] Generally, the main drivers are not ethical concerns of the management but rather their aim to improve their overall corporate image. The internal dimension of CSR relates to how a corporation deals with its employees (protection of labor, qualifications, etc.) and environmentally compatible production processes (waste, pollution, etc.). The external and more important dimension is directed to all other company stakeholders.

The possible actions of Corporate Social Responsibility are various. They cover a wide spectrum from social sponsoring to the complete alignment of corporate management, production, and supplier-relationships according to social and ecological standards. The latter for instance is practiced by *The Body Shop* but also by B2B companies such as *Boeing, Caterpillar, DuPont, GE*, and European aerospace giant *EADS*. *EADS* is conducting workshops for understanding and using the *European Foundation for Quality Management (EFQM) Framework for CSR*. They are using the practical tools, e.g. for self-assessment reporting and apply the output of associated tools to provide added-value to organizations and stakeholders. The objectives of CSR as part of the brand management are:

- Optimization of the stakeholder-values

- Differentiation from competitors

- Create and strengthen confidence of investors

- Consolidation of access to know-how networks and decision makers

A great example of social responsible marketing in B2B is the partnership of *British Airways* with the *United Children's Fund (UNICEF)*. Their campaign is called *Change for Good*. It encourages passengers of *BA* flights to donate spare change in foreign currency from their travels. In the past eleven years, *British Airways* has raised almost US$40 million for *UNICEF*.[116]

Table 4 lists the top-rated B2B companies for social responsibility:

Table 4. Social responsibility rating[117]

Top-Rated B2B Companies for Social Responsibility	
5	Hewlett-Packard
7	Microsoft
8	IBM
10	3M
11	UPS
12	FedEx
15	General Electric

An increasing number of people are requesting information about a company's records on social and environmental responsibility which they take into consideration when purchasing, investing, or making employment decisions. By being socially responsive, companies can become more attractive to prospective customers, high potentials, and investors. How to communicate corporate attitude and behavior toward social responsibility depends on the actual image of the company.[118] *Merck, DuPont*, and *Bank of America* have donated US$100 million or more to charities in a year. Such good deeds can be easily overlooked if not published accordingly. If a company is regarded as being exploitative or fails generally to live up to a "good guy" image, it can even be resented.

Building Brand Through Word-of-Mouth

Nowadays, brands have a life of their own. They are not only what brand managers and marketers want them to be, but tend to develop on their own over time. Word-of-Mouth marketing can have tremendous power. Everyone knows that. Unfortunately, most people are much more likely to talk about something if they are unhappy with it. When Thomas Nicely, a Math professor at Lynchburg College Virginia, noticed a division error in *Intel's Pentium* chip in 1994, the news about it spread very quickly on the Internet and even more quickly when *Intel* tried to belittle the problem. The company got flooded with e-mails and phone calls by concerned customers. The negative word-of-mouth inflation worsened. It reaching its peak when the company was getting about 25,000 calls a day, requesting a no-questions-asked return policy on the microprocessor.

At first, *Intel* refused to take them back but the bombardment with bad press coverage and the sharp drop of its stock price quickly led to a drawback of the company and a change in policy. A write-off to the tune of US$475 million was the cost of this lesson. To avoid a repetition of this disaster, *Intel* has adopted a much more proactive approach to word-of-mouth ever since. It constantly monitors the Internet for possible complaints and **publishes extensive documentation** of bugs in order to maintain the confidence of its customers.[119]

The most important aspect of word-of-mouth therefore is to control bad "buzz" and to try to create positive attention instead. Its success lies in the fact that it is a simple **way of sharing experiences**. The significance of this type of brand development is based on the fact that the advice of people we trust is of major importance to us and it is something we can rely on. This is also the basic mode of **operation with testimonials**.

Famous people praise and endorse certain products that they supposedly use themselves. Even though nobody really believes it, the attention drawn by these famous people does work fine. What is such a testimonial compared to a statement from people you know and trust? If they praise and endorse a certain product, it probably has much more effect on you than the less credible claims of celebrities.

So how can you use buzz to build a brand? The role of word-of-mouth marketing in B2B can be very different depending on the nature of your products and services, customer connectivity, and other marketing strategies applied. One simple rule is that only a superior user experience can activate buzz. An aspirational brand promise may sound great at the beginning but will soon fade if you **create expectations** that you cannot exceed or at least meet. That is also the basic formula for creating Word-of-Mouth marketing: over deliver on your brand promise.

Not every product is a potential target for Word-of-Mouth marketing. Only products and services that provide something interesting and relevant that is really worth talking about can successfully be promoted through Word-of-Mouth. Products have this power to create high involvement among customers if they are[120]

- exciting

- innovative

- personally experienced (e.g. hotels, airlines, cars)

- complex (e.g. software, medical devices)

- expensive.

If your customers are strongly connected to each other, your future business very much depends on their buzz. Take *Cisco* as an example. It always served a tightly connected customer base. They comprise network administrators and information technology managers who are all heavy users of the Internet. The rise of the company merely started by Word-of-Mouth since there was no advertising at first. Since 1984, buzz about *Cisco* has been spreading continuously on the Internet. There are several Internet newsgroups that are dedicated only to *Cisco's* products. Such tight customer connectivity implies that companies have to be very open and direct with their customers in order to avoid negative buzz. If they screw up, their customers will find out very quickly, as the case of *Intel* clearly demonstrated. High-quality products and top service are indispensable as cumulative satisfaction of customers becomes critical.[121]

The most obvious example of this type of branding can be found in the professions of attorneys and medical doctors in many European countries. Since they are forbidden by law to advertise their services, they have to depend on Word-of-Mouth communication to spread the availability and quality of their services.

Recently, the old fashioned Word-of-Mouth method has been enhanced by Internet technology called Weblogs (blogs). They are currently used by only a small number of online consumers worldwide. In the U.S. already more than 50 million visitors of blogs were counted in the first quarter of 2005. They have garnered a great deal of corporate attention because their readers and writers tend to be highly influential.[122] We believe that blogging will grow in importance, and at a minimum, companies should monitor blogs to learn what is being said about their products and services. Companies that plan to create their own public blogs should already feel comfortable having a close, two-way relationship with users. Blogging should be taken seriously in B2B too as the next most influential form of spreading brand influence.

Summary

- **Stop underestimating the power of brands** in B2B! Branding should be the thread running through the subject of Marketing. An important aspect of a successful brand strategy is to completely align it to the business strategy and build lasting brand-conscious customer relationships.

- **Make a consistent impression** with all your stakeholders at every single point of interaction, and do not forget that one of the most important things in B2B brand management is to reduce complexity for the customer.

- **Build a strategic brand architecture** that supports and enhances the type and nature of your company and distinguish between Corporate, Product, and Family Branding.

- The most **common brand strategy in B2B** is a corporate brand in combination with a few product brands. But also, **Ingredient Branding** as a form of multi-stage branding, becomes increasingly relevant for supplies and OEMs.

- The **major communication instruments** in B2B are Direct Sales, Direct Marketing, PR, Specialized Press, Sponsorships, Trade Shows and Exhibitions, Advertising, Sales Promotion, and E-Marketing.

- It is **essential for every brand** to implement a comprehensive and adequate measurement system to gauge and guide brand success.

- It is **crucial to effectively communicate the values of your brands** to your own people; making sure that employees understand these values and thereby leading them to become the best ambassadors of your company and its products.

- Time-strapped decision makers prefer to buy, or at least research, products and services online. Therefore, **Online Branding** is a crucial part of B2B brand building.

- **Social Branding** is a great way for B2B companies to receive high marks for social responsibility.

- **Building Brand through Word-of-Mouth** is a common approach in the industrial world. Recently, this old fashioned method has been enhanced by Internet technology called Weblogs (blogs)

Notes

1   James C. Anderson and James A. Narus, *Business Market Management: Understanding, Creating, and Delivering Value,* p. xiii.

2   Leslie de Chernatony, Malcolm H.B. McDonald, *Creating Powerful Brands in Consumer Service and Industrial Markets,* 1998.

3   Philip Kotler and Kevin L. Keller, *Marketing Management,* 2006, pp. 40-41.

4   Paul Hague, *Branding in Business to Business Markets,* White Paper, B2B International Ltd.

5   Scott Bedbury, *A New Brand World,* 2002, p. 10.

6   Martin Roll, "Understanding the Purpose of a Corporate Branding Strategy," *brandchannel.com* (15 August 2005).

7   Paul Hague, *Branding in Business to Business Markets,* White Paper, B2B International Ltd.

8   James C. Anderson and James A. Narus, *Business Market Management: Understanding, Creating, and Delivering Value,* p. 136.

9   Duane E. Knapp, *The Brand Mindset,* 2000, p. 3.

10 David A. Aaker and Erich Joachimsthaler, *Brand Leadership,* 2000, p. 17.

11 Duane E. Knapp, *The Brand Mindset,* 2000, pp. 14-15; David A. Aaker and Erich Joachimsthaler, *Brand Leadership,* 2000, p. 17.

12 Philip Kotler and Kevin L. Keller, *Marketing Management,* 2006, p. 284.

13 Don E. Schultz, Stanley I. Tannenbaum, and Robert F. Lauterborn, *Integrated Marketing Communications,* 1993.

14 Kevin Roberts, *Lovemarks,* 2004, p. 61.

15 Kevin L. Keller, *Strategic Brand Management,* 2003, p. 522.

16 James C. Anderson and James A. Narus, *Business Market Management: Understanding, Creating, and Delivering Value,* p. 136.

[17] David A. Aaker and Erich Joachimsthaler, *Brand Leadership*, 2000.

[18] Waldemar Pfoertsch and Michael Schmid, M., *B2B-Markenmanagement: Konzepte – Methoden – Fallbeispiele*, 2005, pp. 109-115.

[19] David A. Aaker and Erich Joachimsthaler, *Brand Leadership*, 2000, pp. 103, 127.

[20] Adapted from Backhaus, *Industrieguetermarketing*, p. 389 and Becker, *Typen von Markenstrategien*, p. 494.

[21] Klaus Backhaus, *Industrieguetermarketing*, 2003, pp. 414-415.

[22] Franz-Rudolf Esch, Torsten Tomczak, Joachim Kernstock and Tobias Langner, *Corporate Brand Management*, 2004, p. 8.

[23] Martin Roll, "Understanding the Purpose of a Corporate Branding Strategy," *brandchannel.com* (15 August 2005).

[24] Waldemar Pfoertsch and Michael Schmid, M., *B2B-Markenmanagement: Konzepte – Methoden – Fallbeispiele*, 2005, pp. 112-113.

[25] Web site of *The Dow Chemical Company*, Midland, MI, cited August 2005.

[26] Web site of *ERCO Leuchten GmbH*, Luedenscheid, cited August 2005.

[27] Web site of *Porsche Consulting GmbH*, Bietigheim-Bissingen, cited August 2005.

[28] Dan Morrison, "The Six Biggest Pitfalls in B-to-B Branding," *Business2Business Marketer* (July/August, 2001), p. 1.

[29] James C. Anderson and James A. Narus, *Business Market Management: Understanding, Creating, and Delivering Value*, p. 136.

[30] Charles W.L. Hill, *International Business*, 2003, pp. 422-425; Waldemar Pfoertsch and Michael Schmid, M., *B2B-Markenmanagemen*, 2005, pp. 117-120.

[31] Adapted from Backhaus, *Industrieguetermarketing*, p. 419.

[32] Kevin L. Keller, *Strategic Brand Management*, 2003, p. 282; Alina Wheeler, *Designing Brand Identity*, 2003, pp. 40-41; Duane E. Knapp, *The Brand Mindset*, 2000, pp. 108-109.

[33] Paul Hague and Peter Jackson, *The Power of Industrial Brands*, 1994.

[34] John M.T. Balmer and Stephen A. Greyser, "Managing the Multiple Identities of the Corporation," *California Management Review* (Vol. 44 No. 3, 2002), pp. 72-86.

[35] David A. Aaker, *Building Strong Brands*, 1996.

[36] Alina Wheeler, *Designing Brand Identity*, 2003, p. 41; Anne, B. Thompson, "Brand Positioning and Brand Creation," in: *Brands and Branding*, Rita Clifton and John Simmons (eds), 2003, pp. 90-91.

[37] Gerald Erichsen, "The Chevy Nova That Didn't Go," *about.com* (2005).

[38] Philippe Malaval, *Strategy and Management of Industrial Brands: Business to Business Products and Services*, 2001, p. 187.

[39] David A. Aaker and Erich Joachimsthaler, *Brand Leadership*, 2000, pp. 54-55.

[40] Web site of *United Parcel Service of America, Inc.*, Atlanta, GA, cited July 2005.

[41] Web site of *United Parcel Service of America, Inc.*, Atlanta, GA, cited July 2005).

[42] Vivian Manning-Schaffel, "UPS & FedEx Compete to Deliver," *brandchannel.com* (17 May 2004).

[43] David A. Aaker and Erich Joachimsthaler, *Brand Leadership*, 2000, pp. 50-51.

[44] Frederick E. Webster, Jr. and Kevin L. Keller, "A Roadmap for Branding in Industrial Markets," *The Journal of Brand Management*, (Vol. 11, No. 5, May 2004), pp. 388-402.

[45] Alina Wheeler, *Designing Brand Identity*, 2003, pp. 42-43.

[46] Klaus Fog, Christian Budtz, Baris Yakaboylu, *Storytelling: Branding in Practice*, 2005, p. 15.

[47] Source: http://www.adage.com/century/icon08.html.

[48] Klaus Fog, Christian Budtz, Baris Yakaboylu, *Storytelling: Branding in Practice*, 2005, p. 15.

[49] *Penske System Inc.*, Detroit, MI, cited November 2005.

[50] Klaus Fog, Christian Budtz, Baris Yakaboylu, *Storytelling: Branding in Practice*, 2005, p. 15.

[51] Duane E. Knapp, *The Brand Mindset*, 2000, p. 121.

[52] Klaus Fog, Christian Budtz, Baris Yakaboylu, *Storytelling: Branding in Practice*, 2005, p. 15.

[53] Clay M. Ferrer, "Branding B2B Technology Companies – An Investment For Success," *Techlinks: Community Publishing* (18 October 2000).

[54] Ibid.

55 Schmitz, J. M., "Understanding the Persuasion Process Between Industrial Buyers and Sellers," *Industrial Marketing Management* (Vol. 24), pp. 83-90.

56 Leslie De Chernatony and Malcolm McDonald, *Creating Powerful Brands in Consumer, Service and Industrial Markets*.

57 Dan Morrison, "The Six Biggest Pitfalls in B-to-B Branding," *Business2Business Marketer* (July/August, 2001).

58 Source: Bruhn, *Kommunikationspolitik fuer Industriegueter*.

59 Philip Kotler and Kevin L. Keller, *Marketing Management*, 2006, p. 536.

60 Ibid., p. 537.

61 Robert P. Vitale and Joseph J. Giglierano, *Business to Business Marketing: Analysis and Practice in a Dynamic Environmen*, 2002, pp. 424-425.

62 Ball, B. and Monoghan, R., "Redefining the Sales and Marketing Relationship," Potentials in Marketing (October 1994), pp. 19-20.

63 Philip Kotler and Kevin L. Keller, *Marketing Management*, 2006, p. 537.

64 Kevin L. Keller, *Strategic Brand Management*, 2006, p. 301.

65 Philip Kotler and Kevin L. Keller, *Marketing Management*, 2006, pp. 555-593.

66 Ibid., p. 594.

67 Al and Laura Ries, *The Fall of Advertising & the Rise of PR*, 2001.

68 Lapp Cable, Stuttgart, Germany, cited November 2005.

69 "Cover Story: Game On," *Eventmarketer* (4 May 2004).

70 "Master Yachting Goes Porsche Cup," *firmenpresse.de* (22 August 2005).

71 Karsten Kilian, "Erlebnismarketing und Markenerlebnisse," in: *Psychologie der Markenführung*, Arnd Florack, et al (eds.), 2006.

72 *The McGraw-Hill Companies, Inc.* Reproduced with permission of the McGraw-Hill Companies.

73 Web site of *Covad Communications*, San Jose, CA, cited May 2005.

74 Source: *Wall Street Journal*, 2004.

75 Source: www.intel.com.

76 Philip Kotler and Kevin L. Keller, *Marketing Management*, 2006, p. 585.

77 "BAV – BrandAsset Valuator®," *Young & Rubicam Group*, p. 2.

78 David A. Aaker and Erich Joachimsthaler, *Brand Leadership*, 2000, p. 16.

79 For a comprehensive overview of more than 66 brand positioning and brand evaluation models see markenmodelle.de.

80 Jan Lindemann, "Brand Valuation," in: *Brands and Branding*, Rita Clifton and John Simmons (eds), 2003, p. 34; David A. Aaker and Erich Joachimsthaler, *Brand Leadership*, 2000, p. 16.

81 Source: Interbrand Corp., Berner and Kiley, "Global Brands," *Business Week*, 86-94, 2005.

82 Ibid., p. 34.

83 Watson Wyatt, *B2B Brands and the Bottom Line*, London, September 2002.

84 Web site of *Caterpillar Inc.*, Peoria, IL, cited August 2005.

85 Donald V. Fites, "Make Your Dealers Your Partners," *Harvard Business Review* (March-April 1996), pp. 88-89.

86 Web site of Wal-Mart Stores, Inc., Bentonville, AR, cited June 2005.

87 Dave Ulrich, Steve Kerr, Ron Ashkenas, Debbie Burke, Patrice Murphy *The GE Work-Out*, McGraw-Hill, 2002.

88 David A. Aaker and Erich Joachimsthaler, *Brand Leadership*, 2000, pp. 76-77.

89 Waldemar Pfoertsch and Michael Schmid, M., *B2B-Markenmanagement: Konzepte – Methoden – Fallbeispiele*, 2005, p. 86.

90 Ibid.

91 Waldemar Pfoertsch and Michael Schmid, M., *B2B-Markenmanagement: Konzepte – Methoden – Fallbeispiele*, 2005, p. 65.

92 If you desire further information of the subject of Ingredient Branding we recommend Waldemar Pfoertsch, Intrajanto Mueller, Die Marke in der Marke, Macht und Bedeutung des Ingredient Branding, Springer, Heidelberg 2006, the English language version will be available 2007.

93 Hermann Freter and Carsten Baumgarth, „Ingredient Branding – Begriff und theoretische Begruendung," in: *Moderne Markenfuehrung*, Franz-Rudolf Esch (ed), 1999, pp. 289-315.

94 Nunes, Dull, and Lynch, "When Two Brands Are Better Than One," p. 17.

95 Hermann Freter and Carsten Baumgarth, „Ingredient Branding – Begriff und theoretische Begruendung," in: *Moderne Markenfuehrung*, Franz-Rudolf Esch (ed), 1999, 289-315.

96 David A. Aaker and Erich Joachimsthaler, *Brand Leadership*, 2000, p. 141.

97 Web site of *Infineon Technologies*, cited June 2005.

98 BBDO, "Ingredient Branding in the Automotive Industry – Telematics and CRM," *Point of View 3* (January 2003).

99 Ibid.

100 Nunes, Dull, and Lynch, "When Two Brands Are Better Than One," p. 17.

101 Web site of *Intel Corporation*, Santa Clara, CA, cited October 2005.

102 Bob Lamons, *The Case for B2B Branding*, 2005, pp. 161-163; Web site of *Intel Corporation*, Santa Clara, CA, cited October 2005.

103 Web site of *Intel Corporation*, Santa Clara, CA, cited October 2005.

104 Bob Lamons, *The Case for B2B Branding*, 2005, pp. 161-163.

105 Berner and Kiley, "Global Brands," *Business Week* (1 August 2005), pp. 86-94.

106 Cliff Edwards, "Intel Everywhere?" *BusinessWeek* (8 March, 2004), pp. 56-62.

107 Web site of *Swarovski AG*, Wattens, Austria, cited November 2005).

108 *Swarovski Crystallized™ with Swarovski® Homepage*, cited November 2005.

109 Ibid.

110 *Swarovski Business Homepage*, cited October 2005.

111 Web site of *Swarovski AG*, Wattens, Austria, cited November 2005.

112 Rick Whitmyre, "The 5 Deadly Sins of B2B Marketing," *B2B Marketing Trends* (5 August 2004).

113 Stephen F. Dull, "Was It an Illusion? Putting More B in B2B," *Accenture – Online Insight*, pp. 8-10.

114 Rick Whitmyre, "The 5 Deadly Sins of B2B Marketing," *B2B Marketing Trends* (5 August 2004).

115 If you desire further information on this subject, we recommend Philip Kotler and Nancy Lee, *Corporate Social Responsibility: Doing the Most Good for Your Company and Your Cause* (Hoboken, NJ: Wiley, 2005).

116 Web site of *British Airways Plc.*, Harmondsworth, England, cited July 2005.

117 *EFQM (European Foundation for Quality Management) Framework for CSR* in cooperation with *UN Global Impact.*

118 Philip Kotler and Kevin L. Keller, *Marketing Management*, 2006, pp. 706-708.

119 Emanuel Rosen, *The Anatomy of Buzz*, 2002, p. 16.

120 Ibid., 2002, pp. 25-26.

121 Ibid., p. 27.

122 Jason Rossiter and Waldemar Pfoertsch, *Blogs: The new language of business*, 2006.

CHAPTER 4

Acceleration Through Branding

A journey of a thousand miles begins with a single step.

Confucius

In the previous chapters we provided you with a lot of information about the **basics of branding and brand specialties**. If your mind is now filled with questions like, "How do I implement this? What do I have to do first? How is it different from what I am already doing?" Don't worry – we understand. To talk about something in theory is entirely different from putting this theory into real practice. In answer to your questions, we will now turn to everything that lies ahead of you: The practical implementation of a holistic brand strategy.

In order to achieve **Acceleration Through Branding** brand architects have to be able to see the big picture. A holistic brand approach must reflect corporate values and characteristics if it is to function as the verbalized essence and visual embodiment of what a business stands for.

Creating Value

It is no wonder that so many branding efforts fail. Unless a company has a multi-million dollar budget, it has to know exactly what is important and what needs to be done for the brand to make the effort successful. Many companies tend to focus on profit maximization rather than on shareholder value maximization. We think

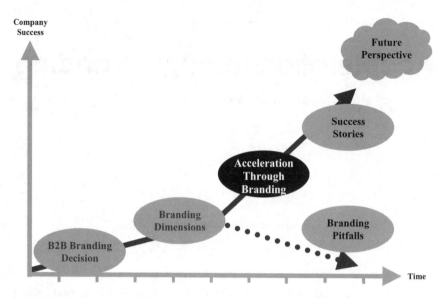

Fig. 39. Guiding principle acceleration through branding

that profit maximization leads to short-term planning whereas any brand building exercise requires a **long term view**. Measuring profit performance using ROI (return on investment) has two problems: First, profits are arbitrarily measured and subject to manipulation; cash flow is more important. Second, investments ignore the real value of the firm, and brands as one of the main value drivers.

A company's real value resides more in its intangible marketing assets: brands, market knowledge, customer relationships, distribution coverage, intellectual property, and partner relationships, as in its balance sheet. These assets are the drivers of long-term profits and they have to demonstrate their impact on **shareholder value** with brand typically being the most important one of them. When management chooses to apply shareholder value analysis to see which alternative course of action will maximize share value, they are on the right track. With a management process in place which goes through the various stages of brand development and brand controlling, one can see clearly how much brand investments contributes to shareholder value.[1]

Many managers are aware of the power of branding, even from their first few years with the company. As J. Justus Schneider, Brand manager of *Mercedes-Benz* admits, "The brand *Mercedes-Benz* is a brand icon, from its founding day till today." Still, the management and the methods of this fascination has to be experienced and learned.[2] The branding process has an aura of execution and uniqueness which lead to much greater business success. To accelerate a brand to the top may take a hundred years as in the case of *Mercedes-Benz*.[3] In the case of *Google*, *eBay* and *Amazon*, it took just a decade to accomplish this. Today's challenge is not only to be known, but to be known around the globe for a sustained period of time. That success is in all cases the result of hard and consistent work.

Brand Building Process

We suggest selecting a brand building approach that incorporates all the relevant processes necessary for building a brand icon. Ideally, the branding initiative comes from top management – the CEO, CMO, or CBO gearing to establish the brand strength, including **brand stability, brand leadership** and **international presence**. Positive guidance from top management and its contribution to the brand building process is indispensable for the effort to be recognized world wide. Unfortunately, this doesn't happen often enough in B2B companies. Quite often, a good amount of convincing work is necessary to bring top management to buy into the idea of branding.

The founders or managers of *Microsoft*, *IBM*, *GE*, and *Intel* had the guts to buy into the idea, and they have been **richly rewarded**. There is no doubt that US-American management has the competency capable of leading their companies to the top. Their brands show excellent clarity, consistency, and leadership. Currently, no other country has so many successful company brands. To guide a brand along these three dimensions for a long period of time is a challenging task. Not too many brands can show consistent long-term success. Only a few brands can in addition **demonstrate brand authenticity**.

Brand building, brand consolidation, and brand expansion need the dimensions of clarity, consistency, and leadership adapted to the surrounding conditions, with special attention to competition and technology. Instead of expecting total consistency across all countries, you should work on the reduction of the differences. Some brands even have to live with paradoxes like being a luxury consumer brand and a quality business brand, e.g. *Mercedes-Benz* with its passenger cars and trucks, *Nokia* with telecommunication systems and mobile phones and *Rolls-Royce* with high-end limousines and aircraft jet engines. Although in many cases the actual development of the brand was based on luck and accidents, particularly in the early days of industrial companies, only an application of solid brand knowledge is creating powerful market leaders today and will do so tomorrow.

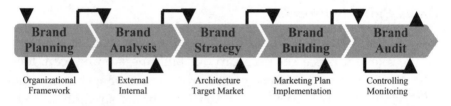

Fig. 40. Sequence of the brand building processes

To get all these dimensions (clarity, consistency, and leadership) in line with a long term view, we suggest the following process, consisting of the following five steps: brand planning, brand analysis, brand strategy, brand building, and brand audit (see Fig. 40).

4.1   Brand Planning

Since brand targets create long-term results, brand planning should always integrate the big picture. Key issues for brand planning therefore include achieving a good balance between **continuity and involvement.** Most companies develop marketing, sales plans, and strategic plans but not brand plans. This overlooked area is often the reason why many brands never reach up to their full potential.

To keep your company and your brand(s) focused, brand planning should be included in future business planning. Big brand changes usually don't happen overnight. You have to induce gradual processes over time rather than have one annual action plan. In order to achieve continuity and involvement, you have to integrate the following processes, steps and procedures within your organization:

Build **a climate of ongoing change**, freeing up management time for brand strategy discussions. (Most managers have a preference for discussing tactics over strategy.)

Have **processes that deliver timely information**, including the reporting of strong and weak opportunity/threat signals about the brand position, the brand identity.

Develop **procedures for rapid breakthrough planning**, based on a profound analysis of the brand situation including size of market, growth potential, distribution channels, market dynamics and trends, customer profiles, current and emerging competition and last, but not least, profit potential.

Have **standard formats for communicating brand plans and changes**. This is where business score cards are very effective. Based on clear business objectives and scenarios they help identifying known and unknown road blocks.

Have strong **implementation processes**. Activities in the overall context have to be de-resourced as well as resourced, and reward and recognition schemes must be adapted. We call this a **Branding Program** which includes current and future brands, appropriate extensions or potentials for incremental growth. All other brand support programs are included here. This action plan for implementation assumes the rollout and long-term management of the brand.

Involve everyone in the planning. One of the main reasons why brand plans fail is that only a clique of people was involved in generating them in the first place. Involvement motivates commitment. In the electronic age, there are some excellent tools which can quickly distribute and solicit information across even the largest companies.

Before we go on, we want to mention some important branding principles that enhance long-term brand success.

Branding Principles

Maybe you have already heard of the "three C's" of branding which refer to the indispensable conditions that precede successful branding. For the purpose of completeness we have added a fourth and fifth branding principle:

- Consistency

- Clarity

- Continuity

- Visibility

- Authenticity

Consistency is the most important branding rule for B2B companies, yet there are still too many companies that fail to provide consistency throughout all relevant touch points. It is necessary for all relevant dimensions, not only concerning the product, but also in the marketing channels, and even in the way the employees answer the phone or respond to a customer complaint. Social responsibility and investment planning are also part of this. Of course, consistency in your brand strategy is not as effective as it could be if the other branding principles are not covered.

Clarity in branding is essential because without clarity there is no true brand. Customers and stakeholders should be able to clearly understand who the company and it's brand(s) are and what they are not. Brand clarity is based on the company's vision, mission, and values, which is easily understood and easy to adopt. They are unique and have relevance for the deciders, users, and sometimes even the public.

The branding rule of **continuity** implies that a company shouldn't change what it stands for just for the sake of change. Strong brands are continuously managed. People rely on them and trust them because they know what to expect.

It is not enough to live up to these rules consistently if you are not always visible to your target audience. Brand **visibility** which increases exposure of the brand to the consumer's eye is important to accomplish a greater brand mindshare. Marketing dollars should be pumped into the best channels, making sure that collaterals are placed at points where customer attention and retention is high.

Finally, brand **authenticity** is directed towards the thinking and acting of everybody in the company with the focus of creating originality and the feeling for the customer to own, use, or direct a unique treasure, even if this takes place subconsciously.

Another important factor many brands are aspiring to is **brand leadership** – to lead the pack. It is the most important factor for long term brand value increase which includes the management of brand expectations, the fulfillment beyond expectations, and the guidance of customers to new heights concerning the company's products and services. In the long run, this could lead to the reinvention of the brand and the company in question.

We agree with Alicia Clegg that "brands that aspire to be contemporary classics have to work on many levels. First and foremost, the product needs integrity, some special quality that sets it apart. But having a 'story' to tell, something that fixes a brand's identity in people's imagination and gets across what it stands for is crucially important too."[4] But we disagree with her statement that "whether the story is made up, or rooted in fact, is beside the point. Like fable in folklore, what matters is that the brand's mythology has the power to intrigue and to draw people in."[5] We contend that the power to create need has to be based on something genuine. Numerous "brand accidents" have shown that **nothing stands the test of time better than the truth**.

4.2 Brand Analysis

Brand building does not begin with the immediate choice of all the various brand elements that need to be defined. Rather, it starts with market research. To conduct thorough market research is one of the most important elements when building a brand. The development of a brand identity should always be supported by a customer analysis, a competitor analysis, and a self-analysis.

Basic decisions related to strategic brand management should always be supported by information relating to the company and the environment it operates in. In chapter 2.2 we talked about the importance of clarifying the **brand relevance** in your respective markets. In most cases, the real challenge is to discover rather than invent what could later be the core values of your brand. Industrial companies can gain significant insights from their close interactions with customers, positioning themselves to effectively help their customers.

To define and formulate a proper **brand mission, personality**, and **brand values** aligned to the corporate vision and mission is mandatory for devising an effective and focused brand strategy. You have to answer the following questions:

- Who are you?
- What is important to you?
- What does your company stand for?
- What is important to your customers?
- What distinguishes you from competition?
- Where and what do you want to be in five years?

The starting point of every brand strategy is to work out what the company stands for. Thorough brand analysis is necessary to give the right answers to all these questions and many more. Internal and external market research is therefore the first step toward creating a brand.

What is marketing research? Well, it is definitely not about compiling a lot of statistics and graphs that are presented once and then laid to rest in a cabinet. If companies do market research they should also be able to analyze and evaluate the results. Many companies waste their efforts in market research because the results are only used to answer one specific question of one specific department (usually marketing). If the company failed to ask the right questions or doesn't even include execution strategies, the market research ends up completely useless.

The questions above only facilitate placing the right questions. To do **effective market research** means you have to know your business, your products and services, your brands, your employees, your competition, and your industry well. Quite often, effective market research can bring up completely new perspectives to companies. When you discover that what customers regard as important is not at all what you think is important, it can even lead to an "ah hah" moment.

> **Brand building starts with understanding the key attributes of your products and services as well as understanding and anticipating the needs of your customers.**

The first step could be the measuring of the "Brand Share of Market", which is calculated as follows: **Brand Sales/Category Sales = Brand share**. This will show your position in relation to the other players in the market and could be used for a brand portfolio analysis, similar to the market-growth market-share matrix. The next step is creating the power of your brand by defining and developing each category:[6]

Fig. 41. Creating brand power

- **Brand Power**, as shown in Fig. 41, consists of four key elements which will be discussed below:

- **Brand Dominance** – The influence or dominance that a brand has over its category or market (more than just market-share).

- **Brand Stretch** – The stretch or extension that the brand has achieved in the past or is likely to achieve in the future (especially outside its original category).

- **Brand Coverage** – The breadth that the brand has achieved in terms of age spread, consumer types, and international appeal.

- **Brand Loyalty** – The degree of commitment that the brand has achieved among its customer base and beyond. It consists of the proximity, the intimacy, and the loyalty felt for the brand.

From the perspective of brand equity, much of the investment spending each year on the creation of brand power should be sought as an investment in consumer brand knowledge. The quality of the investment, not necessarily the quantity (beyond some minimal threshold amount) is critical when building a brand.

Brand equity arises from differences in consumer response to marketing activities. Brand knowledge is what consumers learned, felt, saw, heard, and experienced over time. The differential effect of brand knowledge is reflected in consumer perceptions, preferences, and behavior related to all aspects of the marketing of a brand. **The power of a brand lies in the customer mind set.** Brand equity is therefore a vital strategic bridge from the past to the future and a set of stored values that consumers associate with a product or service. These associations add value beyond the basic offering based on past investments in marketing the brand. They can be captured according to Keller's **Customer-Based Brand Equity** (CBBE) model as is shown in Fig. 42.

The CBBE model implies that a strong brand involves the customer over four steps:

(1) **Deep Broad Brand Awareness** – establishing a proper identity and awareness for the brand

(2) **Establishment of Points of Difference** – creating the appropriate brand meaning through strong, favorable, and unique brand associations

(3) **Positive Accessible Reactions** – eliciting positive, accessible brand responses

(4) **Forging Brand Relationships** – building relationships with customers characterized by intense, active loyalty

Achieving these four steps, in turn, involves establishing six brand-building blocks: brand salience, brand performance, brand imagery, customer judgments, customer emotions, and brand resonance. The most **valuable brand-building block, brand resonance**, occurs when all the other brand-building blocks are established. With true brand resonance, customers express a high degree of loyalty to the brand. They actively seek means to interact with the brand and share their experiences with others. Firms that are able to achieve brand resonance will be able to benefit from the whole spectrum of brand values (e.g. price premiums, high market share).

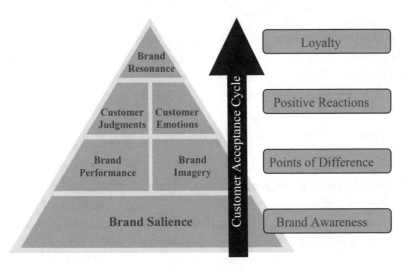

Fig. 42. Customer-based brand equity pyramid (CBBE model)

The key to branding is the triggering of a deep emotional response. This deep **emotional response** is often derived from the key benefit of using the product and the marketer wants to program into us. Many times, however, this deep emotional response has nothing to do with the product itself. It is more important to get a desired emotion linked to the product and thereby to the brand.

4.3   Brand Strategy

The brand is probably the most **powerful communications tool**, yet few organizations consciously create and use a brand identity (positioning statement, category descriptor, brand name, etc.) to market their products or services. According to Juck Peddis, the key to increasing the valuation of your company is in your ability to competitively brand it in the market.

Brand strategy is built on brand positioning, brand mission, brand value proposition (and personality), brand promise, and brand architecture. Chuck Pettis from *TechnoBrands* states[7]: "If people don't remember your brand name, how are they going to find you and buy your product?" The first step in **effectively branding** an offer is to understand exactly what your customers want from you and giving it to them. "If nothing else, I beg you to go out to your customers, tell them why you think they should buy from you, and then ask them what they think," pleads Peddis. But finding out what customers want is only the first step. Peddis also explains that you need to understand how people feel when they successfully use your product and exploit emotions connected to it. "Branding alters people's perceptions of reality." If you can get all this in your strategy, you are on the right track.

The branding strategy for a company can be described as the disposition of the number and nature of common and **distinctive brand elements** that a company applies throughout its organization. But in reality it is much more than just deciding upon the brand architecture. To devise a branding strategy involves the accurate and concise interpretation of the results of the preceding brand analysis.

In addition, when determining the direction of your brand strategy, you have to assess what is feasible and affordable in the first place. And let us state it again: The leadership and management of the brand has to be backed and supported by top management, otherwise it is not possible to really push a brand strategy up to the crest of the wave. Only then can you turn to deciding upon the nature of new and existing brand elements to be applied to new and existing products or the business itself.

The brand strategy is always based on the **brand core**, its **values, and associations**. The products and services are an intrinsic part of the brand as displayed on the left side of Figure 43. The content and the meaning of these dimensions both change over time, and they are guided by the management and its decisions. The definition of the current status and the future perspective are the big challenges of brand strategy building.[8] Consistency between the various aspects of the brand and company authenticity and the pressure from the market environment are **continuously challenging** the management. The need for economic viability and the investments for the brand value have to be considered in every marketing decision.

Mercedes-Benz

New challenges appear once in a while for companies, particularly when they become complacent or neglect their customers. This can happen to even the most prestigious brands, as it did for *Mercedes-Benz* in 1992. This was a year when *Mercedes-Benz* had to take drastic measures to get the brand for passenger cars and trucks back on track. In contrast to the 1980s when *Mercedes* engineering dominated the automobile market, the 1990s saw a demand by customers for smaller, more practical cars. Unfortunately, at this time, *Mercedes* was developing even bigger and bigger cars, culminating in the enormous S-Class of 1992. The demand for its cars decreased, the company failed to achieve its goals and found itself in a deep crisis.

A new CEO started a product initiative for doubling the number of products and started to listen to customers, targeted niche markets and started a branding initiative. The result was the *Mercedes-Benz's*

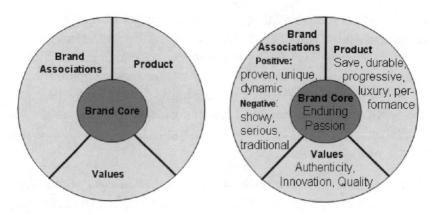

Fig. 43. Brand strategy model & *Mercedes-Benz* brand strategy[9]

new brand that emphasized the brand core with *Enduring Passion*, and became the most valuable achievement of the company that put everything else in line. Having moved away from the pure engineering focus of the company, not even the product design was as powerful as the brand; all advertisements and internal communication had the tagline: "The Future of the Automobile" and the passion had a future.

According to the brand model by Leslie Butterfield the core brand of *Mercedes-Benz* is enduring passion. Brand associations, product and values are shown in more detail on the right side of Figure 43.

Corporate or Product Branding?

One of the early decisions in B2B branding strategy is whether to focus on the corporate or the product brand. Do you want to raise the corporate umbrella or do you want to push product superiority?

Corporate branding employs the **same methodology and toolbox used in product branding**, but it also elevates the approach a step further into the board room, where additional issues around stakeholder relations (shareholders, media, competitors, governments and many others) can help the corporation benefit from a strong and well-managed corporate branding strategy. Not surprisingly, a strong and comprehensive corporate branding strategy requires a high level of personal attention and commitment from the CEO and the senior management to become fully effective and meet the objectives.

There are several benefits for employing a corporate branding strategy that a company can exploit. First of all, a strong corporate brand is no less or more than the face of the business strategy, portraying what the corporation aims at doing and what it wants to be known for in the market place. The corporate brand is the overall umbrella for the corporations' activities and encapsulates its brand dimensions.

Think of *HSBC*. The *HSBC Group* is named after its founding member, The Hong Kong and Shanghai Banking Corporation Limited, which was established in 1865 to finance the growing trade between China and Europe. The bank has recently implemented a successful stringent corporate branding strategy. *HSBC* employs the same common expression throughout the globe with a simple advertising strategy based on the slogan "The world's local bank." This creative platform enables the corporation to bridge between many cultural differences, and to portray many faces of the same strategy. **A corporate branding strategy creates simplicity;** it stands on top of the brand portfolio as the ultimate identifier of the corporation.

The philosophy or basic direction of impact of the brand strategy has to conform to what the company is doing. In many cases the nature of the products or services a company sells limits the decision as to how to brand. Therefore, the decision whether to set the main focus on a corporate or product brand strategy is made easier in B2B than in B2C.

The next important strategic decision is what Constantinos Markides from the London Business School calls:

"To be better or to be different." [10]

He is of the opinion that "to be better" is the more difficult because you have to battle the competition continuously for the next product advantage. To be different is less difficult, in Markides' opinion; it could well be easier to find a way to be different, permanently.

Targeting and Positioning B2B Brands

The development of a positioning strategy is sometimes referred to as the most important discipline in brand management. Brand positioning literally means to "position" your brand in customers' minds in order to create certain desired associations in relation to competitive brands. Ideally, strong brands have a clear and unique position in the target markets. Consider the following automobiles with well-established positions:

- Detroit Diesel: **"well-engineered engines"**
- SGL Carbon Graphite: **"performance"**
- Draeger: **"safety"**

The major goal of marketing is undoubtedly to satisfy the customers' needs and make a profit along the way. Unfortunately, the needs of customers can differ tremendously from industry to industry. Therefore, different approaches are required to meet all the different needs. **Positioning brands** is about finding the right spot in customers' minds in order to create the desired associations. It is therefore absolutely crucial to know who your customers are and where to find them. Positioning always comes after clarifying and segmenting the target market; you just cannot position any product or service without knowing who you are targeting.

To clarify and segment the target market is usually much easier in B2B than in B2C markets. Quite often, B2B companies only have a handful of **important key accounts** that make up for the greater part of their turnover and profit. At the same time, it is also more important to clearly segment your target markets because the possibilities to differentiate one product from another are more restricted in B2B. An **effective segmentation** strategy can also create a competitive advantage in B2B markets.

Many business marketers neglect or poorly perform positioning concepts. Despite of calls for a clear brand positioning, it is often quite difficult to find a common denominator of largely diversified and very complex businesses. Companies that clearly fail at it create positioning statements full of empty phrases that are nothing more than "hot air". They not only lack substance in their positioning but usually also fail to bring their employees to act accordingly.[11]

Applying the "hedgehog concept" of Jim Collins for the brand positioning means that, "It is not a goal to be the best, not a strategy to be the best, not an intention to be the best and not a plan to be the best. It is an understanding of what you can be the best at."[12] This means that your target customer is most attracted to our brand essence, we understand him well and he is in the most profitable growth segment that we want to attract. Positioning is the act of designing the company's offer and image so that it occupies a distinct and valued place in the target consumer's minds. Brand positioning should be so clear, so succinct, and so powerful that once launched, it begins to move people toward your new **evolving brand**. It is all about identifying the optimal place of a brand relative to its competitors in the consumer's mind, and maximizing the company's potential benefit. Brand positioning is the heart of marketing strategy.

The principle of providing a consistent picture also means not changing or diluting the positioning. A brand can only have one true position. An effectively positioned brand communicates its core values to all **stakeholders, internally and externally**.[13] It is crucial to keep a strategic perspective since positioning a brand is not a tactical activity but rather a strategic process aimed at creating a sustainable competitive advantage.

The positioning statement draws on the strongest assets of the brand's equity and clarifies what the brand is all about. It shows the uniqueness and thus the point of difference. It explains why customers should buy and use the company's products and services and not the ones of a competitor. It also defines why the company addresses their needs better than competition. The questions to be answered are:

- Who are you going to give this positioning to?
- Who are you going to market your product to?

- What do they want and need?

- What customer insight is your positioning based on?

The ultimate task for brand positioning is to create the most powerful position you can own and feel passionate about and to direct the passion to the most profitable customer targets. Soni Simpson illustrates this kind of power positioning as shown in Fig. 44 as one "Where deep understanding of your brand equity or essence links directly to a core consumer insight or value."[14]

Fig. 44. Principles of power positioning

Brand Mission

An old saying goes, "If you don't know where you're going, how you will know when you've arrived?" This clearly illustrates how essential it is to articulate a clear brand mission statement that is **aligned with the corporate vision and mission**. Words can be a very powerful tool, but only if there is a true and reliable meaning behind them. Before a company can start to plan and implement a holistic branding approach it must first determine what it actually wants to accomplish.

The starting point of every brand strategy is to work out what the company stands for. For most corporate brands, leadership is an important part of the core brand identity since it can inspire employees and cooperators by setting an inspirational brand level. For customers on the other hand, leadership provides reassurance and security. It also implies high quality and innovative solutions. Leadership can be achieved along many dimensions: competence, innovation, quality, inspiration, success (by market share, etc.).[15]

A brand mission statement is the guiding idea behind the brand. It has to be a clear and ambitious, yet achievable business goal. This enables the brand to obtain authenticity. A brand mission statement is a benchmark for all management and employee decisions. Furthermore, it gives direction to customers, shareholders, and everyone else involved in the company.

Take *SAP* for example. The German business software company provides a range of complex enterprise resource systems (ERP) and related software solutions. In its brand mission statement, *SAP* clearly outlines what it wants to accomplish with its brand: "*SAP* helps make work become a more personally enjoyable and a rewarding experience." It is very aspiring to have a good mission statement that shows the commitment of the company to constantly improve and evolve.[16] The **brand values** that *SAP* wants to reflect are: a global culture, respect for the individual, integrity, partnership, and progressiveness.

Many branding strategies of B2B companies suffer from a lack of focus. It is necessary to focus on one clear benefit that distinguishes the company from the rest. B2B companies should abandon a wordy list of what they would like to be. Charles Mingus, an American jazz bassist and composer once said, "Making the simple complicated is commonplace; making the complicated simple, awesomely simple, that's creativity." [17]

Don't think that a brand mission is only for very large companies. Small and medium sized companies can easily start their own branding strategy. The following brand mission is from Oklahoma Steel & Wire, a mid-sized manufacturer of wires for agricultural and industrial markets with approximately 300 employees.[18]

"Oklahoma Steel & Wire is committed to providing the highest quality products at the most competitive prices possible. We are driven to support our customers and the industry with unsurpassed standards of service and reliability. With these goals and commitments, Oklahoma Steel & Wire maintains an environment that promotes long term growth for our valued customers and the industry."

Brand Value Proposition

Which values are so important to your company that if they disappeared, your company would cease to exist as it is? Many companies disappear every year from the market place, so why does yours survive? Why do your customers trust you? Are you doing something right that other companies are not doing in the same way? What do you stand for?

The value proposition consists of the whole **cluster of benefits the company promises**. It is more than the core positioning of the offering.

CAT's core is "reliable," but the buyer is promised more than just a great machine. Included in the package is a reasonably priced piece of equipment, good service, and a long warranty period. Basically, the proposition is a statement about the resulting experience customers will gain from the company's market offering. The brand depends on the company's ability to **manage its value-delivery system**. The delivery system includes all the experiences the customer will have using the offering.

You also can characterize this as brand personality. It describes the brand as if it was a human being. The personality of a brand can help to provide the necessary differentiation even in a parity market. The personality strongly facilitates brand recognition, making it more interesting and memorable; it moreover stimulates positive attributes such as energy, youthfulness, and responsiveness, which can be very important to many brands.[19]

SAP defines its brand personality as enjoyable, friendly and approachable, honest and responsive, listening and responding, constantly improving.[20] Of course this can only come to life if the customers' perception is the same as was intended by the company.

Brand Promise

Strong brands express the promise behind an organization – the pledge we make to everyone about what they will experience when they do business with the company. The company Advanced Circuits guarantees the "quick turnaround" of custom printed circuit boards. Rackspace web hosting promises to deliver "fanatical support". *FedEx* promises "peace of mind".

A strong, clearly understood brand promise contributes to the momentum of growth. In 1847, John Deere promised, "I will never put my name on a product that does not have in it the best that I have in me." For more than 150 years the John Deer Company remained true to that commitment – building our reputation by building value into every machine that bears our name. So you can count on equipment that's as productive as possible. Up and ready to work when you are. And designed to minimize your daily operating costs, therefore we promise: Nothing Runs like a Deere.

It is necessary to deliver a differentiated brand promise. As companies lose their ability to **differentiate their brands based on functional attributes**, they must focus on process and relationship benefits, such as ease of ordering or responsiveness to customer requests. Thus, frontline employees must understand and deliver the right brand promise to their customers.

Aviagen

Aviagen, a B2B company well-known in farming, transfers its successful business model to lesser successful businesses that it acquires. *Aviagen* has many chicken breeding brands: *Arbor, Acres, L.I.R.,* and *Ross* delivering day old grand parent and parent stock chicks worldwide for the production of broiler chicks. *Aviagen Turkeys* has two turkey breeding brands: *British United Turkeys* (B.U.T.) and *Nicholas* (formally owned by the *Wesjohann* group, Germany), both delivering day old turkey poults around the world, while *C.W.T.* provides hatching eggs for the broiler market (see Figure 45).

Aviagen's business strength has been carefully cultivated by combining their own strength with the strength of the acquired brands. It now controls about one-third of the world's poultry market and has succeeded in turning what once was a local segmented farming business into a world-wide branded corporation.

Fig. 45. *Aviagen* brand portfolio

Brand Architecture

The central role of branding in establishing the firm's identity and building its position in the global marketplace among OEM, VAR (Value Added Reseller) and other market participants make it increasingly imperative for firms to establish a clear-cut brand architecture.

A key element of success is the **framing of a harmonious and consistent brand architecture** across countries and product lines, defining the number of levels and brands at each level. Of particular importance is the relative emphasis placed on corporate brands as opposed to product level brands and the degree of integration across markets. Escalating media costs, increasing communication and linkages across markets, together with the internationalization of OEMs and suppliers, create pressures for parsimony in the number of the firm's brands and a consolidation of the architecture across country markets. Focusing on a limited number of international strategic brands generates **cost economies** and **potential synergies** for the firm's efforts in all markets. At the same time, procedures for managing the custody of these brands have to be established.

There are three major patterns of brand architecture: **corporate-dominant, product-dominant and hybrid or mixed structures.**[21] Corporate-dominant architecture tended to be most common among firms with a relatively limited range of products or product divisions, or with a clearly defined target market, e.g. *IBM, GE, Shell, Caterpillar, AtlasCopco*, and *Lenovo*. Product dominant architecture, on the other hand, is very rare in B2B applications. Typically, they are found among firms which emerged over time with multiple national or local brands, or firms that have expanded internationally through acquisitions or joint ventures. An overview with examples for all three brand architecture patterns are shown in Figure 46.

Most commonly, hybrid or mixed structures can be found, consisting of a mix of global corporate, regional, and national product-level brands, or a corporate endorsement of product brands or different structures for different product divisions. Examples are *Kendrion N.V.* from the Netherlands or *DaimlerChrysler Trucks* with *Fuso* in Japan, *Freightliner, Oshkosh, Dodge*, and *Sterling* in the USA and Canada, *Freightliner* and *Mercedes-Benz* in South America and the original brand in Europe.

Both corporate and product dominant structures are evolving towards **hybrid structures**. Firms with corporate dominant structures are adding brands at lower levels, for example, the house or product level, to differentiate between different product divisions. Product-dominant structures, on the other hand, especially companies emphasizing multiple local (national) brands are moving toward a greater integration or co-ordination across markets through corporate endorsement of local brands.

These companies also vary in the extent to which they have a clearly articulated international brand architecture to **guide this evolution**. Some companies have clearly laid out the different levels at which brands are to be used, the interrelation between brands at different levels, the geographic scope of each brand and the product lines on which a brand is used, while others have few or no guidelines concerning international branding.

There are proven steps to optimize a brand architecture:[22]

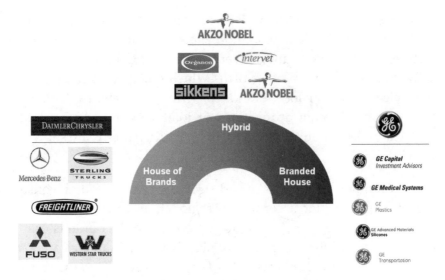

Fig. 46. Examples of industrial corporations brand architectures

- Take stock of your brand portfolio from the perspective of customers. Their view is the foundation for your strategy.

- Do "brand relationship mapping" to identify the relationships and opportunities between brands across your portfolio, checking for these criteria:

  o The perceived or potential credibility of the brands in that space – the perceptual license

  o Whether or not the company currently has or can develop competencies in that space – the organizational capabilities

  o Whether the size and current or potential growth of the market is significant enough to merit exploitation and investment – the market opportunity

- Mine the opportunities where all three criteria are met or use these innovative strategies if all criteria do not intersect:

  o "Pooling" and "trading"

  o Branded partnerships

  o Strategic brand consolidation

- o Brand acquisition

- o New brand creation

- Continuously emphasize the portfolio-wide thinking and business-wide implications of brand-oriented decisions. Consider creating a brand council.

When managed strategically and used as a structure to anticipate future business and brand needs, concerns, and issues, a clearly defined brand architecture can be the critical link to business strategy and the means to optimize growth and brand value.

4.4 Brand Building

Brands must not only be started. They must be built over time and modified over time.[23] Consider the *Tyvek* material invented by *DuPont*.

Tyvek

DuPont scientists, who have invented so many materials, including *Duco* lacquers, *Teflon* coating, *Corfam*, and *Nylon*, succeeded in creating a form of synthetic paper by shredding and processing nylon fibers. After sustained trial and error, they stabilized the concept and introduced *Tyvek* material in 1961. Under the corporate brand umbrella *DuPont – The miracle of science DuPont* heavily supported the marketing efforts.

In 1967, *DuPont* came up with *Tyvek* envelopes. As a communications symbol, *DuPont* used a medieval-looking metal box to emphasis the strength and durability of the new product solution (see Figure 48). *DuPont* approached large corporate accounts and offered them unique solutions. After fifteen years, the envelopes and other products based on the *Tyvek* material began to turn a profit. Today, the *Tyvek* envelope is the world's leading solution in demanding conditions of weather, weight, and content for surface and air mail – all without traditional raw wood material from the forest (see Figure 48).

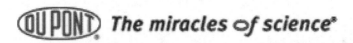

Fig. 47. *DuPont* logo and claim

High-Performance Protection

Tyvek® envelopes are made from DuPont™ Tyvek® brand protective material, a material so strong and durable it easily withstands even the most grueling conditions.

It's light. It's water-resistant. It's even puncture- and rip-resistant. In fact, it's virtually indestructible because *it isn't paper*, it's Tyvek®!

And when you're sending something important, that's exactly what you want your envelope to be.

Tyvek® envelopes. Protect What's Inside™.

Fig. 48. *DuPont*'s advertisement for *Tyvek* envelopes

In the case of *Tyvek* envelopes, *DuPont* moved through four steps: (1) establishing the proper brand identity, which established breadth and depth of brand awareness, (2) creating the appropriate brand meaning through strong, favorable, and unique brand associations, (3) eliciting positive, accessible brand responses, and (4) forging brand relationships with customers that are characterized by intense, active loyalty. The sum of all communications and customer experiences resulted in a distinctive image in their mind based on perceived emotional and functional benefits.

Tyvek is not just one of the most protective materials ever created; it is also very versatile and accommodating. Just about every type of business, from professional firms to educational institutions, from trade groups to government organizations rely on *Tyvek* envelopes. Here is a particularly interesting example:

"Students at *Northwestern University* in Evanston, Illinois don't carry simple IDs. They carry smart cards – plastic cards that let them

Fig. 49. Northwestern University student card cover

obtain cash at ATMs (Automatic Teller Machines), pay for food on campus, use college copiers or laundry facilities, gain access to buildings and more. Needless to say, the magnetic strip on the cards contains a lot of information. This means that once the University Services Wildcard Department inputs these data on all 17,000 student cards, the last thing it wants to do is have to input it all over again. But that was exactly the daunting prospect they faced every year (due to damage to the cards) – until Northwestern switched to Card Sleeves of *DuPont Tyvek* that protected the magnetic strips on the cards.

Successful brands don't stand still. They are continually built. According to the CBBE model, as shown in Figure 50, brand building involves four logical steps[24]. Their development must be based on a solid brand strategy and a consistent brand architecture:

1. Establishing the proper brand identity.
   Identity: Who are we? → Deep, broad brand awareness

2. Creating the appropriate brand meaning.
   Meaning: What are you? → Unique brand associations

3. Eliciting the right brand responses.
   Response: What about me? → Positive, accessible reactions

4. Forging appropriate brand relationships with customers.
   Relationship: What about you and me? → Intense, active loyalty

According to Keller, brand awareness consists of brand recognition which can be defined as the "customer's ability to confirm prior exposure to the brand when given a brand as a cue" and brand recall the "consumer's ability to retrieve the brand from memory when given the product category, the needs fulfilled by the category, or a purchase or usage situation as cue."

Building **brand strategy** must always be based on the **brand core**, its **values, and associations**. As we have shown (see Figure 43) the products and services are an intrinsic part of the brand. The content and the meaning of these dimensions may change over time, and have to be guided by the management and its decisions.

The other key element of success is the framing of **brand architecture** across product lines and a country, defining the number of levels and brands at each level, a harmonious and consistent system, in line with the strategy is required.

Therefore the "brand image is created by marketing programs that link strong, favorable, and unique associations to the brand in the customer's memory." These associations are not only controlled by the marketing program, but also through direct experience, brand information, word-of-mouth, or with the brand's identification with a certain company, country, distribution channel, person, place, or event. The CBBE model is built by "sequentially establishing six 'brand building blocks' with customers" that can be assembled as a brand pyramid, based on the brand strategy and architecture as shown in the Figure 50.[25]

Brand salience relates to the awareness of the brand. **Brand performance** refers to the satisfaction of customers' functional needs. **Brand imagery** *arises from* the satisfaction of customers' psychological needs. **Brand judgment** focuses on customers' opinions based on performance and imagery. **Brand emotions** are created by the customers' emotional responses and reactions to a brand. **Brand resonance**, finally, is based on the relationship and level of identification of the customer with a brand.

Achieving success in building your brand is a process that takes time and patience. "Branding is a long-term initiative that is predicated on building a relationship, based on trust, respect and consistency"[26]

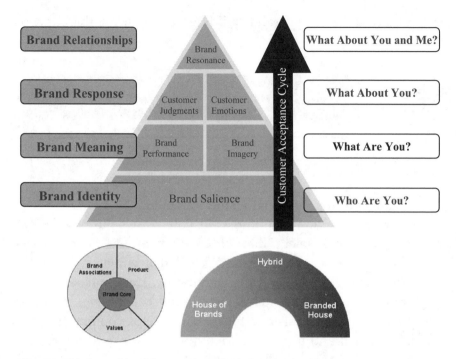

Fig. 50. The brand building pyramid with brand strategy and architecture

as Roger Giffin points out. It takes dedication and persistence – and most importantly, a **Brand Champion**; someone who takes responsibility to make sure that the 'brand promise' is always fulfilled. We know that when companies go through this process, they get clarity and a perspective. After completing the process, they find it easier to work on the media strategy, creative decision-making, and the revisiting of the strategic business plan.

Kevin Clancy, head of the marketing strategy firm Copernicus, has a different approach to brand building. We suggest using such an approach if you can start a branding concept from scratch; this may apply when you

- start a new business venture or when a company is
- spun-off from a larger unit or when you have to
- live with a new identity.

He outlines a five step brand building approach for this kind of situation:[27]

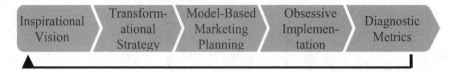

Fig. 51. Kevin Clancy Copernicus's 5 step brand building process

1. **Create your inspirational vision statement**

   Your brand vision identifies your enterprise's purpose for existing beyond solely that of creating profits. It reveals a broader, deeper, "built-to-last" view that enriches the enterprise, its customers, and the community. Determine also your brand personality. It helps your brand come alive. It makes your brand accessible and touchable. It helps you to differentiate yourself and it provides depth and dimension to your enterprise. If strategically sound, it delivers credibility and likeability. Some brands have a personality that triggers charisma – trust that goes from loyalty to advocacy. Work also on your brand character which is about the culture of the brand. It is the value system that directs every aspect of the enterprise, its principles, attitudes, and characteristics. It is the commitment made to customers, associates, and suppliers.

2. **Transformational strategy**

   In thinking of the relationship between your brand and your customer, it is necessary to adopt a more transformational, cross-functional approach in understanding the entire value chain. By moving from market segments to strategic segments the valued customer could be reached through a clear defined value proposition (what to offer), and for the distribution of an appropriate value network (how to deliver). A transformational strategy could also be achieved by radical business innovation which moves away from market driven to market driving.[28] Market drivers are visionary elements, creating new markets and redefining categories, rather than focusing on obtaining market share in existing markets. They also include the development of **a transformational brand image.** There are two aspects of brand image – how you want to be seen, and how you are seen. The challenge is to direct, shape, and focus on how customers see you. Yet, how the customers see your brand is not just what their eyes see, but what they think and **feel**. The eyes and the brain create an array of impressions, past and present, real and perceived, rational and emotional. Brand image is what is physically in front of customers' eyes and senses, and what the brain does with that information.

3. Model-based marketing planning

The short life cycle and fast decay in revenue, combined with the rapid and frequent introduction of new products, make successful marketing an extremely challenging management task. With new product and services often involving large investments, the potential to improve decision-making in the industry would appear to be considerable. This means moving away from traditional marketing planning models. Many of these models were based on a "numbers game" notion where top management, via a process of setting objectives, could summon those below to develop strategies capable of achieving these objectives. Objectives were set in order to motivate and to control performance. It is important to move to the use of sophisticated planning tools such as *DuPont*'s ratio analysis or value-based planning models including economic value added (EVA) and simulare discounted cash flow methods.

4. Obsessive implementation

Being 100% consistent in delivering the brand experience is critical to the long-term success of your brand. Every time you change or mix the message to your customers or every time you don't deliver the promise, you chip away at what you are trying to achieve and are ultimately proving the brand is not to be trusted.

5. Diagnostic metrics

For successful brand strategies the best-designed and most effective brand diagnostic metrics have to be in place. They should provide a link between brand strategy and business strategy. These metrics, based on **Business Intelligence (BI)** methods, will show how the brand can be better managed while providing the rationale for more effective brand and business resource allocation.

The result will be that the business as a whole can show the benefits of having a consistent approach for measuring the brand's overall performance. With this knowledge in place, the further fine-tuning of the branding and business strategy can progress to new heights.

Brand Portfolio Management

The 1990s boom years resulted in a proliferation of products and brands. As a result, corporations must ask "how should we **allocate existing financial** and **human resources** among our brands to grow shareholder value?" Firms experiencing the largest gains in brand equity saw their ROI average 30 percent; those with the largest losses saw their ROI average a negative 10 percent[29]. Message: focus on getting the most from existing brands through better organizing and managing brands and brand inter-relationships. Different business strategies require different brand architectures. The two most important types are:

- **"Branded house" architecture** – employs a single (master) brand to span a series of offerings that may operate with descriptive sub-brand names. Examples: *Boeing*, *GE* and *IBM*.

- **"House of brands" architecture** – each brand is a stand-alone; the sum of performance of the independent brands is greater than under a single master brand. Examples: *General Motors* and *Marriott International*.

Neither type is better than the other. Some companies use a mix of both. The key is to have a well-defined brand portfolio strategy.

Brand portfolio management is not just a marketing issue. It directly affects corporate profitability. Ill-defined and overlapping brands lead to erosion in price premiums, weaker manufacturing economies, and sub-scale distribution. In a slowing economy, the problem of an underperforming brand portfolio is even more acute: While adding brands is easy, it becomes difficult to harvest the value in a brand or to divest it.

Effective brand portfolio management starts by creating a fact base about the equity in each brand and the brand's economic contribution. The application of analytical tools, such as the five precepts of portfolio power (shown later), can inform decisions about individual and collective brand strategies from targeting and positioning to investments, partnerships, and extension opportunities. Linking the intangibles of brands to hard financial metrics allows companies to exploit the full potential of their brands and thereby gain a competitive advantage.

Successful brand portfolio managers embed branding decisions into each aspect of the company's business design, from customer selection to the internal organizational system. They use divisional or business unit brands as part of creating and protecting unique business designs within the company. At the same time, they recognize the need to minimize the complexity and cost in managing a portfolio.[30]

Marriott

Take the example of *Marriott International,* a company that has excelled in its field. The *Marriott* group manages 2,100 lodging properties in almost 60 countries. While the lodging industry grew at less than 6% annually during the 1990s, *Marriott's* growth rates exceeded 10%. Similarly, the company's profitability showed an 18.4% growth rate, three points higher than the industry as a whole. Many factors have contributed to *Marriott's* success, including sophisticated revenue management and centralization of many common processes such as purchasing. But *Marriott's* managers have also developed a clear understanding of where they can and cannot take their brand (see Figure 52).

Fig. 52. Selection of *Marriott International, Inc.*, brand portfolio

Fact-based insights of the *Marriott* management, grounded in an understanding of both brand equity and the economic contribution of their brands to corporate profitability, form the foundation for a winning brand portfolio. Consequently, the Marriot organization acted on those insights, with everyone behaving in ways that advanced the cause of the whole portfolio, not just of individual brands. Brand portfolio management requires developing the links between intangibles and hard financial metrics. Proceed by applying these **five precepts of portfolio power**:[31]

1. **Align the brand portfolio with the business design.**
   Embed branding decisions into each aspect of the company's business, from customer selection to the internal organizational system. The evolution of brand strategy at Citigroup is used to illustrate this precept.[32]

2. **Consider building a brand pyramid.**
   Individual brands within a portfolio become far more powerful when they are interrelated, as *Kraft Foods* has demonstrated[33]. Without a coordinated holistic portfolio strategy each brand cannot be tailored for a distinct level of the pyramid. The pyramid model requires constant vigilance and defense against attacks of its base. Use economic measures that reflect incremental costs, allowing the higher levels to cover the core costs. Manage the base of the pyramid as a low-cost business design, with production eventually moved to low-cost countries.

3. **Grow winners and harvest losers**.
   While adding brands is easy in prosperous times, in a slower economy, a concentration of investments on smaller groups of

power brands is recommended. *Unilever's* practice with their brands is cited to show how rigorous they were in cutting or repositioning weak brands[34].

4. Play the cards you are dealt.
Rather than stretching a brand until it snaps, build a new brand or buy a brand. This is based on a clear understanding of where the company can and cannot take its brands. *Marriott's* practices have been used before to illustrate this point.[35]

5. Counter the tendency to make brand decisions in a decentralized, ad hoc manner.
Establish brand management functions with management guidelines that outline when, how, and where a brand should be used. Reward managers for making decisions that benefit the entire portfolio, rather than for building one brand at the expense of another. Coordinate marketing's focus on demand generation to drive sales and to guarantee brand focus on longer-term image building to achieve sustained growth.

Fact-based insights, grounded in an understanding of both brand equity and a brand's economic contribution to corporate profits, form the foundations for a winning brand portfolio.

4.5   Brand Audit

Companies should periodically audit the performance of their individual brands. You need to agree on the objectives of the audit, and then you can start collecting data, identifying participants, scheduling interviews, and setting a findings review session.

The brand audit aims to assess the strengths and weaknesses of a given brand or brand portfolio. Typically, this consists of an internal description of how the brand has been marketed (named "brand inventory"') and an **external investigation**, through focus groups, questionnaires, and other consumer research methods, to identify what the brand does and could mean to consumers (called "brand exploratory"). The final step would be the analysis and interpretation of the results.

We know that the strongest brands are often supported by formal brand-equity-management systems.[36] Managers of these brands have a written document – a **Brand Equity Charter –** that spells out the company's general philosophy with respect to brands and their inherent brand equity (e.g. what a brand is, why brands matter, and why brand management is relevant to the company). This charter also summarizes the activities that make up brand audits, brand tracking, and other brand research procedures; specifies the outcomes expected of them and includes the latest findings gathered from such research.[37]

Finally, you have to bring your brand to the acid test. The **Brand Score Card** measures the performance of your brands in relation to customer priorities. In general, there are four dimensions of brand measurement that tend to bind the customer to the brand:[38]

- The functional performance of the underlying product or service
- The convenience and ease of accessing the product or service
- The personality of the brand
- The pricing and value component

The combination of these attributes often provide a well-rounded picture of how well the brand asset is growing and how much untapped cash flow is waiting to be unlocked. Brand attributes should be monitored in tracking studies conducted in waves every six or 12 months. The **advanced B2B companies** like *GE, IBM,* and *Accenture* are today migrating towards "continuous" brand tracking, with smaller samples fielded every other month. Our suggested brand audit should be a customer-focused exercise that involves a series of procedures to assess the health of the brand, uncover its sources of brand equity, and suggest ways to improve and leverage its equity.

The brand audit can be used to set a **strategic direction** for the brand. Are the current sources of brand equity satisfactory? Do certain brand associations need to be strengthened? Does the brand lack uniqueness? What brand opportunities exist and what potential challenges exist for brand equity? What is the current status of the brand architecture? [39]

A **compliance audit** goes a step beyond this: A bottom-up audit of the individual brands allows an assessment of how well each brand functions as part of the overall brand architecture of the firm. The key steps of the compliance audit are:

(1) collection of information that establishes how the brand has been used in each country that it is marketed in

(2) assessment of deviations from its established position in the structure and reasons

(3) evaluation of the brand's performance

A **strategic audit**, in contrast, refers to a top down audit, conducted on multiple levels. If the end-result of the strategic audit is that the firm's brand architecture no longer fits underlying drivers, steps should be taken to revise the firm's architecture so that it reflects the new realities of the marketplace.

Using these audits, a company can develop a marketing program to maximize long-term brand equity. Future results need to be monitored and necessary corrective action taken.[40]

Brand Metrics

The best-designed and most effective brand metrics can only be developed if the link between brand and business strategy is clearly understood. These metrics will show how the brand can be better managed while providing the rationale for more effective brand and business resource allocation. If properly implemented, the business as a whole can reap the benefits of having a consistent and measured approach for gauging the brand's overall performance.[41]

Business Intelligence (BI)

Business Intelligence solutions can help to solve some brand metrics problems. Data mining is the most common BI technology today. It helps corporations to quickly analyze and make sense of massive amounts of information stored in databases throughout the enter-

prise to identify sales opportunities, supply senior management
with data for decision-making, and provide intelligence used in
other decision-making processes. New tools and technologies are
now emerging that bring the value of BI to **marketing, branding
and corporate communication professionals** by tapping into the
often overwhelming amounts of unstructured information.

There are two approaches for extracting business intelligence from
unstructured information:

- **Key Word Searches (KWS)**
  This approach is as simple as it sounds – identifying mentions
  and coverage of a company and its brand based on a key word
  alone. The approach is feasible for smaller companies, where
  their **media coverage and that of competitors** can easily be
  identified, analyzed, and checked for accuracy. However, it
  presents a significant challenge for larger organizations and
  those who have greater media coverage to identify what is real,
  and what it all means.

- **Natural Language Processing (NLP)**
  The second approach uses NLP.[42] It is one of the most highly
  accurate methods available, with extremely low numbers of
  false positives. The best NLP solutions use **information extrac-
  tion technologies** that combine statistical and semantic analysis
  to quickly scan through thousands of unstructured documents
  to identify those that are truly relevant. The technology deci-
  phers how words within a sentence relate to one another. It can
  determine whether your company is the focal point of an article, or a passing reference. It can determine what messages are
  being associated with your brand, and whether your company
  is being viewed as a technology leader, or behind the times.
  Unlike simple key-word based approaches, NLP technology
  can be leveraged to automatically discover important information about companies, people, products, and competitors, cutting down research and analysis time dramatically and
  opening up business opportunities that you might have overlooked.

By tying the BI approach into a larger **communications management strategy** in which companies use a single integrated platform to create, execute, and measure their marketing and communications programs, companies can do a better job of measuring brand perceptions. They can quickly benchmark themselves against their competitors, and identify who is writing about them and about the market. They can determine if they have more visibility in the trade and business press as well as in online or broadcast media. They can see which messages are strongly associated with a particular company, how long certain branding messages maintain visibility and exposure – and which die quickly. They can see, immediately, how a competitor is perceived, and how they are responding to your messages.

With **accurate and rapid information,** companies can **make knowledge-based decisions** more quickly. For instance, if the initial impact of a major brand re-launch is less than expected, immediate action may be required. When using traditional approaches, companies have no idea that their strategies are not working until months later. But when using NLP-based BI technology, quick strategy changes based on solid data and metrics are possible. Perhaps more importantly, a communication measurement and analysis solution that incorporates NLP technology allows companies to truly justify their marketing and communication expenditures, establish a compelling ROS (Return On Sales) in months, not years, and demonstrate the **effectiveness of their strategies**, both at a tactical and strategic level. Not only will they be able to explicitly identify how much coverage certain campaigns generated, and how that **coverage impacted visibility** and **brand perception**, but they will also be able to better determine the impact on larger strategic goals.

After you have implemented your brand strategy, identified your brand, and launched your branding efforts, you will want to measure your ROBI (Return On Brand Investment). "Do You Know Your ROBI?" It is a useful resource.[43] Davis outlines eight qualitative and quantitative ROBI metrics.

- **Brand knowledge** (qualitative) – provides detailed data on the level of awareness, recall, and understanding of the brands.

- **Brand positioning understanding** (qualitative) – identifies how well different customer segments understand the brands' positioning as well as their customer service, personal contact, expertise and selling messages targeted at them.

- **Brand contract fulfillment** (qualitative and quantitative) – determines whether the brands are fulfilling their promises in the marketplace.

- **Brand personality recognition** (qualitative) – determines how well the brand's personality is being communicated to internal and external audiences and how well it actually is understood and remembered.

- **Brand-driven customer acquisitions** (quantitative) – tell how many new customers are attracted with the brand portfolio management efforts and who these customers are.

- **Brand-driven customer retention and loyalty** (quantitative) – measures the number of customers who have been lost because of the implemented brand portfolio strategies.

- **Brand-driven penetration and frequency** (quantitative) – measure the number of existing customers who are buying more products or services as a result of the brand portfolio management.

- **Financial brand value** (quantitative) – measure the price premium the brands can command over their competitors and the earnings attributable to the brands strength.

Based on the results of measuring the brand portfolio management, marketers can **adjust** their **strategies** correspondingly. Since the findings might affect all branding aspects, the firm should get cross functional teams involved from the start so that the adjustments can be made instantly. The measurement scores will help determine how the firm is performing today and highlight areas to focus on in the future.

Many companies probably won't want or need to do all. If you have to concentrate your efforts, the following three will provide the most important brand metrics: **Brand Positioning Understanding, Brand-Driven Customer Acquisitions,** and **Brand-Driven Customer Retention** and **Loyalty**. With this set of metrics in place, managers can work toward four objectives:

- Measuring the brand's performance against the portfolio strategy

- Ensuring that the brand is sustaining the firm's focus

- Developing consistent communications

- More effectively allocating resources to build the brands in the future

Reevaluating Brands

A good brand strategy should last as long as it is the **best strategy possible**. To change and re-brand simply for the sake of change probably won't produce the results you wished for. To kill a great brand strategy because someone in marketing got bored before the market did, not only wastes a lot of money, time, and effort but can be harmful as well. Top management or the Chief Marketing Officer (CMO) must provide discipline and leadership in order to resist change only for change's sake.

People rely on things they know and trust – if you change something, this trust probably will be challenged and consequently either reinforced or weakened. **Re-branding** or **brand juvenation** efforts should not be undertaken lightly.

UPS

Let's have a look at the re-branding of *UPS* again. The company wanted to show its **evolution** and **draw customer attention** to all that they have to offer.[44] Over the years the company continued to expand across the globe and introduced a portfolio of new services in a diverse spectrum of interrelated business areas. It had been developing and acquiring new capabilities to improve and broaden its market offerings.[45] Yet, the UPS brand was still regarded as synonymous with ground delivery by trucks, at least in the United States. It was almost unknown to the majority of UPS customers that the company heavily invested in its airborne delivery services, establishing the eleventh-largest airline in the world, delivering 2 million packages and documents every day.

In 2001, UPS acquired Mail Boxes Etc. (MBE). MBE provided an enormous opportunity for enhancing UPS's already extensive 70,000 access points, which included other retail partners, further supported by UPS branded drop boxes. In the course of these changes, the question was whether to re-brand all MBE franchisees or not. After extensive market testing over almost two years the company made the decision to re-brand the stores.[46] The result of these tests in traditional branded MBE stores, co-branded stores, and UPS-branded stores showed that the **deciding factor** was less about price than about the power of the UPS brand. The UPS store locations outpaced all the other test stores.[47]

Consequently, all franchisees of the MBE locations in the U.S. were given the opportunity to re-brand their shops into The UPS Store, and over 90 percent did agree to it (and which can be considered a very high participation rate in the franchising industry).[48] If a brand no longer fully expresses the company's capabilities, it is time for a change. It was quite obvious that the UPS brand was lacking certain attributes. The new UPS brand better reflects the broader scope of its business dealings.

The change of UPS's visual identity is regarded to be one of the most significant corporate identity transformations in American history. The scale of the whole project was huge. The following numbers demonstrate the gigantic scale of the project. The new logo had to be put on more than 88,000 vehicles, 257 airplanes, 1,700 facilities worldwide, 70,000 drop-off and retail access points, more than 1 million uniform pieces and more than 3 billion packages annually.[49] The estimated cost of the re-branding exercise was tagged at approximately US$20 million for the first year.

If you want to change or **broaden the perception** of a brand it is not enough to present a new logo to your customers and the public. It is necessary to start the process inside out. *UPS* did a great job in integrating the re-branding within the context of a solid and holistic brand strategy. For years, the employees of *UPS* had embraced and lived the brand. In order not to alienate them during this process, the company executed a massive internal and external launch program that explained the reason for the new look.[50]

The **communication elements** that were used to support the re-branding efforts were mainly television and print campaigns. Using different approaches for the United States and the rest of the world, *UPS* focused on communicating its expanding capabilities beyond package delivery.[51] Beginning with the 2002 Winter Olympics in Salt Lake City, *UPS* started the communications push for the stretching of its brand. At that time, they introduced the very successful "What Can Brown Do for You?" campaign which lasted for over two years. To broaden the view of its customers, it showed *UPS* as a logistics and supply chain company, rather than a ground delivery service expert. In 2003, with the logo change, they added the corporate tagline: "Synchronizing the world of commerce." Although many critics were considering it quite a risky brand stretch, the *UPS* brand has shown no signs of flagging since the start of the **repositioning approach**.[52]

That the re-branding exercise really did pay off is shown by the increasing willingness of the world business community to leverage on the advantages offered by *UPS* through its diverse spectrum of market offerings and total supply chain solutions. In 2003, the non-package revenue of the company increased by almost 100% to US$2.7 billion. In the Asia-Pacific region the export volume rose nearly 10% in the fourth quarter of 2004. Consequently, the transportation issue was shifting from the shipping room to the boardroom as trends in outsourcing of logistics functions to third parties such as *UPS* were gaining grounds.[53]

Summary

- The brand building process consists of brand planning, brand analysis, brand strategy, brand building, and brand auditing.

- **Brand building starts** with understanding the key attributes of your products and services as well as understanding and anticipating the needs of your customers.

- **Mastering brand stability, brand leadership,** and **international presence** calls for a structured sequence of the brand building process.

- The first thing you have to do when building your own brand is to **articulate a brand mission** that reflects what you want to accomplish with it. Secondly you have to add a coherent set of brand values and a brand identity. All the visual elements of the brand, the brand name, logo, and slogan, should be developed accordingly to create a unique visual identity that reflects what the company stands for as well as what its attitude and culture is all about.

- The **power of a brand lies in the customer mind set** – brand equity is therefore a vital strategic bridge from the past to the future and a set of stored values that consumers associate with a brand. These associations add value beyond the basic product functions due to past investments in marketing the brand and they are captured in the Customer-Based Brand Equity (CBBE) model.

- **Brand analysis** helps to define and formulate a proper brand mission, define a brand personality and set brand values. Aligning to the corporate vision and mission is mandatory for devising effective, focused, and distinctive brand elements that help develop a long-term brand strategy.

- The "three C's" of branding refer to the indispensable conditions that precede successful branding. For the purpose of completeness we have added a fourth and fifth **branding principle**: Consistency, Clarity, Constancy, Visibility, and Authenticity.

- A **brand strategy** should not be changed just for the sake of change. Re-branding or brand rejuvenation efforts have to be carefully evaluated in terms of necessity and success probabilities. Companies with many unstructured and maybe even diluted brands need to refocus their brand which is almost the same work as building a brand from scratch.

- Brand strategy consists of developing a strong mission, positioning, brand promise, and value proposition.

- Successful brands don't just sell products; they communicate **clear values** stretched across a number of products.

- A key element of success is the framing of a harmonious and consistent **brand architecture** across countries and product lines, defining the number of levels and brands at each level.

- Brand auditing seeks to measure the strengths and weaknesses of a brand and the overall brand portfolio. The Brand Score Card measures the performance of your brand in relationship to customer priorities. Based on internal and external analysis, compliance and strategic audits should be conducted regularly. Other brand metrics could be implemented such as Business Intelligence, key word search or Natural Language Processing.

- Fact-based insights, grounded in an **understanding of both brand equity and a brand's economic contribution** to corporate profits, form the foundations for a winning brand portfolio.

- **Over time every brand needs re-evaluation**, fine-tuning, and re-branding.

Notes

1 The 17 B2B companies listed on the Interbrand ranking of the 100 best global brands of 2005 had an average of 20,1 % of market capitalization; Source: Robert Berner and David Kiley, "Global Brands," *Business Week* (July 2005), pp. 86-94.

2 Remark by J. Justus Schneider (Head of Mercedes-Benz Brand Communica-tion) in the Introduction to Leslie Butterfield, *Icon of a Passion – The Development of the Mercedes-Benz Brand*, 2005.

3   "Recognition of Signs and Logos," Analysis for the Olympic Committee 1995, *Today* (20 July 1995).

4   Alicia Clegg, "The Myth of Authenticity," *brandchannel.com* (15 August 2005).

5   Ibid.

6   Iain Ellwood, *Essential Rand Book: Over 100 Techniques to Increase Brand Value* (London: Kogan Page, 2002); Stedman Graham, *Build Your Own Life Brand! A Powerful Strategy to Maximize Your Potential* ... (New York: Free Press, 2001), p. 200.

7   Chuck Pettis, *TechnoBrands: How to Create & Use Brand Identity to Market, Advertise & Sell Technology Products*, American Management Association, December, 1994.

8   Leslie Butterfiled (2005), p. 191.

9   Leslie Butterfield, *Icon of a Passion – The Development of the Mercedes-Benz Brand*, 2005), p. 66, 109.

10 Constantinos C. Markides, *All the Right Moves: A Guide to Crafting Breakthrough Strategies* (Cambridge, Ma. 1999).

11 Christian Belz and Klaus-Michael Kopp, „Markenfuehrung fuer Investitionsgueter als Kompetenz- und Vertrauensmarketing," in: *Handbuch Markenartikel*, Manfred Bruhn (ed) 1994, pp. 1577-1601.

12 Jim Collins, *Good to Great. Why Some Companies Make the Leap and Others Don't*, 2001.

13 Paul Temporal, "What Is Positioning?" *brandingasia.com* (April/May 2000).

14 Soni Simpson, Adjunct Professor, Stuart School of Business, Illinois Institute of Technology (IIT) Chicago, during her lecture in Spring 2005.

15 David A. Aaker and Erich Joachimsthaler, *Brand Leadership,* 2000, p. 67.

16 Web site of *SAP AG*, Walldorf, Germany, cited June 2005.

17 thinkexist.com/quotes/charles_mingus/ (cited July 2005).

18 Web site of *Oklahoma Steel & Wire Co., Inc.*, Madill, OK, cited November 2005.

19 David A. Aaker and Erich Joachimsthaler, *Brand Leadership,* 2000, p. 51.

20 Web site of *SAP AG*, Walldorf, Germany, cited June 2005.

[21] Sylvie Laforêt and John Saunders, "Managing Brand Portfolios: How the Leaders Do It," *Journal of Advertising Research* (September/October 1994), pp. 64-76.

[22] Michael Petromilli, Dan Morrison and Michael Million, "Brand Architecture: Building Brand Portfolio Value", *Strategy & Leadership*, Volume 30 Number 5, 2002, pp. 22-28.

[23] Andrew Pierce, Hanna Moukanas, and Rick Wise, *Brand Portfolio Economics – Harnessing a Group of Brands to Drive Profitable Growth,* Mercer Management Consulting, Inc., 2002.

[24] Building Customer-Based Brand Equity, March 2001, Kevin Lane Keller, Amos Tuck School of Business, Dartmouth College. An excerpt from an article in *The Advertiser*, October 2002.

[25] Based on Kevin Lane Keller, Strategic Brand Management: *Building, Measuring, and Managing Brand Equity*, Upper Saddle River, Prentice Hall, 2003.

[26] Roger Griffin, Associate Partner the Custom Fit Communications Group, seen January 7, 2006, http://www.customfitonline.com/news/branding001.htm.

[27] Kevin J. Clancy and Peter C. Krieg, *Counterintuitive Marketing Achieving Great Results Using Common Sense*, Free Press, New York 2000. See also http://www.copernicusmarketing.com/about/docs/intellectual_pro perties.htm.

[28] Nirmalya Kumar Marketing as Strategy: *Understanding the CEO's Agenda for Driving Growth and Innovation*, (Boston: Harvard Business School Press, 2004), pp. 245-255.

[29] Michael Petromilli, Dan Morrison and Michael Million, "Brand Architecture: Building Brand Portfolio Value", *Strategy and Leadership* 5, 2002.

[30] Andrew Pierce, Hanna Moukanas, and Rick Wise, "Brand Portfolio Economics: Harnessing a Group of Brands to Drive Profitable Growth," *Viewpoint* (No. 1, 2002), Mercer Management Consulting Inc.

[31] Andrew Pierce and Hanna Moukanas, "Portfolio Power: Harnessing a Group of Brands to Drive Profitable Growth," *Strategy & Leadership* (Vol. 30 No. 5 2002), pp. 15-21.

[32] Andrew Pierce, Hanna Moukanas, Rick Wise, 2002, p. 5.

[33] Silvio M. Brondoni, *Brand policy and brand equity*, Symphonya, Emerging Issues in Management, Milano, Istituto di Economia d'Impresa, 2002, examples at pp. 16 -18.

[34] Catherine Gorrell, Quick takes, *Strategy & Leadership*, Oct 2002, Issue 30, p. 5.

[35] Andrew Pierce and Hanna Moukanas, "Portfolio Power: Harnessing a Group of Brands to Drive Profitable Growth," *Strategy & Leadership* (Vol. 30 No. 5 2002), pp. 15-21.

[36] Kevin L. Keller, "Manager's Tool Kit," The Brand Report Card, *Harvard Business Review* (February, 2000), p. 147.

[37] Kevin Keller recommends the brand equity report, because it not only describes what is happening within a brand but also why, we would like to use a Brand score card with multi- dimensional factors.

[38] Patrick LaPointe, "The Picture of Brand Health," *CMO Magazine* (December 2005).

[39] Laurel Wentz, "Brand Audits Reshaping Images," *Ad Age International* (September 1996), pp. 38-41, and Susan P. Douglas, C. Samuel Craig and Edwin J. Nijssen, "International Brand Architecture: Development, Drivers and Design," *Journal of International Marketing* (Vol. 9 No. 2 2001).

[40] Philip Kotler and Kevin L. Keller, *Marketing Management*, 2006, p. 43; Patrick LaPointe, "The Picture of Brand Health," *CMO Magazine* (December 2005).

[41] Laurel Wentz, "Brand Audits Reshaping Images," *Ad Age International* (September 1996), pp. 38-41.

[41] Scott Davis, "Brand Metrics: Good, Bad and Don't Bother," *The Canadian Marketing Report* (26 January 2004).

[42] For more information go to http://www.aaai.org/AITopics/html/nat-lang.html.

[43] Scott M. Davis, *Management Review* (Vol 87 (9) 1998), pp. 55-58.

[44] Vivian Manning-Schaffel, "UPS & FedEx Compete to Deliver," *brand-chan-nel.com* (17 May 2004).

[45] Web site of *United Parcel Service of America, Inc.*, Atlanta, GA, cited July 2005.

[46] Larry Bloomenkranz, "Evolving the UPS Brand," *Design Management Review*, vol. 15, no. 2 (Spring 2004), pp. 68-73.

[47] Connie R. Gentry, "Building on Brand Awareness, " *Chain Store Age* (July 2003), pp. 36-37.

[48] Larry Bloomenkranz, "Evolving the UPS Brand," *Design Management Review,* vol. 15, no. 2 (Spring 2004), pp. 68-73.

[49] Web site of *United Parcel Service of America, Inc.,* Atlanta, GA, cited July 2005.

[50] Larry Bloomenkranz, "Evolving the UPS Brand," *Design Management Review,* vol. 15, no. 2 (Spring 2004), pp. 68-73.

[51] Web site of *United Parcel Service of America, Inc.,* Atlanta, GA, cited July 2005.

[52] Sean Callahan, "Look What Brown Has Done for UPS," *BtoB's Best* 2004 (25 October 2004), p. 26.

[53] Pang H. Yee, "Rebranding Pays off for UPS," *thestar online* (17 May 2004).

CHAPTER 5

Success Stories of B2B Branding

Few things are harder to put up with than a good example.

Mark Twain (1835-1910)

In this chapter, we are going to describe several examples of successful brands of industrial companies that illustrate how brand strategy is put into action.

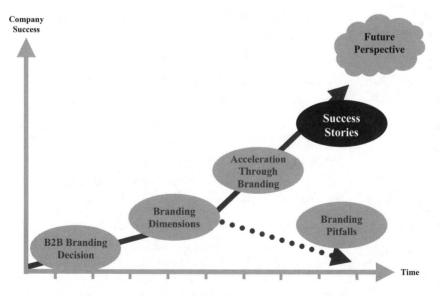

Fig. 53. Guiding principle success stories

The eight cases are:

Table 5. Selected Case Studies

Case	Principle
FedEx	**From a House of Brands to a Branded House** "How *FedEx* communicates one brand promise in B2C and B2B in several businesses."
Samsung	**Leveraging the brand from B2C to B2B** "How to successfully leverage B2C brand strength to B2B business."
Cemex	**Dual branding to create brand equity** "*Cemex* dual branding concept of branding for B2B clients and individual branding for B2C clients with specific country needs."
IBM	**Successful turnaround through brand communications** "Strengthening *IBM* brand by an integrated marketing communication approach."
Siemens	**Branding for cross-selling initiatives** "Effective and efficient brand communication of *Siemens'* cross-business activities."
Lanxess	**Brand communication of a spin-off** "Successful build up of brand positioning and alignment of communication activities to lead the business into independence."
Lenovo	**Building a global Brand from China** "Leveraging the excellent reputation on quality and services of *IBM's* PCs to *Lenovo's* own brand."
Tata Steel	**Branding steel based on customer focus** "How *Tata Steel* successfully branded its products and moved to high value added products (through internal Marketing focused on customers)."

5.1 FedEx

From a House of Brands to a Branded House

Federal Express was founded in 1973 by Frederick W. Smith. He literally invented the concept of overnight delivery, thereby creating a whole new market where previously there was none. Starting off with only fourteen small jets at its disposal, *FedEx* today has more than 560 aircrafts – making them the largest all-cargo air fleet in the world.[1] The total daily lift capacity of their fleet exceeds 26.5 million pounds. Within 24 hours it travels approximately 500,000 miles. With the 2.5 million miles the *FedEx Express* couriers log a day; it is equivalent to 100 trips around the earth.[2]

A need that already has been identified rarely provides companies with big business opportunities. The **greatest opportunities** arise when you detect a **completely new need** that your customers didn't even recognize themselves until you offered a solution to them. That is the success story of *FedEx* with its overnight delivery system.

The company was named "Federal Express" because of the intended associations with the word "Federal" since it expressed an interest in nationwide economic activity. Another trace to the name is the proposed contract with the Federal Reserve Bank, which the company hoped to attain at that time. Although the proposal was denied, the name "Federal Express" was chosen since Smith believed it was a **particularly good one** for their purposes. It draws public attention to the business and facilitates name recognition.[3]

While the ability to **identify an unidentified need** provides a great business opportunity, it tends to remain useless if a company fails to come up with a new and innovative way of meeting it. The delivery of a new service can be quite tricky. *FedEx* solved it brilliantly by its hub-and-spoke distribution system. This innovation lies at the heart of the *FedEx* network and is only one example of various other innovative solutions in this area. The effective integration of its ground and air system is another case where the company proved its willingness to do things differently.

Soon after its foundation, the company managed to become the premier carrier of **high-priority goods** in the marketplace, setting the industry standard for their operations. Considering the fact that there was no other company with a comparative market offering at that time, this is not really surprising. Nonetheless, the company did not generate any profit until July 1975. By the end of 1995 the company was well established, with an astonishing growth rate of about 40 percent annually. Gradually new competitors appeared, attracted by this appealing economic potential. In 1983, the company made business history by being the first American company reaching the **financial hallmark of US$1 billion** in revenues within ten years of start-up **without mergers or acquisitions**.[4]

By building out its **core competencies** in logistics *FedEx* has definitely produced a **competitive advantage**. When *UPS*, its main competitor, successfully invaded the airborne delivery system in 2001, *FedEx* responded with counteroffensive defense. In order to challenge *UPS* in its own home turf it invested heavily in ground delivery service while still building out its special overnight services, such as extended pickup hours and Saturday delivery.[5]

FedEx Brand

The idea of express networks that first emerged 150 to 200 years ago in the United States still constitutes the core of the *FedEx* brand. These networks were established to move something very important under someone's custodial control and have it delivered within a certain time. This basic principle of a general delivery service lies at the heart of the *FedEx* business. Transportation, logistics, and movement of goods – anything that suits this **basic principle** fits the *FedEx* **brand**. The focus of the brand, though, rests on what it identifies: **express networks**. General but yet powerful associations are security and reliability. It provides customers with peace of mind, nurturing their sense of security by using the brand.[6]

Over the years, customers adopted the shortened name *FedEx* to speak of the company and its services. Actually the term has been used as a verb, meaning the equivalent of "sending an overnight shipment". To "FedEx" something is **common terminology**. Thankful for this cue from its customers, the company officially changed its brand from *Federal Express* to *FedEx* in 1994. This can be regarded as the first **evolution of the company's corporate identity**.[7]

In the early 1990s the company was then expanding into global markets and wanted to modernize its corporate brand. Soon, the company realized that **more than a cosmetic face-lift** was needed for its dated purple logo. In order to do it right *FedEx* started a **complete overhaul of the corporate identity** from the visual design to the corporate name to the names of everything that it offered – from services to drop boxes to shipping containers. Research findings at the time revealed that many customers didn't really understand what *FedEx's* services were because the naming was quite confusing. In some cases *FedEx* used acronyms that didn't gave them any clue at all. In order to clarify the naming system and to keep it simple the company implemented a system that relies **solely upon the** *FedEx* **brand** in **addition with real words to describe the operating company**, product or service explicitly. The re-branding efforts created a successful brand portfolio of services and products with names that have become timeless.

In 2000, the company implemented the second evolution of the company's corporate identity when it changed the name to *FedEx Express* in order to **better position** the business in the overall *FedEx* Corporation portfolio of services. Just like it was the case for *UPS* changing its logo, the re-branding signified an **expanding breadth** of the company's market offerings. It simply had to move away from being just an overnight delivery service business, which can be compared to *UPS* moving away from being just a ground delivery service business.

The brand promise of *FedEx* that secured its place in customers' minds and hearts is the guaranteed next-day delivery **"absolutely, positively by 10:30 a.m."** With the intention to create a more diversified business including a portfolio of different but related businesses, the company invested heavily in a number of acquisitions and realignments.

With the acquisition of *Caliber System Inc.*, for instance, the *FedEx Corporation*, originally called *FDX Corp.*, was formed in January 1998.

House of Brands   **Branded House**

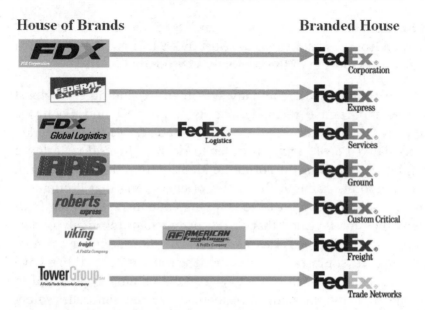

Fig. 54. From a house of brands to a branded house[8]

In a move to integrate the company's portfolio of services and become a Branded House, all *Caliber System Inc.* subsidiaries were re-branded.[9]

Today's *FedEx* is directed by *FedEx Corporation*, which leads the various companies that operate according to the business motto "operate independently, compete collectively and manage collaboratively," under the *FedEx* brand name worldwide. This way it ensures that all companies can benefit from the *FedEx* brand as it is one of the world's most recognized and trusted brands. In 2004, the *FedEx Corporation* acquired the privately held *Kinko's Inc.* and later re-branded it *FedEx Kinko's*. It is therefore the only acquired brand the company chose to keep as an official subbrand with its own equity in the brand portfolio.[10]

Fig. 55. *FedEx Kinko's* as the only independent subbrand[11]

Communicating the Brand

FedEx regards its own operations as one of the best channels of communications they have. The close integration of their information systems and transportation systems with those of their customers makes it even more difficult to switch to alternative market offerings. One of the first things they see on the screen when they turn on their PC is *FedEx*.[12]

While most brands focus either on businesses or on consumers, *FedEx* keeps them both on its radar screen. The primary target is the B2B world, but in order to ensure that its ubiquitous brands maintain its leadership status they also build its master brand inside the B2C universe.

All communications contribute to developing the *FedEx* brand image and reputation. Advertising, direct mail, sponsorships, corporate identity sales force, couriers and information systems are used. **Maintaining its reputation** and its **brand image** is a **top priority concern**, since it is one of the most valuable things the company has. As CEO, Frederick W. Smith regards guarding and championing the brand as an important part of his job.[13] Major branding decisions are usually made by him, the Vice President of Marketing, and the **Director of Global Brand Management**. Market research is used to validate and provide guidance for execution.[14]

Over the years, *FedEx* had several taglines: *America, you've got a new airline, Absolutely, Positively, Don't worry. There's a FedEx for that, Our office is your office* and *Relax, it's FedEx*. The last one was so successful that they launched a new advertising campaign in 2005, still using this previous tagline. Communication elements comprise TV, print, radio and online ads. The campaign is targeted at small businesses and delivers the central message that the portfolio of *FedEx* services will help them to meet their needs.

The launch campaign for the *FedEx Kinko's Office* and *Print Centers* in July 2004, incorporated TV spots, print, radio, direct mail and online elements around the slogan *Our office is your office*. It was targeted especially at small businesses and had to reflect the one-stop resources offered by the centers. *FedEx* has some kind of signature style about its ads that is rooted in its rich heritage of humor in advertising. [15] The TV spots used a series of hilarious slices of small-business life and were wonderfully wry and perfectly cast to deliver a key point. News that is delivered in an entertaining fashion tends to be more memorable for people. The humor in the advertising campaign also has positive effects on *FedEx's* sense of self-confidence. The target audience of small business owners' response to the spots was overwhelmingly positive.[16]

The average core customers of *FedEx* are primarily males between the ages of 25 and 55. One central goal of communications is to place the brand wherever this **target group frequents**. That's the reason why the company extended its sponsorship of the National Football League for three years. It was also driving the decision to join forces with *Joe Gibbs Racing* in 2005.[17] *FedEx* is sponsoring the #11 *FedEx Chevrolet* during the 2005 *NASCAR* season. The *FedEx Racing* campaign with the headline "Every Day Is Race Day" will be supported by TV, print and online ads.[18]

Sponsorships are used quite intensely at *FedEx*. Qualities like speed, teamwork, and precision in building the largest express delivery company in the world are held up high. These same qualities are prominent in their **sponsorships**, resulting in rather natural and complementary relationships.[19] The company regards this marketing tool a great opportunity to drive business and even **integrates the sponsorships** as an anchor point throughout the marketing mix, not the other way around. Certain events are used as content useable in media, promotions, employee incentives, and online. Examples include NFL-themed promotions, Orange Bowl-flavored retail incentives, and PGA-related TV spots. The company uses sponsorships to invade new markets and penetrate new areas, resulting in high growth rates.[20]

Sometimes companies get very lucky because their company and/or brand are included in movies simply for plot reasons. *FedEx* lucked out in 2003 when they benefited tremendously from product placement at no cost because the company and brand were featured in the major motion picture *Castaway* starring Tom Hanks. Actually, you could say that this was a **two hour** *FedEx* commercial that people even paid to see. There were plenty of Fed Ex trucks, Fed Ex posters and Fed Ex planes; you can imagine how much favorable exposure *FedEx* received from this.[21]

5.2 Samsung

Leveraging the Brand from B2C to B2B

Samsung is a Korean industrial group with a product portfolio ranging from electronics, finance and construction to other services. It successfully internationalized its business from local to global. *Samsung* is headquartered in Seoul, South Korea. It is ranked as number 20 of the 100 most valuable brands worldwide carried out by *Interbrand* in 2005. This is an increase of **more than 100% since 2000 with brand value rising from US$5.2 billon up to US$12.5 billion**. In 2005 the company had 175,000 employees and an annual turnover of US$43.6 billon. Innovation and premium branding helped *Samsung* to achieve profits of US$10.5 billion the same year.

Exporting dried fish and vegetables *Samsung* was founded in 1938 and started large scale manufacturing in the late 1950s in various industries. In 1978, *Samsung Semiconductor* became a separate entity producing for the domestic market. With the development of a 64K DRAM (Dynamic Random Access Memory) VLSI chip (Very Large Scale Integration electronics **chips**) it expanded globally. In the financial crisis in 1997, *Samsung* was facing US$20 billion in debt and had to slim down the company by more than 100 non-essential businesses in a restructuring process. It kept only 47 affiliated companies and strategically re-focused on four technical components: displays, storage media, random access memory (RAM) and processors.

The restructuring process led *Samsung* also to focus on core businesses. It restructured its business into four strategic business areas – Home Network, Mobile Network, Office Network and Core components – that support network products. *Samsung* implemented a clear mission and vision across all core businesses:

Vision: **"Leading the Digital Convergence Revolution"**

Mission: **"Digital e-Company"**, i.e. a company that leads the digital Convergence Revolution through innovative Digital Products & e-Processes.

Also, *Samsung* focused on developing pioneering products and technology in semiconductors, telecommunication devices and home appliances field, which on the long-term made *Samsung* a most competitive total solution provider in digital convergence.

The strategy to **develop new markets and new approaches** has led *Samsung* to become a brand-led technology innovator. Its specialty is to focus on its customer needs and to adapt quickly to changes in consumer preferences.

Simultaneously to the reorganization of its business units, *Samsung* established an intensive internal **change management process** – where marketing activities were bundled under one Corporate Center. The aim was to implement a holistic marketing strategy instead of individual marketing plans to strengthen its market power and to increase brand strength with high quality and innovative products. *Samsung* had to face the following challenges:

- Create one **global brand and marketing strategy** establishing a clear brand vision and brand values to leverage brand's success across B2C and B2B businesses.

- Concentrate communication **from customer to stakeholder perspective** as communication to non-customer stakeholder groups becomes more and more important having a strong direct brand impact.

- Increase communication planning **from cost to investment perspective along the entire brand screen.**

- Expand position on chip/semiconductor market via cutting-edge technology and concentrate communication **to digital consumers.**

Clear Brand Positioning

Samsung's aim to build a clear brand positioning followed a structured approach. First, *Samsung* established a brand mission according to the overall mission of the company. The mission reflected the core values of the brand – being close to the customer, consider customer needs and deliver innovative solutions.

Second, *Samsung* developed a distinctive value proposition to foster its single brand strategy. The value proposition gave further detail on the brand mission and explained how *Samsung* aimed to concentrate on a clear focus towards customer orientation and its promise to innovate best-in-class technology. Moreover, the value proposition accentuated some emotional aspects the brand wanted to communicate. The increased emotionality was then brought to life in *Samsung's* image campaign.

Looking back, in the 1990s, **Samsung was the brand you bought if you couldn't afford Sony or Toshiba**. But this image should change a lot. The strategy was changed from a low cost and low quality image to a price premium and market leader. *Samsung* aimed at providing leading-edge, stylish products.

Samsung established its brand as a **brand known for the most fun and stylish models** ranging from cell phones to flat-panel plasma TVs. Additionally, *Samsung's* ability to produce almost any kind of digital technology products, monitors, MP-3 players, TVs and printers allowed the company to be mostly independent from main component suppliers.

In a third step, *Samsung* deepened its single brand strategy via introducing a new corporate identity program. It aimed to **strengthen competitiveness** by bringing the attitudes and behavior of all employees in line with *Samsung's* desired perception by the public. *Samsung's* corporate logo was redefined to reflect *Samsung's* determination to become a world leader[22].

The *Samsung* name was then written in English, expanding its global presence throughout the world. The name was superimposed over a

Fig. 56. The new Samsung logo

dynamic, new logo design, giving an overall image of dynamic enterprise. The elliptical logo shape symbolized the world moving
through space, conveying a distinctive image of innovation and
change. The first letter, "S", and the last letter, "G," partially break
out of the oval to connect the interior with the exterior, showing
Samsung's desire to be one with the world and to serve society as a
whole.

The new logo was developed in the Corporate Marketing Center.
Brand campaigns were handled from the Headquarters, apart from
country specific adaptations and the media mix. *Samsung* began
making a **strong push to build a reputation on digital convergence**
from the late 1990s, **using international competitions** to gain fast
recognition. In 2001 *Samsung* won the first spot on the IDEA (Industrial Design Excellence Award) list jointly with *Apple Computer Co.*
and was the sole winner in 2002[23].

The new marketing strategy led to a US$400 million worldwide ad
campaign "digitAll-everyone's invited". The image campaign became more emotional: For the first time *Samsung's* new ad campaign by Berlin Cameron/Red Cell told an emotional story, relating
Samsung's products to every day situations. This was a change from
its rather product oriented communication strategy and a move towards the image creation by its products. *Samsung* established a
controlling tool to measure the effectiveness and efficiency of its
communication activities and to identify improvement potentials
on each step of the customer relationship path. Since *Samsung's*
concentration on a single brand strategy, the amount of global marketing spending summed up to €2 billion (2004)[24].

Additionally, *Samsung* created an **own universe for its campaign** situated in the *Time Warner Center* in New York and supported by an online-world www.samsungexperience.com.

Excursions: The *Samsung Experience* is a remarkable 10,000-square-foot interactive emporium of virtual reality experiences and technology. The permanent venue is located on the third floor of The Shops at Columbus Circle in the *Time Warner Center*. *Samsung* has created a range of experiences, each of which ties the *Samsung* brand and technology to the experiences of everyday life. The site features hundreds of *Samsung* products in unique technology demonstrations such as a virtual world in a 360 degree interactive simulation, a map of the city that can be manipulated with hand gestures, and a digital fashion collection created by one of New York's hottest designers.

The *Samsung Experience* is not a store and is always free to visitors. Visitors are invited to relax and learn how the latest devices can enrich their lives. Content from *Samsung's* many partners, including MIT Media Lab, Parsons School of Design, *Napster*, *Microsoft*, *Time Warner*, Lincoln Center, and Sprint PCS, helps add to the experience.

"*Samsung Experience* is digital convergence in its purest form – where you can see, hear, touch and create the art of the possible," said Dong Jin Oh, CEO of *Samsung Electronics North America*. "Our hope is that the venue will become a great educational resource, communicating the life-enhancing benefits of digital technology without the pressures of a sales environment."

Samsung is also pioneering an innovative loaner program. Visitors to the *Samsung Experience* will be able to take a hard-disk based camcorder with them to shoot video around New York City. Once they return, they can edit the footage at kiosks inside the Experience, burn their movies onto DVDs, and return home with a digital souvenir. Visitors are also able to use *Samsung Napster MP3* players to download songs off *Napster* to CDs, and also download ring tones to their cell phones. Images embedded in the venue's giant interactive map of the city can be transferred to customize postcards and create personalized artwork.

Additionally, *Samsung* will host technology seminars and tutorials at the *Samsung Experience*, as well as product launches and special events. "Digital technology doesn't need to be confusing and overwhelming. The *Samsung Experience* will help people learn how to take control of digital devices and use them to improve the quality of their lives," said Peter Weedfald, *Samsung Electronics* North America senior vice president-marketing. "As a digital convergence leader, *Samsung* is the perfect company to meet this need."

"This is a major strategic play for Samsung," said Stephen Baker, NPD Techworld's Director of Industry Analysis. "By creating a direct consumer presence without relying on resellers, *Samsung* **builds not only brand awareness**, but also greater **appreciation for digital technology** overall. Everyone wins – especially consumers and retailers, who benefit from better understanding of what digital living is all about." Early in the design and planning process, *Samsung* recognized that its ultimate brand expression required many pioneers of the digital convergence revolution to achieve a total immersion experience. *Samsung* enlisted a number of its long-time partners and recruited new converts as well as to collaborate in achieving the "art of the possible."

"Our products, great as they may be, are just the enabler – ultimately, this is not about products, but about the experience," said CEO Oh. "Working closely with content providers and other leading digital brands is the most gratifying part of what we've accomplished, and enables us to create the deepest, most satisfying expression of the new digital lifestyle."[25]

Communication to All Stakeholders

For companies operating in the B2B sector a focus in communication on high impact groups is increasingly important to successfully establish brand transfer. That is why, *Samsung* set up a comprehensive program to ensure consistent communication to all stakeholders considering the different roles of the brand. *Samsung* identified three high impact groups:

- **Staff and customer base:** brand's role to build trust and foster identification

- **Target customers/financial community/broad public:** brand's role to build trust platform, to trigger analyst expectations, to build goodwill platform (corporate citizenship)

- **Talents/gatekeepers/opinion leaders:** brand's role to build "preferred employer" position, build goodwill platform

Within this program, *Samsung* signed a deal in 2000 with *Lucent Technologies* to supply internet phones and, in 2001, *AOL Time Warner* and *Samsung* agreed upon mutually promoting their brands within a strategic marketing agreement.

Since 1998 *Samsung* has been an **official sponsor of the Olympic Games**: Nagano (1998), Sydney (2000), Salt Lake City (2002) and continues its sponsorship until 2008. During the Games *Samsung* provides athletes, organizational staff and journalists with especially developed mobile phones promoting *Samsung*'s products and delivering its promise of being an innovative and flexible company.

With the Olympic Games *Samsung* gained quick, cost-effective global exposure. "I convinced the company we had to have a single message," says Kim. Its brand awareness increased after each Olympics about 2% and had a huge impact on the quick rise of the brand. Brand value increased since 2000 until 2004 about 100%.

For its target customers, *Samsung* established both in B2C and B2B the **concept of hero products**. It means that each *Samsung* subsidiary has to define at least one hero product, e.g. mobile phone, TV or digital camera, which has – based on local or regional market research – **potential to become a blockbuster**. *Samsung* very closely involves its target customers in the development/research process via generating feedback on its B2B online platforms.

Comprehensive Communication Planning

To achieve business impact, a common planning/monitoring across disciplines is needed with a **brand management via value creation**

and innovation rather than simple cost controlling. *Samsung*, when switching its strategy towards a premium brand, started to move its planning towards communication activities which have impact on each step of the customer relationship path, i.e. from awareness to purchase to loyalty.

Two major directions of impact towards **high-end distribution channels** and an **emotional approach** for its campaign were *Samsung's* strategy. In its latest campaign, *Samsung* cemented the company's new up market image by promoting its products in high-end distribution channels.

Expand Position on New Chip/Semiconductor Market

Despite several challenging moments for the semiconductor industry, such as the recession in early 1990s and early 2000, **Samsung aggressively increased its investments** in the business unlike the rest of the industry which laid-off workers to cut cost. **This preemptive investment strategy** helped *Samsung* to gain market share and to meet the rapidly growing demand for 4 megabyte chips after 1994 in the global market. *Samsung* became the number one memory chipmaker in 1993.

By pursuing twin goals of **leading-edge technology** and producing **one generation-old products** in the niche market of memory chips, *Samsung* successfully avoided risks of failing in the market. They laid out Flash memory where text, photos, sound and screen can be saved in the small-sized chips. *Samsung's* market share of memory chips has been growing continuously from 10.8% in 1993 to 28% in 2004, but it still follows *Intel* in the non-memory sector.

In 2000, *Samsung* asserted that digital consumers, a growing importance of business networks and technical devices would create new demands for semiconductors in the future. *Samsung* recently announced its plans **to beat *Intel* in computer chip sales** and to make a better partnership with it at the same time. Synergy effects will be drawn when all three core elements of investment, leading-edge technology and the unique digital products work together within a dynamic business interaction.

Samsung's vice president Yun Jong-yong stated that the company will try to **become one of the top 3 electronics firms by 2010** in terms of quality and quantity and will therefore try to raise its brand value and revenues in its semiconductor business over *Intel*. Despite tough competition *Samsung* and *Intel* both plan on building better platforms to improve combined business opportunities.

Samsung is already **leading the electronic market** in some product segments, such as in the set-top box as leading product in home networking. In late September, 2005, ***Samsung Electronics* announced a US\$33 billion investment to add new production lines in *Hwasung*, *Gyunggi-do* by 2012**. It will be the **largest semiconductor cluster** and create about 12,000 jobs. *Samsung's* expects to achieve total sales of US\$61 billion when the project is completed.

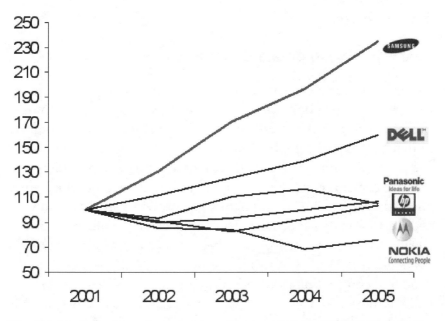

Fig. 57. *Interbrand* brand equity development 2001-2005 (indexed; 2001 = 100)[26]

Besides being successful in this particular project *Samsung* increased its overall brand equity tremendously. Compared with the peers *Dell, Panasonic, HP, Motorola* and *Nokia, Samsung* doubled its Interbrand equity.

The conclusions we can draw are that *Samsung* successfully followed a **one brand strategy by establishing one global value proposition**, one logo and one consistent brand message *Samsung* communicated the same values across all businesses to all stakeholders, and followed a clear focus towards an emotional approach to increase brand image. *Samsung* followed also a preemptive investment strategy to comply with digital consumers demand and applied communication measures in an effective and efficient manner, and they **consistently communicated their promise** to offer innovative products perfectly tailored to customer needs.

5.3   Cemex

Dual Branding to Create Brand Equity

Amazon.com founder, Jeff Bezos, has been quoted as saying he would like to position his company to be able to sell anything – except concrete.[27] Although the cement business is a **commodity industry** characterized by low growth, high asset requirements and unpredictable demand, *Cemex* defies one's expectations regarding cement. *Cemex* (NYSE: CX), a cement company located in northern Mexico, has undertaken a fast growing process in the last decade to become the **most profitable cement company in the world**. A clue for its success has been its accurate corporate brand strategy. In 2003 & 2004, *Cemex* received the first place spot on the Reader's choice brand recognition of the *brandchannel.com* for Latin America.[28] The *Cemex* brand success was only possible through a **strong brand strategy developed** by the marketing team at *Cemex*.

Company History

Founded in 1906, *Cemex* started its dynamic growth in the 1990's, and in less than 10 years moved from No. 28 to No. 2 in the global cement industry. *Cemex* reported that 2005 net income was more than quadruple 2003's net income. *Cemex* sold in 2005 more than US$15.3 billion (2004 US$8.2 billion) with a profit of US$3.6 billion (2004 US$1.3 billions), the most profitable company in its industry.[29]

Cemex operates in more than 50 countries and has commercial relations in over 90 nations. *Cemex* is engaged primarily in the **production, distribution and marketing of cement**, ready-mix products and aggregates. To provide these world-class products and services to its customers, *Cemex* combines a deep knowledge of local markets with its global network and information technology systems. Known as a "digital leader", *Cemex* has applied IT and e-business ideology to this traditional low-tech industry, **thus transforming the rules of the game** on most of the markets where it is present. With the acquisition of *RMC*, *Cemex* is on the way to the global leadership position.[30]

However, being a technology leader is only part of the success of *Cemex*. The *Cemex Way* is strongly focused in **developing the right behaviors and values of all *Cemex* people** to integrate the worldwide knowledge on products, customers and operations. This knowledge is used to develop a robust process that shows the most efficient practices, creating a business system easy to deploy in the integration of new acquisitions around the world.

As described by the company, its business model is made of the following elements: (1) **focus on its core business** of cement, ready-mix concrete and aggregates (2) provide its customers with the **best value proposition** (3) grow profitably through **integrated positions** across its industry's value chain (4) **allocate capital effectively** (5) and continuously **improve their operating** efficiency and productivity.[31]

The Importance of Brand management for Cemex

Cemex CEO Lorenzo Zambrano had a distinctive vision of the industry. For him the cement industry was really a **culture industry, not a cyclical commodity industry**. This is the reason why brand positioning plays a significant role in the company's market share. In many of the company's markets, cement is sold as a **brand-name product in bags**. This is particularly true in fast growing developing economies, where cement is the most commonly used building material, and **brand positioning plays a major role in market share**. The *Cemex* brand holds a leading position in countries like Mexico, Spain, United States, Venezuela, Dominican Republic, Costa Rica, Panama and a significant presence in Colombia, Egypt, several Asian nations and West & East European countries. These countries have major infrastructure needs and a relatively low per-capita cement consumption, which translates into important growth potential.

Branded cement is one of the main building blocks of *Cemex's* success. And consumers associate *Cemex* brands with strength, durability and tradition – the very essence of a good cement product. This has enabled *Cemex* to **differentiate its products** and **build customer loyalty**. In these volatile economies brand loyalty is a critical intangible asset, so that the self-construction sector continues buying the product through tough and prosperous times. Brand loyalty is perceived by *Cemex* as a **sustainable competitive advantage**, and therefore customer satisfaction is a top priority. *Cemex* believes that a diligent brand management is required to serve customers distinct preferences worldwide.

The Corporate Brand Strategy at Cemex

Cemex has developed a **transnational brand strategy**, with individual brands for each of the local products, but all of them under the umbrella of the corporate brand. Historically, *Cemex* uses it grassroots products to create brand equity to its **corporate brand**, and then uses their corporate brand to expand its value to new products. This is achieved by a continuous endorsing of the product brands.

First the promotion is focused on the local well-known product. When the consumer is used to seeing the corporate brand, then marketing is focused on building the **corporate image**.

Figure 58 shows two sponsored jerseys of the local soccer team of Monterrey, Mexico. The first picture shows in the center the logo of the *Cemex* cement brand sold in the area, and in small letters the corporate *Cemex* logo. A jersey worn some seasons later shows the corporate logo of *Cemex* in the center and the local *Cemex* cement brand small.

Fig. 58. *Cemex* branding through sport promotion

Creating a strong corporate brand has been the most cost-efficient advantage for *Cemex*.[32] The **brand equity** is easily carried into new products and services. By continuously endorsing brands, **both segments – B2C and B2B –** are maintained with a dual branding concept. The individual brands in each country allow *Cemex* to adapt to the specific functional needs of the consumer and price constraints of the market. And the corporate brand vigor allows *Cemex* to maintain a strong link to their B2B direct clients, the distributors and service users. Keeping a strong brand recognition among its direct customers as well as the end consumer is crucial for the company's continuous growth.

Cemex is interested in maintaining a strong corporate brand and few individual brands covered by the corporate brand. Due to its wide international expansion, each geographic business unit portrays the *Cemex* logo with the country name. Under each country, it uses the *Cemex* logo to describe or endorse its main products or services including all the *Cemex* cement brands and *Cemex Ready Mix* (concretos). The corporate brand is also used to endorse other B2B units such as *Cemex Capital*.

The *Cemex* brand is used to certify the quality of the product or service. However, it is never used as a brand by itself on a product or service. For example: Cement *Cemex*, or the usage of the logo elements on the product logo only. In that way the corporate brand is protected from possible correlations or limitations to a specific area of business.

In the 2004 annual report *Cemex* declared: "the *Cemex* trademark is more than just a logo, slogan or mission statement; it is **a promise we make to our customers** to deliver outstanding service and top quality products"[33]. And today the *Cemex* brand is synonymous with strength, prestige and stability in all the markets where present. A company is not just evaluated by its financial results, but also by its human resources competences, environmental sound policies, and social responsible behaviors. And that has been achieved by *Cemex*, creating a corporate brand not only appealing to the customer but to all the stakeholders. Through a strong brand they had been able to create a more appealing look to investors, attract better human talent, **increase the market value of the company**, be a magnet for better associates, and obviously increase sales on their products.

Their best way to create the strong brand image is **through everyday actions undertaken** by the company. So that is why we can say that each employee of *Cemex* has been responsible for the creation of the current image. To do so, *Cemex* continuously communicates through its internal IT channels any change in corporate direction; and *Cemex* keeps a tight and limited usage of the logo, name and business colors. This is particularly important, to keep the pace with the aggressive business mergers and acquisitions, but still creating a homogeneous internal and external business image.

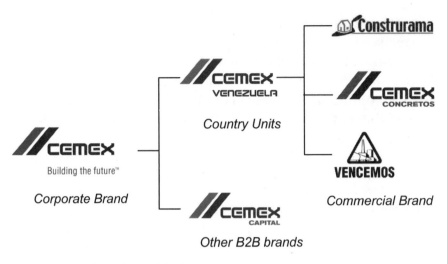

Fig. 59. *Cemex* brand portfolio[34]

As stated by *Cemex*, the values nurtured into its image are collaboration, integrity and leadership. And some of the identified attributes in the corporate brand include: global company, customer focus, investor focus, and technology innovation. The values and attributes of the *Cemex* brand are easily recognizable throughout the company activities and decisions.

Collaboration: Most of the business carried by *Cemex* is B2B through selling to its distributors and not to the end customer. *Cemex* showed its strong collaboration commitment by building and licensing a brand to its major distributors. *Construrama* is now the largest construction materials chain in Latin America. It is a win-win proposition for *Cemex's* customers and distributors. On one hand, it offers distributors a number of advantages that they couldn't realize on their own such as brand recognition, access to products and services at competitive prices, training programs, best industry practices and marketing support from *Cemex*. And to the end consumers, it offers guaranteed quality and uniformed service. *Cemex* gains customer loyalty at both levels, and builds up an image of collaborative enterprise.

Integrity: *Cemex's* commitment to integrity and social responsibility is manifested through social programs such as "Patrimonio Hoy".[35] This program is designed for low income families who do not have the discipline to see a building project through. A family can construct at approximately three times the traditional rate and at four-fifths of the traditional cost. By 2003, *Cemex* had 26,000 families as members, and over 100,000 had passed through *Patrimonio Hoy*. Initiatives like this strengthen the company image; but just as importantly, the payment rate was 99.6%.

Leadership: By applying technology to the issues that matter most to customers, *Cemex* has strengthened their leadership brand image. Named the *Cemex Way*, they have offered their clients improved service, more efficient distribution, simplified business transaction, and 24/7 access to real-time account information. The live electronic storefronts around the world enable clients to place orders and purchase products online, as well as to track their account states.

Global company: The challenge of managing a brand on all fronts and across acquisitions is overwhelming, but *Cemex* has managed it wisely. All its acquired subsidiaries have been renamed successfully. To protect the brand from a bad reputation, *Cemex* buys a company, works to turn it around, and when it has a stable situation, renames it under the *Cemex* umbrella. Such is the case of *Cemex* Thailand, bought in 2001 and renamed in 2002 after deep management structure reorganization and a considerable improvement of its processes, systems and product quality. In a similar way, *Cemex* Spain was renamed in 2002 after a 3 year long process of image refurbish. The 3 Spanish business units: concrete, aggregates and ready-mix concrete products were renamed also to *Cemex Hormigon*, *Cemex Morteros* and *Cemex Aridos*.

Customer Focus: *Cemex* combines a deep knowledge on local markets with its global operational network. In this way, *Cemex* can offer solutions tailored made to satisfy the particular needs of its clients. Whenever possible, these solutions are marketed and sold under a brand that endorses the *Cemex* logo, thus adding equity to the corporate brand. For example, in 2003 *Cemex* Costa Rica discontinued its 30-year-old "Cempa" brand, and introduced the "Sanson" brand offering two different types of cement, for structural construction and for minor construction. This re-branding enhanced customer brand recognition. Other examples include the *Titan* brand in Dominican Republic for concrete block producers (2002), *Vencemos* in Venezuela for do-it-yourself constructors (2003), and *Al-Fanar Type II* cement in Egypt for coastal construction (2004), all under the *Cemex* umbrella. *Cemex's* brands are now positioned as the leading cement brand in Upper and Lower Egypt, with 50% share of mind in their selected markets. An additional example of customer focus and brand development is the "Island" brand of *Cemex* Philippines who won in 2004 the *Philippines National Shoppers Choice Award* as the preferred brand among more than 100,000 consumers surveyed countrywide.[36]

Cemex Capital is a credit branch who gives financial support to the business customers of *Cemex* subsidiaries. The support is not limited to the procurement of *Cemex* products, but also to finance working capital, overall business growth of distributors, and loans for construction companies. Created in 1997 under the *Cemex* corporate brand umbrella, *Cemex* capital offers credit at a lower cost than the commercial banking.

Cemex's CEO, Lorenzo Zambrano, believes that many other companies could use technology in a more effective way. So he launched

Fig. 60. *Cemex:* from stags to bags

Neoris, a business consulting company that is based on *Cemex's* **successful management capabilities**. This subsidiary is part of the B2B portfolio of *Cemex*, and although its brand has been set aside of the influence of the central *Cemex* brand, it is solidly supported by the corporate image. Neoris has sales above US$150 Million, with one quarter of customers outside *Cemex*. Its main consulting services include: IT consulting, outsourcing and management services, and investment in emerging technologies.

Cemex has opened the eyes of many industries in Latin America and throughout the emerging economies on the importance of an accurate brand strategy and management as contributing to a corporation's success. The *Cemex* corporate brand serves as an umbrella that encapsulates the vision, values, personality, positioning and image of the company. It has created a strong relationship with its key stakeholders. And finally, it has been decisive for the proper development of its B2B initiatives as a strong contributor to B2B success.

5.4   IBM

Successful Turnaround Through Brand Communications

When talking about the **most valuable brands** in the world *IBM* is always included. According to the well-known Interbrand ranking, the *IBM* brand is one of the **top five of the world's** most valuable brands, only surpassed by *Coca Cola* and *Microsoft*. Considering the hard times the company had to go through only a few years ago, literally walking on their last leg, this is an amazing success story. The company has not only managed to prevent the demise of a once great corporation and come back to business but it came back even better and stronger, reviving the glow of the old times.

IBM is one of the companies with a very long and rich history. It incorporated already in 1911 as the Computing-Tabulating-Recording (C-T-R) Company and was formally renamed **International Business Machines** Corporation in 1924. Starting out as a manufacturer of machinery ranging from commercial scales and industrial time recorders to meat and cheese slicers along with tabulators and punched cards, it has undergone massive transformations over the years.[37] We regard the refocusing of the global *IBM* brand as an excellent example of how to **manage B2B brands** and furthermore as one of the cornerstones of the successful turnaround of the then struggling company. So let's have a look at those changes and how *IBM* managed to rebuild and strengthen the *IBM* brand as we all know it today.

Crisis Time for the IBM Brand

IBM was performing very well in the 70s and early 1980s. They were renowned for their own strong corporate culture and employee selection procedures. High value had been placed on consensus-based decision making, which, however, turned out to be a tremendous weakness in the fast-moving mini computer industry of the late 1980s and 1990s. Slow and bureaucratic processes are not particularly conducive to corporate risk taking which was necessary at that time, and still is today. Back then the world made first steps towards a commercial environment where rapid decision making and entrepreneurial risk taking are indispensable. If the culture of a company discourages and complicates such behavior, it easily and quickly can drop out of the running. This happened to *IBM* when it found itself outflanked by then-small companies like *Atari, Apple, Commodore, HP, Compaq Computers, Osborne, Tandy,* or even *Microsoft.*[38]

The following numbers clearly circumstantiate this: In 1981, *IBM* introduced its first PC and managed to increase its market share to 41 percent by 1985 – only three years later the market share had dropped to 28 percent. The blame for this loss was partly seen in *IBM's* **unfocused marketing strategy** that left their brand vulnerable to cheap competitors' clone products.[39] In 1993 finally, the struggling company hit its negative peak by producing an US$8 billion loss, which many marketer even regarded as the final nail in the slow-moving mainframe behemoth's coffin. The *IBM* brand and global brand image was in deep trouble as well. The brand had not only lost its strength from previous years, but almost became irrelevant. Critics began to see *IBM* as an elephant, and some as a dinosaur.

Today, *IBM* is leading the pack again. It practically owns e-business and solutions and **dominates technology services**, which now account for almost half of its revenues and more than half of its profits. Most incredible is the fact that many customers, employees, stakeholders, and Wall Street now describe *IBM* as nimble.[40] It is not by chance that the very **successful turnaround** of the struggling *IBM* has been attributed in part to the rigorous refocusing of their well known global *IBM* brand and branding strategy.

Redefining IBM

In 1993, the former RJR Nabisco CEO and former president of American Express, Louis V. Gerstner, Jr., took over *IBM*. Lou Gerstner set out to transform *IBM* from a lumbering hardware manufacturing company to a customer-focused service business. This redefinition from a product oriented to a customer and market oriented "builder of networks" also implied a renewed attention to brand management and advertising.[41]

One of Gerstner's first decisions was to **shift huge amounts of resources to rebuild the *IBM* brand**. The company chose to dial up its **master brand.** This required serious adjustments for the product-marketing teams. The umbrella quality reputation that the *IBM* name provides for all of its products and services is far more valuable than specifications of individual products. An organization like *IBM* can **provide customers with numerous synergies and benefits.**[42] During the 1990s, *IBM* extended its brand portfolio relevance to take advantage of a market opportunity in information technology services and the Internet. Great market opportunities aligned to *IBM's* core competencies were further drivers of the subsequent brand repositioning.[43]

As part of the **strategy to reinvigorate the *IBM* brand** the company fired its 70 global agency partners and consolidated all its global advertising business with *Ogilvy & Mather (O&M)* in 1994. This **consolidation resulted in integrated and more effective marketing communications** and **uniform branding** at a much lower total communications cost. Since then the company strongly invested in marketing and brand building which enabled them to make over the *IBM* brand image.[44] The new *IBM* was positioned as a company that understands the needs of its business customers and that can provide a total portfolio of products, services and consulting advice. The **360-degree marketing communications** strategy developed by *O&M* included TV, print, outdoor, events, sports sponsorships, online and non-traditional media to communicate its brand positioning.[45]

The company understood that in order to achieve real change they had to reach not only their customers but also and maybe even more importantly, their employees. Therefore the company developed advertising aimed at changing the perceptions of both sets of constituents. To educate and empower their employees was one of the major steps towards the new *IBM*.[46]

Part of *IBM's* massive **reorganization strategy** has been to put 235,000 employees into 14 customer-focused groups such as oil and gas, entertainment, and financial services. This way a big customer will be able to cut one deal with a central sales office to have *IBM* computers installed worldwide. Under the old system, a corporate customer with operations in 20 countries had to contract with 20 little Big Blues, each with its own pricing structure and service standards.[47] At *IBM*, new reps receive extensive initial training and may spend 15 percent of their time each year in additional training. *IBM* has now switched 25 percent of the training from classroom to e-learning, saving a great deal of money in the process.[48] Frontline employees can spend up to US$5,000 **to solve a customer problem on the spot**.[49]

The **global brand manager** (GBM) was an individual charged with creating a global brand strategy that leads to strong brands and global synergy. At *IBM*, the slot was called **Brand Steward**[50], reflecting the role and position of building and protecting brand equity.

> *"One of IBM's key media strategies is to **deploy traditional media in radically new ways**. For example, IBM is using video online to communicate its brand message to an audience of IT and business decision-makers. It has partnerships with ESPN.com, CNN.com and other Web sites to deploy interactive video interviews with key IBM executives and other content to **connect with its target audience**. When we are trying to reach loyalists for a given server platform, it wouldn't be economical to deliver the message using traditional TV. IBM also uses sports sponsorships and huge events to build its brand. As the technology provider for the U.S. Open tennis tournament this year, IBM delivered real-time scoring on a **large interactive billboard** in Times Square, as well as on traveling vans in New York. It is a real live demonstration of our business consulting and technology expertise".*[51]

During the middle to late 1990's, when many firms were **attempting to be relevant to the Internet** and the emerging network world of business, *IBM* was a trend driver with its e-business position. The company ultimately spent over US$5 billion building the **eBusiness "label"** after its introduction in 1996, and related all its business units to that context.[52]

Sam Palmisano, who became the new CEO of *IBM* in 2003, had a difficult act to follow. *IBM* had achieved a dramatic turnaround under Lou Gerstner during the 1990s, in part by making the synergy and technology of the organization work for the customer. Palmisano's strategy was based on a **new value proposition**: *On Demand*. The core idea was that IT systems and resources would be available on-demand, when needed. All *IBM* **business units were charged with delivering the value proposition**.[53] In 2003, *IBM* created in addition another subcategory, eBusiness on Demand, which means that firms would develop an IT system that would encompass suppliers, customers, and partners and deliver information and computer resources on demand, when needed. The creation of responsive products and services throughout the firm to **meet this set of customer needs was unreachable by competitors**.[54]

This other big shift was the enlargement of the service offerings. Currently, almost half of *IBM's* annual revenues come from global services. To fulfill its service promise, *IBM* has had to develop new skills and become more customer focused. The US$3.5 billion acquisition of PriceWaterhouseCoopers Consulting in October 2002 has further provided valuable strategic and operational expertise.[55]

Today *IBM* has left the field of personal computer production. The last part of the huge industrial project of the last decade has been sold to one of their joint venture partner in China. *Lenovo* paid US$1.25 billion for the other part of the JV and the distribution system and the distribution rights of the *IBM* brand for the next 5 years. The exit of the foremost leading PC manufacture shows that *IBM* has learned from its mistakes.

IBM Campaigns

The *IBM* brand essence, "magic you can trust" **captures the inspirational aspect of their products and services**, combined with the trust generated by the company's heritage, size, and competence. Because of its varied markets however, *IBM* uses several taglines: "Solutions for a small planet" is relevant for a customer seeking solutions and inspiring to those with a **global vision**, while "e-business" positions *IBM* as the dominant choice for those seeking help with e-commerce. *IBM* used the e-business subbrand to make an association it owned, technological leadership, more dynamic, relevant and contemporary.[56]

In 2001 *IBM* and *Ogilvy & Mather* were awarded a gold trophy in the Computer Software category for the *Software Evangelist* campaign. The campaign, designed to promote *IBM's* e-business software, included television and print ads. It also marked the first time *IBM* touted itself as a software provider. The campaign tag line was "It's a different kind of world. You need a different kind of software." The campaign helped *IBM* become the number one provider of "middleware" – a "fundamental building block for e-business" – and contributed to the company's US$13 billion in software revenue during 2000.[57]

IBM Enters the Small Business Marketplace

For years the perception many business people had of *IBM* was that of a big business, white shirts and doing things the corporate way. Realizing that small businesses thought of *IBM* as irrelevant to them, the company decided to **break down that perception by providing services that appealed directly to small businesses**. *IBM* managed to successfully re-brand itself for the small business marketplace

IBM counts small to midsize businesses as 20 percent of its business and has launched Express, a line of hardware, software services, and financing, for this market. *IBM* sells through regional reps as well as independent software vendors and resellers, and it supports its small-midsize push with millions of dollars in advertising annually. Ads include TV spots and print ads in publications such as *American Banker* and Inc. magazine.[58]

Many companies are systematically measuring customer satisfaction and the factors shaping it. *IBM*, for instance, **tracks how satisfied customers are with each** *IBM* **salesperson** they encounter, and makes this a factor in each salesperson's compensation.[59] *IBM's Business Partner* program provides a great example of how to get comparable **third-party leverage in a B2B complex purchase model**. *IBM's PartnerWorld* program provides extensive support to the channel in key value-added areas such as marketing and sales, education and certification, technical support, and customer financing. Partners can access this support on-line, over the telephone, or through their channel sales manager. All of these investments are designed to help the channel understand the *IBM* brand and better promote *IBM's* products and services, even though many *IBM Business Partners* also partner with *Sun, Dell*, and *EMC*.[60]

Visionary companies hold a **distinctive set of values** from which they do not deviate. *IBM* has held to the principles of respect for the individual, customer satisfaction, and continuous quality improvement throughout its history.

5.5   Siemens

Branding for Cross-Selling Initiatives

Siemens is one of the world's **largest electrical engineering and electronics companies**, and one of the **oldest industrial brands** (see chapter 2). It was founded more than 157 years ago. In fiscal year 2005, *Siemens* had approx. 461,000 employees, sales of €75.554 billion and a net income of €3.058 billion. Company businesses are focused on six key areas: Information and Communications, Automation and Control, Power, Transportation, Medical and Lightning and Business Services. *Siemens* activities are influenced by a variety of regional and sector-specific factors, e.g. some businesses are subject to procedures with long lead times (up to 10 years) like Power Generation or Medical Solutions. Other factors are regional adaptation requirements such as electrical standards (UL-listing for the USA, CE in Europe, etc.) and some are subject to short-term business requirements such as the durable consumer goods or mobile phones. The company's traditional strengths are **its power of innovation, its strong customer focus, its global presence and its financial solidity**[61].

The new, the US-trained CEO Klaus Kleinfeld has started a new campaign: *One Siemens*, a program designed to get company units to cooperate better to win business. At age 40 Kleinfeld got the chance to put the theory into practice. *Siemens* sent him in January, 2001 to the USA, first as chief operating officer then, a year later, as CEO of New York-based *Siemens Corp.* Under Kleinfeld, units including Medical Solutions and Power Transmission & Distribution joined together to supply diagnostic equipment, software, telecommunications, and power to a new hospital being built in Temple, Tex., for *Scott & White Healthcare System.*

In 2004, *Siemens* decided to set up several company programs and initiatives to increase the effectiveness and efficiency of its business. Within these programs, *One Siemens* is part of the *Siemens Management System (SMS)* initiative focusing on innovation, customer focus and global competitiveness[62]. Within *SMS*, *One Siemens* is a global, company-wide strategy to improve market penetration and drive growth in new fields by enhancing cooperation across the entire organization. Focused primarily on large-scale infrastructure projects, *One Siemens* bundles the comprehensive expertise in order to create complete, customized solutions for selected industries. It is an integral part of the global cross-selling initiative and builds a framework for regional activities to act as one *Siemens* by applying:

- a systematic approach
- to generate incremental business
- across business groups.

One Siemens is a globally rolled-out initiative. Local entities had to implement the program in their market. At this point, we want to show how *Siemens USA* **understood the challenge and how they managed to improve communication effectiveness and efficiency**[63].

For the U.S. market an own legal entity under the label *Siemens One* was founded in 2001 to provide customers with customized, comprehensive solutions. *Siemens One* is involved whenever a potential project could involve multiple *Siemens* operating companies. *Siemens One* provides customers with **one interface to multiple** *Siemens* **operating companies**, facilitating an efficient and cost effective manner for dealing with *Siemens*.

Its purpose is to stimulate incremental sales by a) coordinating efforts to develop and sell integrated solutions under the *Siemens* brand that involve technologies from multiple *Siemens* operating companies to current and potential customers (= leveraging technologies and the competence of a solutions provider) and b) **systematically realizing cross-selling** opportunities within existing accounts across *Siemens* operating companies (= leveraging the customer base). The customer decides on the level of "single source" he wants from the spectrum of a **single point of contact/single contract/single billing/single point of accountability** to individual components from separate *Siemens'* operating companies and business partners.

Main Purpose and Challenges

A joint project with *Siemens Corporate Communications* and *Siemens USA* was established with the aim to improve communication effectiveness and efficiency of *Siemens USA*. The main achievement is to create a stronger impact of communication on *Siemens One*'s business performance. *Siemens USA* faced three communication challenges:

1. Increase benefit-orientation of communication vis-à-vis customers and other stakeholders

2. Reduce complexity of existing messaging, sharpen stakeholder adequate message content and leverage global communication concepts (e.g. global value proposition)

3. Develop concepts for effective external and internal communication of cross-group activities (*One Siemens*)

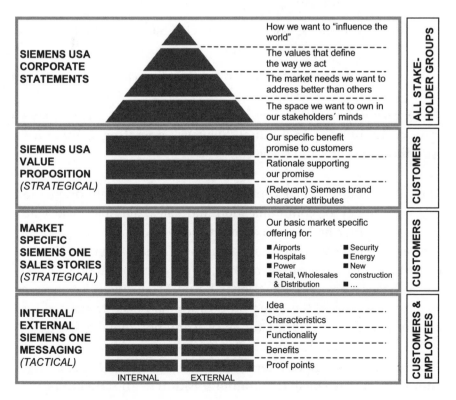

Fig. 61. *Siemens:* framework for a consistent message hierarchy[64]

The process to increase **communication effectiveness** and **efficiency** has been set up in three phases:

One: Establishment of message hierarchy to base communication on a consistent communication framework.

A framework with four levels was developed to establish a consistent message hierarchy based on three key requirements, which were clarity, consistency and continuity.

1st level: Corporate statements communicated to all stakeholders describing *Siemens USA's* "reasons for being" with its levers vision, mission, business drivers and positioning.

2nd level: *Siemens USA* Value Proposition communicated to the customers.

3rd level: Market specific *Siemens One* sales stories communicated to all customers.

4th level: Specified internal and external *Siemens One* messaging.

Two: Development of value proposition to reflect *Siemens USA* ability to bundle individual *Siemens'* operating companies' products, systems and services.

The value proposition concept helped to increase benefit-orientation and consistency of communication and sales activities. The value proposition first had to be communicated internally as a basis for future communication and sales activities. It had to ensure that the benefit promise was consistent with other communication concepts, i.e. SMS activities and the Global Value Proposition. To increase customer relevance, the value proposition had been translated into market specific sales stories, for vertical and horizontal markets.

Three: Development of internal and external messaging and sales stories to ensure consistent communication to all stakeholders.

The messaging was clearly structured in key elements: idea, characteristics, functionality, benefits and proof points. The market specific sales stories had to be aligned and refined with Market Sector Teams and were to be used as basis for customer-specific activities. For internal messaging the main relevant facts on *Siemens One* were aggregated as a **basis for specific internal communication messages**. Moreover, to maximize the impact of the internal messaging, a concept was developed how to best communicate these messages, as e-mail and intranet may not be the best vehicles to convey these messages.

Example of "Airport" Sales Story

Market Specific Challenges

The airport business today is facing an increased number of challenges: On the one hand airports have to differentiate themselves in the marketplace with compelling offers to attract valuable passengers, concessions and airline tenants and thereby secure and increase their revenues; on the other operating procedures have to be optimized to handle the increased number of flights, people, baggage and cargo, to avoid staff overload and to improve cost-efficiency. Moreover, all kinds of safety concerns related to airplanes and the public spaces in the airports have to be addressed successfully.

Relevant Technologies

Technological solutions that meet the increasing end-customer demands and help to realize synergy potentials, require the integration of different technologies:

- Transportation Systems – to bring people to the airport
- Parking Garage Guidance Systems – to guide people to free parking lots
- Electronic Visual Information Display Systems – to provide people with relevant gate, flight & baggage information
- In-line Baggage Security Screening – to screen all baggage for explosives
- High-Speed Baggage Transport & Sortation – to move baggage between check-in, planes & baggage claims

- Baggage Handling Systems – to handle baggage at make-up and baggage claim
- Graphical Baggage System Monitoring – to control the process of baggage handling
- Cargo Handling Systems – to move cargo between cargo facilities and airplanes
- etc.

General Business Drivers

To succeed in this highly complex environment solution providers are needed that can reduce this complexity, integrate different technologies, and ensure that the solutions are compatible with existing systems and pay off in terms of an improved performance. In addition, solutions should not only best fit the business' current needs, but also facilitate exploitation of future opportunities. Accordingly the solution provider's commitment has to last for the solution's whole lifecycle in order to support the utilization of the technology over time and to protect the investment.

Customer Specific Needs

Besides these general needs, challenges and resources largely vary between different players in the airport business, e.g. airport management, airlines and service companies. Each customer requires a tailor-made, best total solution for his specific situation.

The example of *Siemens One* in the U.S. served as pilot in order to guarantee a successful global roll-out of the *One Siemens* concept in the long-term. In the US two major learning blocks were derived: First, a clear and strong process management is needed and second the content of the global value proposition has to highlight the benefits of cross-group business activities.

1. The process: Strategy development should start with strongly aligning communication, sales and marketing departments with the **target group customers and the** regional and market specific requirements. The value proposition development should be led by a global implementation team with Corporate Communications, business group and regional communication and sales people. The business drivers are then to be validated in each region.

2. The content: The value proposition for *Siemens USA* aims to strongly reflect the benefits of cross-business leverage. The customer familiarity with relevant product portfolio is the basis for cross-group business. **Cross-business communication** requires supplying strong examples. *Siemens USA* could already state a success story: *Scott & White Healthcare System.* The U.S. healthcare provider's new 381-bed hospital – slated to open in Temple, Texas in the fall of 2006 – illustrates *Siemens'* ability to **bundle systems and solutions** from Medical, Communications, Building Technologies, Automation & Control and Power/Transportation into one innovative, customized package. These systems and solutions include advanced medical imaging and diagnostic equipment, comprehensive IT systems like *Soarian™*, fully integrated voice, data, video and nurse call systems, building control technologies and energy supply systems to integrate the Scott & White network.

Only a few years later the overall success of the activity could be tracked. Using the Interbrand brand equity analysis we could prove that *Siemens* compared with its peer *GE* had an increase from 2001 to more than 600 index points.

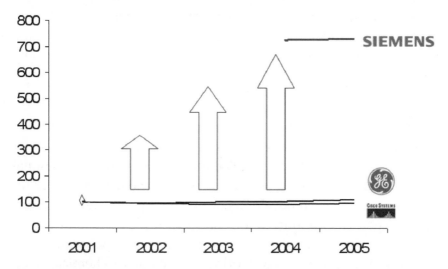

Fig. 62. *Siemens, GE* and *Cisco* Interbrand brand equity development 2001-200 (indexed; 2001 = 100)[65]

With no thought *Siemens* had to catch-up, *GE's* extraordinary performance in the last 30 years changed the whole situation in the industry, but now *Siemens* saw its chance and focused on its core competences and the increase of the customer equity. The immediate result could be seen in the brand equity increase.

5.6 Lanxess

Brand Communication of a Spin-off

> *Our credo is impact in place of image. At Lanxess, we understand communication and brand strategy as an investment, which has to contribute substantially to the company's success.*

Mr. Sieder, Senior Vice President, Head of Corporate Communications

Bayer is known to be a **traditional and global company**, which experienced a lot of strategic changes recently due to a different and changing market environment. *Bayer* focused for a long time on its traditional lines of business of chemistry, agricultural products and pharmaceuticals. After taking the cholesterol lowering medicine Lipobay off the market in August 2001, its business plummeted dramatically. Under these circumstances *Bayer* had to **undertake major structural and strategic changes**. In the end, the company decided on a new strategic orientation of its product portfolio, which led to a spin-off of the chemical sector.

Bayer founded a new chemical company **in record time**. In the beginning its business activities were carried out under the name of *NewCo*. On 18th of March in 2004, on the occasion of the annual press conference, *Lanxess* was introduced as the new name resulting from an intensive development process by the board of directors, Corporate Communications and employees. The aim was to build within one year – with a lot of energy and motivation – an authentic brand for a new worldwide operative chemical company. On 1st of July in 2005, former *Bayer Chemicals* was officially renamed as *Lanxess*.

The second step to **independence and autonomy was completed with the initial public offering**. But the new strategic direction wasn't without any risks, because some parts of the business were considered as rather poor in performance. *Lanxess* proved able to advance and push ahead sales and so far its ambitious plans have been realized, e.g., re-organisation of the company's structure to improve overall efficiency and the IPO at the beginning of 2005. *Lanxess* proactive attitude is expressed throughout its corporate values within the Corporate identity "courageous, capable, and lively" and throughout the company's brand promise "energizing chemistry".

In order to guarantee *Lanxess'* business success, cost efficient business processes had to be designed and implemented. The new company's main goals were **independence, competitiveness and profitability**. Future corporate communications and thus future alignments of branding strategy had to follow these main goals in a value and market oriented manner. The company put a high emphasis on setting up a profit oriented corporate communication program. The different globally linked business units were more or less connected with coordinated communications – and marketing activities surpassing national and local boundaries. Thus the global situation and the economic situation of *Lanxess* made a central concentration of communication activities inevitable. This alignment assumed the **coordination of all communication activities** of the different countries under one central lead, the use of cross country synergy effects and the consideration of regional conditions, following the well-known principal "Think global, act local".

As a structural solution *Lanxess* established **communication hubs** in Europe, USA, Asia, South America and India, where various national markets with similar influencing factors were combined under one region. This top down approach facilitated a dialogue on local levels to identify communication needs of individual entities and to communicate these to the headquarters. Vice versa the headquarters could inform local entities on communication content, processes and structures. Local entities could still align communication activities with other countries.

The *Lanxess'* organizational approach allowed for a **concentrated communication structure** which guarantees a market and customer specific communication strategy. The company is now able to communicate easier to the different markets and to customer specific needs. After creating a high level of awareness, the branding strategy since 2005 focuses on essential market needs. *Lanxess* decided to conduct customer interviews in order to identify strengths, weaknesses and main challenges to compare to its main competitors. The identification of relevant strategic issues and a strategic image build up should help to strengthen *Lanxess* position in the future.

Lanxess **brand positioning** and its communication goals are carried out in three steps:

Analytical phase: Serves mainly to develop a first hypothesis for future brand positioning and to develop a communication focus.

Strategy phase: Carries out an approximation of target positioning regarding core branding and brand attributes. Carried out are core messages for each target group. These have implications for planning and budget allocation.

Roll-out phase: Develops a plan to implement measures and is followed by planning the detailed communication mix and the budget allocation.

Today, *Lanxess* has carried out for most parts the roll-out phase. A quick build up of its brand awareness to relevant stakeholders such as investors, customers and the public already play an important and sustainable part.

The brand still has to optimize its potential across various image dimensions and a highly diversified value proposition. Until now, customers' brand perception is still affected by the company's history.

To become a leading brand *Lanxess* had to overcome a **multitude of challenges:**

- Worldwide aligned communications and marketing activities
- Branding strategy in alignment with company's goals
- Creation of a worldwide consistent and integrated brand image
- Performance-oriented brand strategy focusing on customer needs
- Attainment of brand leadership

Corporate communications, which have been built up since the foundation of the company **with great accuracy**, has already helped *Lanxess* to attain brand leadership. Due to targeted PR-measures, such as international coverage of the spin-off, a first branding success was achieved within less than a year: brand awareness almost doubled. Public introduction and positioning of the new CEO helped stakeholders to affiliate an individual face to the company. Prompt creation of corporate design, conception of advertising campaigns and a webpage were further steps leading to brand uniformity and uniqueness.

Lanxess is going to gain further expertise while systematically carrying out analyses processes on a regular basis. This guarantees a continuous feedback from target customers as well as a frequently optimized budget allocation. *Lanxess Corporate Communication* has already established an excellent mix between company's strategy and market orientation and between globalization and local strategies.

5.7 Lenovo

Bridging East and West to Build a Global Brand

Lenovo is an innovative, international technology company formed as a result of the acquisition by the *Lenovo Group* of the *IBM* Personal Computing Division. As a global leader in the PC market, *Lenovo* develops, manufactures, and markets cutting-edge, reliable, high-quality PC products and value-added professional services.

Founded in 1984 as *Legend Group Ltd.*, a spin-off of the Chinese Academy of Science, with a seed capital of US$25,000 and a group of eleven scientists led by Mr. Liu Chuanzhi, *Legend* was the first company to introduce the PC concept in the People's Republic of China. *Legend* was also established to distribute computers such as *HP, IBM, AST,* and *Compaq* in 1984. Since 1997 the company has been the leading PC brand in and around China with annual revenues (as of May 2005) of approximately US$3 billion.[66]

Lenovo brand PCs have been the best seller in China for seven consecutive years. In 2003, the former *Legend Group Limited* launched its new brand *Lenovo* to cater to the group's future business development and laid the groundwork for its **expansion into overseas market**.

Subsequent to the acquisition of the *IBM* PC division, they now have 7.8% of the world PC market. *Lenovo* PCs also ranked number one in the Asia Pacific (excluding Japan) market with a 55% market share at the end of 2005[67]. With the integration of the *IBM* PC division, more than 10,000 employees from *IBM* joined *Lenovo* with a resulting climb in sales to US$12 billion (2005). *Lenovo* paid US$650 million cash and US$600 million in shares in the *IBM* transaction. Much of this value clearly stems from the *IBM* brand, both removing it as a competitor and acquiring it, rather than its tangible assets such as the equipment and existing operations. *Lenovo* group management team currently owns 42% of the company's stock, *IBM* 13.4% and *TPG, General Atlantic* and *Newbridge Capital* 10.2%. *Lenovo* was listed on the Hong Kong Stock Exchange in 1994 and is a constituent stock of the Hang Seng Index. It's American Depositary Receipts (Stock code: LNVGY) are also being traded in the United States.

The new company formed the third **largest PC enterprise** in the world. Stephen Ward, a former *IBM* Senior Vice President (SVP), and first Chief Executive Officer (CEO) of *Lenovo* post-acquisition announced[68] "that new products will be launched under the *Lenovo* brand worldwide. The new *Lenovo*, boasting the world-famous laptop brand *ThinkPad* and the well-known brand *Lenovo*, will have more than one third of China's PC market and hold a leading position in the world PC market".[69] The former CEO Yang Yuan-ping stepped down and became the Chairman of the Board. At the end of 2005, William Amelio from *Dell* Asia was nominated to become the new CEO with the task to improve the already excellent operational performance. In becoming such a stronghold in the Chinese market, specific competitive advantages contributed to *Lenovo*'s success:

- **Strong brand recognition** in China. The corporate brand name *Lenovo* acts as an umbrella for several sub-brands of corresponding product lines.

- **Good relationship with government and educational institutes**. The Chinese Academy of Sciences was the biggest founding shareholder of *Lenovo*, undoubtedly a big benefit to the firm.

- **Highly efficient operations**. In terms of supply chain management, *Lenovo* achieves a lead time of 3 to 5 days on the average for order fulfillment, 2 days shorter than the 7 days promised by Dell.

- **Diversified distribution channels**. With an in-house sales team, *Lenovo* can cover large enterprise clients itself. By coordinating with the Value-Added Resellers (VARs), small and medium size customers can be reached. Through business partners-owned chain stores and franchised shops, *Lenovo* can penetrate into both the urban communities and rural sectors. Additionally, they operate multiple internet shops.

- **Market leadership** in China with more than 30% market share and broad product portfolio for both consumer and commercial segments.

Lenovo's business performance has proved that the group has **deep insight into the China** (PRC) IT market and clear grasp of user needs. A significant part of *Lenovo*'s success has been its **ability to retain leadership** in **supply chain systems**. The close relationship with the upstream suppliers, most of them Taiwan electronic companies, and own manufacturing facilities in the mainland of China, lead to a rapid inventory turnover. *Lenovo* has already penetrated the local market deeply with the help of over 6,000 retailers and distributors. They cover business and individual clients. With a specific approach which *Lenovo* calls **relationship-model and transaction-model they treat these client groups separately and thoroughly.** *Lenovo* has also built up strategic alliances with international technology giants such as *Intel* and *Microsoft* to improve their position in the application markets.

The Lenovo's Brand Development Before the IBM PCD Acquisition

Lenovo's brand story really started in 1992 when it started to **promote its corporate name** *Legend (Lianxiang)* and created the concepts of *Legend 1+1, Household Computer* and *Economic Computer*. In the early 1990s, the company launched an advertising campaign with the slogan "What is the world going to be if we stop dreaming?" It had a good impact on the Chinese public who viewed the slogan as romantic. An internal survey conducted in 1991 indicated that 12.9% of the customers learned about *Legend* from this slogan, and 7.6% of them bought the *Lenovo* PC because of it. Through a series of **marketing campaigns** such as *Legend Computer Express* and *Grand Training Program* in the summer of 1991, *Legend* broadened awareness and recognition of its brand name, thus building a loyal customer base. By being the first major company for personal computers in China, the company set up leading industry examples and became the dominant PC brand nationwide.

In the early 2000s, *Lenovo* was facing pressure from slow growth on demand, intensive competition, diversified customer requirements, and commoditized products and markets. In order to respond to this challenge, the company divided individual clients into **three segments**: starters, mainstreamers, and senior players. To better target these new market segments it introduced **new subbrands** such as *Tianjiao, Fengxing,* and *Jiayue*. With these subbrands, *Legend* delivered different associations of easy life, passion, and harmony. These associations allowed these subbrands to provide not only functional benefits but also additional self-expressive benefits to different customers.

In 2003, the company changed its brand name from *Legend* to *Lenovo* for the **purpose of internationalization**. They took the "Le" from *Legend* to honor their roots and added "novo," the Latin word for "new," to represent the innovation at the core of the company. The new name represents the innovative and legendary company more accurately.

During this period, *Lenovo* focused on **incorporating emotional values** into the brand, portraying this through the metaphor of brand personality traits such as honest, innovative, passionate, and easy-going. *Lenovo* selected **brand personalities** consistent with the emotional values of the brand and the target consumers' lifestyle so that consumer and brand personalities were brought into alignment.

The same year, some key issues guided the decision to develop the new branding theme "Only if you dream ..." First, a successor to the romantic "world and dreaming" theme was long overdue. Second, the cost of creating a new branding theme and transitioning customers to it, although huge, was within the capacity and will of *Lenovo*. Third, the 联想 (*Lenovo*) equity and program, rather than being wasted, could be leveraged by link with the new theme. With this new branding theme, *Lenovo* positions its brand as: **integrity, innovation, professional service and easiness**.[70]

The Lenovo Brand's Role Pre-acquisition: Corporate Brand vs. Subbrands

The research about the power of subbrands[71] in the area of computers and related products indicates that the equity of subbrands in the high-tech area is remarkably weak in comparison to corporate brands.[72] In fact, less than 12% of respondents even knew that *Vaio* was made by *Sony*, even though by attitude measures, *Vaio* is one of the strongest notebook brands. This finding is consistent with a much earlier not published *Compaq* study that found its *Presario* brand having less equity than expected.

Why do subbrands in the high-tech area have such low equity?[73] First, corporate brands, such as *Dell, HP,* and *IBM* are very intensely and extensively promoted, especially during the early days of the category. Second, subbrands have generally failed to develop a point of sustainable differentiation and as a result, lack a brand personality and a substantial reason to exist. To tackle this problem, the central brand group at *Lenovo* took control of the proliferation of new brands. A business unit had to demonstrate to the brand group that a **new subbrand had reason to exist**. If they could demonstrate its sustainability, they could use a subbrand. The *Lenovo* brand worked for both industrial customers and consumers. The *Lenovo* persona was approachable but also serious, competent, and successful – very compatible with the corporate world as well as appealing to individuals.

Taking Advantage of Corporate Brand Name

The *Lenovo* brand became a **corporate brand** and a **master product brand.** The role of the *Lenovo* corporate brand, like many corporate brands, is first to provide trust and credibility to the *Lenovo* offerings based on the size, capability, heritage, and success of the organization over time. Second, because *Lenovo* represents the organization that stands behind its products in spirit and substance, it can be a credible endorser that works at both a functional and emotional level. On the other hand, the use of *Lenovo* corporate brand as a master brand maximizes such brand portfolio goals as **generating leverage, synergy and clarity**. It also evokes the power and uniqueness of the corporation as an organization, thereby creating differentiation for the product brand.

The *Lenovo* brand played the major driving role in nearly all of the firm's offerings in that it drove the purchase decisions and defined the user experience. The major *Lenovo* subbrands (*Tian* series desktop computers, *Soleil* and *Xuri* notebook computers, *Wanquan* series servers) largely played a descriptive role, serving to define the scope of the *Dell* product footprint. The *Lenovo* product brands *Fengxing, Jiayue, Tianjiao* and *Yangtian* desktop computers, *Tianyi, Xuri* and

Soleil notebook computers, *Wangquan* servers also played a descriptive role, but, targeted different market segments and initiating an upward technology shift.

Overall, the *Lenovo* brand plays **the major driver role in nearly all of the firm's offerings** in that it drives the purchase decisions and defines the customer's experience.

Brand Management After Acquiring IBM PCD

After *Lenovo* and *IBM* completed the acquisition of the PC unit of *IBM*, they marketed the birth of the third largest PC enterprise in the world. *Lenovo* got access to *IBM's* powerful global brand through a five-year brand licensing agreement with strictly defined limitations. To retain the customer base and to **develop new markets**, *Lenovo's* upcoming challenge is to leverage the excellent reputation for quality and service of *IBM's* brand. Despite the fact that *Lenovo* is allowed to use *IBM* in the coming 5 years, but only on products, *Lenovo* has taken over *IBM's Think* family brands including *ThinkPad* and *ThinkCentre*, which are the symbols of technical innovation, reliable quality and professional service. "The halo effect of the *IBM* brand allows *Lenovo* a broader range of options while its existing operations in China allow it to keep costs down. Thanks to *IBM*, *Lenovo* can have its cake and eat it too. The *IBM* **brand brings kudos to** *Lenovo*. It removes a barrier to *Lenovo's* products - particularly outside of China. *Lenovo* now seems more reliable, more trustworthy. Even to customers who are fully aware that the product is no longer "made" by *IBM*, a stamp of approval from such a highly respected company means a lot in any market."[74]

Lenovo, which as a brand name is popular in the domestic market, can be developed to dominate in some emerging markets like India and Russia and fill in the SMB and consumer market *IBM* left. Logically, **brand transfers** mean *Lenovo* would take a two-pole action: retaining *ThinkPad* and *ThinkCentre* brands, and developing other *Lenovo* branded products for different market segments geographically and demographically.

However, the firm will not light-heartedly adopt a co-branding strategy or stick a co-brand logo like *Lenovo-IBM* to its products. It is sufficient for both companies to show that they are working together. They have announced a "commitment to ongoing operational cooperation, not merely in terms of *IBM* distributing *Lenovo* products, but each company acting as preferred partner to the other. Both companies have committed to supporting each other: *Lenovo* with PC products to complement *IBM's* high-end servers and mainframes; *IBM* with customer relationships, service and support. An ongoing association between the two companies will bring fresh markets and new customer relationships to be leveraged."[75] In addition, using the *IBM* and *ThinkPad* brand means for *Lenovo* a significant licensing fee. With only the co-brand logo, *Lenovo's* image would always be in the shadow of *IBM*, and the brand recognition on its own is hard to be built once the brand licensing agreement expires. Logically, brand transfers mean *Lenovo* would take a **two-pole action**:

1. Emphasize the heritage of **technology innovation, sound quality and service** from *IBM* to *Lenovo* by launching advertising campaigns with the combination of corporate names of *Lenovo* and *IBM* (noticeable only on products pictures), and retain *ThinkPad* and *ThinkCentre* brands. *Lenovo* can build the corporate image of technology leadership, high quality products and excellent customer service.

2. **Differentiate the product attributes in terms of performance, price, and targeted market segments** by adopting the *Think* family brands and *Lenovo's* new 3000 product lines to different product classes and to different market segments from small business to consumers and geographically. The enterprise clients, who are willing to pay the premium price, should be served with *Think* series of laptops and desktops. Small and medium enterprises and small office/home offices (SOHO) can accept *Lenovo's* 3000 products for a high ratio of performance to price. The mass consumer market would be covered with *Lenovo's* consumer products.

Fortunately, *Lenovo*'s management in the new global headquarter takes such factors into account, and they carefully consider in their strategy how to build *Lenovo* into a strong master brand known for innovation, customer service and high quality. As the company builds up the *Lenovo* **brand globally**, they are carefully watching consumer's awareness, preference and other metrics to determine when the right time is to switch over from the *IBM* brand to *Lenovo*. Also scheduled for change is the *Access IBM* button on the top row of the *ThinkPad*, which allows a user to connect directly to *IBM's* service desk. In the future, it will be labeled *ThinkVantage*.

In May 2005 *Lenovo* selected *Ogilvy & Mather*, one of the largest global marketing communications networks, to handle worldwide brand advertising for *Lenovo*. The campaign would include a range of media channels, including online ads, event sponsorships and perhaps television, in addition to print. The initial newspaper advertisement that *Lenovo* ran showed a man sitting in the shovel of a backhoe, working on a laptop computer. "How do you build new technology?" it says. "Start by building a new technology company." The text-heavy spot goes on to explain the fusion of *IBM's* PC division into *Lenovo*.

Building Brand as Icon and Company

In the stage of brand as personality, the *Lenovo* brand has become more than the PC. It represents values which go beyond the functions of a PC, and acts as an efficient communicator of the personality of the owner. The challenge for *Lenovo* now is to **develop the brand further to make it accepted widely** so that the *Lenovo* brand can be used to stand for something beyond itself, in short, to **make it an icon**. This would enable the customers to own the brand because they would understand and use its symbolic properties. At this point, the symbolic value of *Lenovo* brand expands to include categorical meanings as well as self-expressive ones. Categorical meanings symbolize customers' group membership, social position, status and locate the individual in social-material terms.[76]

To reinforce the symbolism, *Lenovo* frequently uses some physical symbol to denote the brand. Its *Lenovo*, *ThinkPad* and *ThinkCenter lenovo* ThinkPad. ThinkCentre.

Fig. 63. Corporate and product logos

logos can work for this purpose. These become shorthand means of identifying symbolic brands no matter what the local culture is. They're aiming for one tagline worldwide; "New World. New Thinking."

At the same time, some changes are happening to customers and markets. First, it can be assumed that customers are interested in more than the brand. They hold **corporations accountable** for individual brand actions and may boycott any transgressor's brand portfolio. Furthermore, they will use the new communication channels to broadcast any wrong doings to other consumers. Increasing consumer cynicism may demand that *Lenovo*'s senior management formulate clear views about the values the firm adheres to and ensure that everything the firm does ties into these values.

Second, **growing penetration of the Internet** will allow more customers to find out what they want **to know about the** *Lenovo* **brand**. Some consumers will become less receptive to mass market communication and will demand more open and specific communication. More efficient and flexible electronic data capture also enables *Lenovo* marketers to **gain a deeper appreciation** of small groups of consumers' buying behavior, offering the opportunity for a new set of relationships to be forged between customers and *Lenovo* brand.

Third, markets are likely to become **more splintered, as needs-based segmentation** becomes more common. *Lenovo*'s possible response could be a greater number of subbrands or descriptors designed to meet the needs of smaller and smaller segments as the firm did before.

Fourth, no longer do managers think of only the **physical product; rather, they think of products plus services**. The era of the service industry has arrived and it has a major impact on how firms create value for their customers. The *Lenovo* brand can deliver not just a computer brand, but a computer brand with regular maintenance and integrated solution service through a series of communications directed from *Lenovo* to individual consumers. It is the service component that enhances *Lenovo*'s ability to create value, differentiate itself, and energize the *Lenovo* brand.

Lenovo has started a process of building a brand as an icon and they have been re-thinking *Lenovo*'s brand to include the service element. This means a re-structuring of communications at all the diverse points of contact that occur between stakeholders and the firm and careful selection and training of staff about the brand. Through the *Lenovo* brand, management must explicitly consider what values they are communicating, how they can include customers in the creation of added value, and how they can maintain consistency of message.

The Olympics Sponsorship

The right sponsorship, handled well, can transform a brand. Respondents to a Sponsorship Research International (SRI) survey on the effectiveness of Olympic sponsorship said such things as: "**The Olympic emblem on products means they are famous and world-class**" and "I feel more favorably toward a product because it is from an Olympic sponsor." This survey confirmed that such sponsorship has a positive effect on product image and by extension, corporate image.[77]

In March 2004, *Lenovo* joined *The Olympic Partner (TOP) Program* of the *International Olympic Committee (IOC)* as the first Chinese company to become the computer technology equipment partner of the *IOC* for the period from 2005 to 2008. The sponsorship of the Olympics has the potential to influence the *Lenovo* brand in several ways.

Lenovo has managed to win out in stiff competition with high-profile multinational corporations for the right to be an Olympic partner. **This bolsters a positive image of** *Lenovo* **as a global corporation,** which helps to strengthen the foundation for overseas operations and exports. *Lenovo*'s ongoing Olympic sponsorship is also elevating the image of China and Chinese companies, and instilling pride in all Chinese people for being involved in the Olympic Games.

At the most basic level, the TOP program provides credibility and **associations of being a leader in computer technology**. Considering the required computing capability and system stability, the Olympics would not use *Lenovo* if it were not superior. Thus, the TOP program can provide the ultimate in relevance and communicate more about the brand than product advertising could ever say. Meanwhile, there are more subtle possibilities. By choosing *Lenovo*, a customer can receive self-expressive benefits, as it is a way to associate oneself with the world's top athletes and teams.

However, the potential of an Olympic sponsorship is not being taken for granted by *Lenovo*. The company has been successful in creating links around the sponsorship with a host of brand-driven activities including promotions, publicity events, website content, newsletters, and advertising over an extended time period. *Lenovo* is well aware of how important the Olympics are as a marketing tool, and is maximize the communication effect that will be created during the Games. Furthermore, famous athletes have been selected as *Lenovo* brand ambassadors in specific activities, conveying a brand image that stresses friendship and humanity. In addition, *Lenovo* is supporting various foreign national teams to elevate their corporate image in important markets outside the host country.

It is clear that a number of **critical brand portfolio decisions** have been made at *Lenovo*. The new *Lenovo* brand enables the firm not only to retain the existing customer base in China's market and worldwide served with *IBM's Think* products, but also to address competitive threats and enter new markets. The relationships between brands are particularly important in defining new and transitioning business arenas. While the master *Lenovo* brand will provide an essential synergetic force in the portfolio, the subbrands like *ThinkPad* and *ThinkCentre* will inherit the reputation and recognition of *IBM* brand.

After **successful integration** by overcoming cultural barriers and streamlining operational processes, the re-born *Lenovo* filled its brand image with new values. Moreover, it influenced the market environment and actually defined product categories. In doing so, *Lenovo* positioned itself as a **differentiated brand leader, building a bridge from East to West. They have in fact created the first global brand, "Made in China".** PCs and laptops are just the beginning. *Lenovo* also manufactures and distributes mobile phones in China. We can be sure to see more brand developments and marketing success through brand building in these other product areas in the near future.

5.8 Tata Steel

Branding Steel Based on Customer Focus

As one of India's most successful companies, *Tata Steel* also represents a great example of a strongly branded B2B company. In 2001 and 2005, *Tata Steel* was ranked the **world's best steel company** in studies carried out by World Steel Dynamics Inc., USA (*WSD*), a leading steel information service provider. The rankings were based on a set of different criteria, ranging from cash operating costs to stock market performance of the respective past three years. In 2005, *Tata Steel* outpaced 23 other companies that have been identified as world-class steel makers. Among them, businesses like the French *Usinor*, the American *Nucor*, the South Korean giant *Posco*, *Nippon Steel*, as well as the Russian giant *Severstal*.[78]

Company Background

Established in 1907 by J.N. Tata in Jamshedpur, Bihar, in the eastern part of India, the company began production in 1911 with a capacity of 0.1 million tons of mild steel and continued to grow steadily over the years. By 1958, half a century later, its capacity had increased to 2 million tons. The company followed organic as well as inorganic ways of growth, acquiring companies in the process. In 1973, the company acquired some flux mines and collieries. Ten years later *Tata* bought the *Indian Tube Co. Ltd.*, a manufacturer of seamless and welded tubes and in 1991, it acquired the ferrochrome units of OMC alloys Ltd. Today, it produces a wide range of products. *Tata Steel* is part of the *Tata Group*, one of India's largest and most respected business conglomerates.[79]

In the early 80s, the company started a **five stage modernization** program for its steel plants which ultimately made the company Asia's first and India's biggest Integrated Steel Producer (ISP) in the private sector, a decade later. By 2000, eight divisions of *Tata Steel* were ISO 14001 certified and the company had already completed four phases of the modernization program by investing over 60 billion INR. By April 2001, *Tata steel* was the world's lowest cost producer of steel with operating costs of hot metal (liquid stage) being US$75 per ton.

At this time, the company also started the fifth stage of the modernization program, in which focus was laid upon attracting, developing and retaining its human resources, under its Performance Ethic Program (PEP). It consisted of two basic elements, creating a new organizational structure which aimed to **create growth, flexible decision making processes and accountability**, and the introduction of **performance management systems** which would focus on reward systems linked to performance and self development opportunities of all the employees equally. The company also initiated a Total Productive Maintenance (TPM) program to reduce breakdown time, readjustments, accidents, errors and product rejections, starting from its bearings division and later implemented to all the plants across the company.[80]

In August 2001, B. Muthuraman took over as managing director of the company and he devised a new program known as Vision 2007, which aimed at making the Economic Value Added (EVA)[81] of *Tata Steel* positive by the year 2007, which the company achieved in the first year of the inception of the program itself!

At first this number was negative, and the return from their business was less than the cost of capital. Than in May 2005, *Tata Steel* declared its annual financial results ended on March 31st, 2005. *Tata Steel* declared a profit after tax (PAT) of 34.741 billion INR (€659,7 million) over a turnover of 158.77 billion INR (€2,995 billion). This was an increase of 99 percent and 33 percent in last years PAT and turnover respectively. The company also reported a rise of 37 percent in the export revenues over previous financial year. It already owns a subsidiary in Sri Lanka and has taken the first significant step to **build a global business** by investing in Singapore based *Nat Steel* to acquire 100 percent of its steel business in Singapore and its regional steel subsidiaries and associated companies in China, Malaysia, Vietnam, Thailand, Philippines and Australia at an enterprise value of US$486.4 million.[82]

Branding Steel

The profitability of the steel industry in India is generally linked to business cycles, reaping profits when economy is going well and eroding them when it is in depression. In the late 1990s, the Indian steel industry was experiencing a glut in the market which strongly affected the profit margin of all related companies. To reduce its dependence on the external environment and business cycles, *Tata Steel* adopted a strategy which stressed the following two points: **branding its products and moving to high value added products.**[83]

The company soon realized that a strong customer focus is essential if any branding approach was to be successful. It soon began to introduce internal campaigns in order to bring the customer-centric message to its employees. In the late 1990s, the company launched several internal marketing programs to emphasize customer focus and service. The programs had taglines such as, "**customer first – her haal mein**" (Customer comes first in any case), "**customer first – her haal mein, her saal**" (customer comes first in every case, every year), "**customer ki kasam – hain taiyaar hum**" (We pledge to the customer that we are ready for him). These are the mantras behind *Tata Steel*'s success. This transfer from producer logic to customer logic was seen as the path to influence customer behavior for mutual gain.[84]

Before jumping on to the brand wagon, *Tata Steel* set up a **branding task force** in January 2000 to explore the possibilities of branding

Tata Steel products. Only three months later, the task force evolved into a brand management department. Within this department they created the distinct sub functions "market development"', "order generation" and "order fulfillment"' which were computerized, enabling *Tata Steel* to reduce its customer response time significantly. The company also initiated the concept of **"customer account managers"** who were authorized and empowered to solve specific customer grievances immediately. The company furthermore sought to increase customer interaction in order to better understand customer needs and to explore new and improved ways to meet these needs and expectations.[85]

Tata's second area of key focus was to shift into the domain of high value added products. In April 2000, *Tata Steel* launched its first branded product, along with the commissioning of its CRM plant. *Tata Shaktee* is their brand for galvanized corrugated sheets. Eight months later the company introduced its second brand, *Tata Tiscon* (re-bars) for rods used in the construction industry.

In February 2003, *Tata Steel* launched another product brand *Tata Steelium*. By September 2003, *Tata Steel* had three products as well as three generic brands in its brand portfolio, as *Tata Pipes*, *Tata Bearings*, and *Tata Agrico* (hand tools and implements) and *Tata Wiron* (galvanized wire products).

"To beat the industry trend in a situation of over supply we need to move away **from selling commodities into marketing brands**. Even as we will continue to leverage and take to greater heights the value of the *Tata* brand there will be efforts to create new images and associations for our services our product in current as well as new businesses"[86]

The leader of the company had decided that branding the commodity steel would provide them a unique selling proposition in a great way. Branding Steel would help *Tata Steel* in two big ways:

> **It would help stabilize the flow of revenues even during business downturns, and it would make premium pricing possible.**

Table 6. *Tata Steel* logos[87]

Similar development could be noticed in other steel companies around the world. *Usinor Steel*, today part of *Arcelor Steel* conglomerate established in 2000 a clear set of product brands which propelled their sales to new heights.[88] *Tata* went on a similar road. Because the corporate brand *Tata* was already associated with various products and attributes the company decided not to put the main focus on it but to create subbrands with separate identities, supported by the **corporate brand as co-driver**. At that time the *Tata* group was involved in a wide range of product and service categories ranging from automobiles to software and was one of the biggest industrial houses of the country.[89] They had learned from the European competition that specialty product offerings and strong brand associations had guarded the market against the low cost importers from the Far East.

Tata Steel wasn't the first company to **brand its steel in India**. Other steel companies are hoping to keep their bottom-line healthy by producing branded steel in their furnaces that customers will ask for by name. But *Tata* was pushing ahead with its ambitious plans to ensure that larger quantities of its steel are branded in the coming years.

At the beginning, one of the major obstacles *Tata Steel* had to overcome was its inexperienced marketing personnel. Their knowledge
of branding techniques was quite limited and moreover, many of
them had doubts about the feasibility of branding steel. As a solution they started several training programs for them and organized
seminars and workshops where experienced people from other sectors came and spoke to employees regarding various issues related
to branding. It also formed separate marketing teams for its "long"
and "flat" products, keeping in view, the different approaches required for both. The positioning reinforces especially the brand's
leadership position, both in the market place and in the minds of
the Indian consumer.

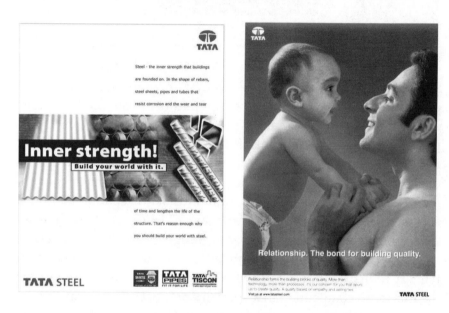

Fig. 64. *Tata Steel* print advertising, source: www.tatasteel.com

The communication tools used for the brand launches were primarily **print ads and outdoor advertising**. Yet, they also created TV
commercials that portrayed signs of happy customers and employees
reveling in the concern the company had for them. "We also make
Steel" was the punch line that signaled the triumphant finale of that
TV ad. They also began to **engage in community welfare programs**.

They were instrumental in controlling AIDS in the state of Jhark-hand, by their AIDS awareness initiatives.[90] Many such programs for community and employee welfare put *Tata Steel* well ahead in terms of Corporate Social Responsibility practices in the industry.

Around 60 per cent of *Tata Steel*'s products are sold through con-tracts – quarterly, half-yearly or annually – and so these products are naturally protected from price fluctuations. It is, therefore, the remaining 40 per cent that are subject to price fluctuations. This is where branding becomes important. *Tata Steel* is spending between 1 per cent and 1.3 per cent of brand-related turnover to establish the brands, and it pays off. The company claims that as a product ex-ample, *Tata Agrico* currently commands a premium of 15 per cent over competing brands. Company sources say there are plans to in-crease *Agrico's* market share even further than 25 per cent. Keeping customers is only one side of the picture. At another level steel companies have come to believe that branding can create a greater level of awareness and interest at the shop floor level. The theory is that if workers know where their products are headed and what they will be used for, it creates a higher level of commitment.

Value Management

Tata recognized earl on that their employees were essential assets in the course of becoming more customer-focused. Therefore it adopted a program of **Retail Value Management**, under which the company provided training to sales people recruited by the retailers to help increase sales. In a region in northern India, for instance, sales teams trained by the company approached local architects and convinced them of the advantages of using more steel, resulting in a doubling of the market share of *Tata Tiscon* in that region.[91]

One of the most important things in branding is to know who you are actually messaging to. One of the major implications that Tata undertook in the course of their branding efforts was a concise tar-get group check and distribution revamp. The company was ac-tively involved in both B2B and B2C areas. The B2B customers were mainly automakers *Maruti, Telco* and *Ford*, who with their knowledge of steel helped the company to focus on product quality on a holistic way, negotiating for specifications and discussing the advantages of using different grades of steel.

When *Tata Steel* scrutinized its customer base, it revealed the quite common Pareto effect in the allocation of total sales related to customers. Only 200 large industrial customers were providing the big chunk of its total sales – 80 percent – while the remaining 20 percent were contributed to by around 5,000-6,000 smaller customers. The **logical consequence was to adopt different sales strategies for B2B and B2C**. For the 200 key accounts that made up for 80 percent of the sales, the company started an extensive **Customer Value Management** program. Under this program they allocated a whole team consisting of people from various departments of the company to one customer.[92]

Future Prospects

From the beginning, the branding initiative of *Tata Steel* showed impressive results. *Tata Steel*'s corporate sustainability report for 2003-04 states that the sale of branded products increased by 84 per cent. This resulted in a share of branded products as a percentage of total turnover of 22 percent in that fiscal year. The future expectations and prospects of the company are also very positive. Today, *Tata Steel* is already one of the best branded names in steel industry and has already started initiatives in the co-branding arena with high end customers like *Ashok Leyland* and *Telco*.[93] Looking to the future, *Tata Steel* has announced that the company would be focusing on **co-branding initiatives** with its high-end customers such as *Telco, Ashok Leyland*. Company sources say that initially *Tata Steel* would be focusing on the automobile sector; later the co-branding initiative will be expanded to the consumer durables sector also.

Just recently, in November 2005, *Tata Steel* and *BlueScope Steel* announced that they have agreed to enter into a partnership and form a new Joint Venture company in India. The 50/50 Joint Venture Company will build a new business across India and South Asia that will manufacture zinc/aluminum metallic coated steel, painted steel and rolls formed steel products, and deliver pre-engineered buildings (PEBs) and other building solutions. The new company will offer a comprehensive range of branded steel products for building and construction applications.[94]

The steel industry has been racing along at a surprisingly high speed during recent years, largely due to the huge buying from China. *Tata Steel* has also done extraordinarily well as the industry moved upwards, but the next big challenges are already seen on the horizon: **global reach with global branding**. The world number two *Mittal Steel* has successfully reached out to orchestrate a hostile takeover of *Arcelor*. The newly created European giant is the largest and most global steel producer and brand.

Summary

- The selected B2B brand cases demonstrate that brand building in its various forms supports corporate success in a dramatic, measurable way.

- After establishing a **seamless, reliable express delivery worldwide,** *FedEx* focused on **developing its corporate image and reputation**. Maintaining its superior brand image was the top priority only next to establishing a brand house for sustaining their competitive advantage.

- *Samsung* successfully followed a one brand strategy by establishing one **global value proposition with an emotional approach** to increasing brand image for their B2C products and transferring that image back to their B2B business areas. *Samsung* also followed a pre-emptive investment strategy to comply with innovative consumer demand and applied communication measures in an effective and efficient manner.

- *Cemex* introduced **branding management** to successfully place itself in Mexico, its home market, and is now expanding around the globe. The *Cemex* corporate brand serves as an umbrella that encapsulates the vision, value, personality, positioning and image of the company. Having been decisive in the proper development of their B2B initiatives, *Cemex* serves as **branding role model** for many companies in Latin America and throughout emerging economies

- After Lou Gerstner reinvented *IBM*, achieving a dramatic turnaround during the 1990s, Sam Palmisano's task was to strengthen the synergy and technology of the organization so that it would work for their customers. Palmisano's strategy was based on a new value proposition: *On Demand*. The core idea was that IT systems would include customers and suppliers, information and computer resources and would be available on-demand when needed. All *IBM* business units were charged with delivering this value proposition. In addition, the business model was transformed into that of a service company where hardware is only the starting point of a business relation.

- *Siemens'* new value proposition and business organization *Siemens One*, with focus on cross-business leverage, proved that cross-business communication works. This new brand-minded leadership transformed the world's largest electrical engineering and electronics companies, and one of the oldest industrial brands to a corporate power house through cross-selling initiatives.

- *Lenovo's* attempt at building a global brand from China was successful after the **integration of the *IBM* PC division**. By overcoming cultural barriers and streamlining operational processes, *Lenovo* filled its brand image with new values. The possibility is strong that *Lenovo* will define new product categories and expand its brand leadership into new regions in the near future

- *Tata Steel* has fulfilled its set corporate goals and has been very successful in branding commodity steel in India. By segmenting, focusing, and streamlining operations, *Tata* has become the preferred supplier in the region. The next big challenges are already on the horizon; global reach with global branding.

Notes

1   Frederick W. Smith, "Federal Express: The Supremely Packaged Ware-house in the Sky," in: *Brand Warriors: Corporate Leaders Share Their Winning Strategies*, Fiona Gilmore (ed) 1997, pp. 217-218.

2   Web site of *FedEx Corp.*, Memphis, TN, cited June 2005.

3   Ibid.

4   Ibid.

5   Charles Haddad, "Ground Wars," *BusinessWeek* (21 May 2001), pp. 64-68; Charles Haddad, "FedEx: Gaining on Ground," *BusinessWeek* (16 December 2002), pp. 126-128; Kevin Kelleher, "Why FedEx Is Gaining Ground," *Business 2.0* (October 2003), pp. 56-57.

6   Frederick W. Smith, "Federal Express: The Supremely Packaged Ware-house in the Sky," in: *Brand Warriors: Corporate Leaders Share Their Winning Strategies*, Fiona Gilmore (ed) 1997, pp. 217-228.

7   Web site of *FedEx Corp.*, Memphis, TN, cited June 2005.

8   Source: www.fedex.com; www.answers.com.

9   Web site of *FedEx Corp.*, Memphis, TN, cited June 2005.

10 Ibid.

11 Source: www.fedex.com.

12 Frederick W. Smith, "Federal Express: The Supremely Packaged Ware-house in the Sky," in: *Brand Warriors: Corporate Leaders Share Their Winning Strategies*, Fiona Gilmore (ed) 1997, pp. 227-228.

13 Ibid., p. 228.

14 Alina Wheeler, *Designing Brand Identity*, 2003, p. 143.

15 Mary E. Podmolik, "FedEx Campaign Touts New Unit,"*BtoB Online* (25 October 2004).

16 "Best Creative Winner: FedEx," *BtoB's Best 2004* (25 October 2004): 30.

17 Mary E. Podmolik, "FedEx Campaign Touts New Unit."

18 Web site of *FedEx Corp.*, Memphis, TN, cited June 2005.

19 Ibid.

20 "Cover Story: Game On," *Eventmarketer* (4 May 2004).

21 Warren Berger, "That's Advertainment," *Business 2.0* (March 2003), pp. 91-95.

22 "The Power Shift", Business Korea (1 October 2005).

23 Web site of IDSA, IDEA (Industrial Design Excellence Award) 2002.

24 "Das hat in der Branche einen Urknall ausgelöst", Frankfurter Allgemeine Zeitung (7 July 2005).

25 www.samsung.com, Press release (April 2004).

26 Interbrand „Global Brands" brand equity rankings 2001-2005.

27 Adrian J. Slywotzky and David J. Morrison, "Concrete Solution – Company Operations," *The Industry Standard* (28 August 2000).

28 *Brandchannel's* 2004 Readers' Choice Award. www.brandchannel.com.

29 "Cemex Provides Guidance for the Fourth Quarter of 2005," Cemex Corporation (16 December 2005).

30 "Cemex to Acquire RMC," *Business Wire* (27 September 2005).

31 "Building for Future Generations," Cemex Corporation (26 January 2005).

32 "Making Cement a Household Word," *Los Angeles Times* (January 2000); Los Angeles Times reports on Cemex´s vision to turn its bags of cement into a brand-name consumer product, and reviews its path leading to global diversification.

33 "Another Great Year: Annual Report 2004," Cemex.

34 Source: www.cemex.com.

35 Maria Flores Letelier, Fernando Flores and Charles Spinosa, "Developing Productive Customers in Emerging Markets," *California Management Review* (Summer 2003).

36 *BusinessWorld* (December 2004), p. 21.

37 Web site of *IBM Corp.*, White Plains, NY, cited September 2005.

38 Charles W.L. Hill, *International Business: Competing in the Global Marketplace*, 2003, p. 460.

39 Greg Farrell, "Building a New Big Blue," *USA Today* (22 November 1999); Tobi Elkin, "Branding Big Blue," *Advertising Age* (28 February 2000).

40 Michael Dunn, Scott M. Davis, *Building the Brand-Driven Business: Operationalize Your Brand to Crive Profitable Growth*, (San Fransisco, CA: Jossey-Bass, 2002), p. 23.

41 Greg Farrell, "Building a New Big Blue," *USA Today* (22 November 1999); Tobi Elkin, "Branding Big Blue," *Advertising Age* (28 February 2000).

42 David A. Aaker, *Brand Portfolio Strategy*, 2004, pp. 204, 135.

43 Michael Dunn, Scott M. Davis, *Building the Brand-Driven Business: Operationalize Your Brand to Crive Profitable Growth*, p. 43.

44 Greg Farrell, "Building a New Big Blue," *USA Today* (22 November 1999); Tobi Elkin, "Branding Big Blue," *Advertising Age* (28 February 2000).

45 Kate Maddox, "IBM's Strategy Keeps It in and on Demand," *BtoBonline* (25 October 2004).

46 Michael Dunn, Scott M. Davis, *Building the Brand-Driven Business: Operationalize Your Brand to Crive Profitable Growth*, p. 239.

47 Dwyer, "Tearing Up Today's Organization Chart," pp. 80-90.

48 Philip Kotler and Kevin L. Keller, *Marketing Management*, 2006, p. 621.

49 Ibid., pp. 705.

50 David A. Aaker and Erich Joachimsthaler, *Brand Leadership*, 2000, p. 322.

51 Kate Maddox, "IBM's strategy keeps it in and on demand," *BtoB online* (25 October 2004).

52 David A. Aaker, *Brand Portfolio Strategy*, 2004, p. 118.

53 Ibid., p. 81; Spenser E. Ante, "The New Blue," *Business Week* (17 March 2003), pp. 79-88.

54 David A. Aaker, *Brand Portfolio Strategy*, 2004, p. 118.

55 Spencer E. Ante, "The New Blue," *Business Week* (17 March 2003), pp. 80-88; "Is Big Blue the Next Big Thing?" *The Economist* (21 June 2003), pp. 55-56; Brent Schlender, "How Big Blue is Turning Geeks into Gold," *Fortune* (9 June 2003), pp. 133-140.

56 David A. Aaker and Erich Joachimsthaler, *Brand Leadership*, 2000, p. 86.

57 Kevin L. Keller, *Strategic Brand Management*, 2003, p. 293; www.effie. org.

58 Philip Kotler and Kevin L. Keller, *Marketing Management*, 2006, pp. 210.

59 Ibid., pp. 145.

60 Michael Dunn, Scott M. Davis, *Building the Brand-Driven Business: Operationalize Your Brand to Crive Profitable Growth*, p. 149.

[61] "Siemens – Global network of innovation", *The Wall Street Journal* (Nov. 2005).

[62] "Siemens One", Annual Report 2004.

[63] "Increasing communication effectiveness & efficiency of Siemens in the US", *BBDO Consulting* (May 2004).

[64] "Increasing communication effectiveness & efficiency of Siemens in the US", *BBDO Consulting* (May 2004).

[65] *Interbrand* „Global Brands" brand equity rankings 2001-2005 Siemens not included in Interbrand Top 100 rankings 2002 + 2003.

[66] In HK$m 22.555. in June 2005.

[67] Further IDC information about *Lenovo* is available at http://www.idc.com/getdoc.jsp?containerId=prUS20051406 January 26, 2006.

[68] In 2006 the link is rerouted to *Lenovo*'s homepage, using IBM URLs, see http://www.pc.ibm.com/de/*lenovo*/news/2005/1_Mai_2005.html?de.

[69] "*Lenovo* completes IBM acquisition deal," *chinaview* (May 2005), available at http://news.xinhuanet.com/english/2005-05/01/content_2904 126.htm.

[70] The MBA student Kong Lihua provided the research for this case study. Kong Lihua's master thesis was about: Making Brands Go Global - Chinese Companies' Brand Management, Pforzheim University 2006.

[71] See: Leveraging the Brand in: David A. Aaker Building Strong Brands New York: The Free Press, 1996.

[72] Brandt, Marty/Johnson, Grant, *PowerBranding - Building Technology Brands for Competitive Advantage* (San Francisco, 1997).

[73] Questions also asked in Daniel Arber, *Markensysteme: Der Einfluss der Branche auf ihre Gestaltung,* Inauguraldissertation, Faculty of Bern University, 1999.

[74] Chris Grannell, "IBM – reboots," *Brandchannel* (February 2005), available at http://www.brandchannel.com\features_profile.asp?pr_id=217.

[75] Ibid.

[76] M. McEnally, "The Evolving Nature of Branding: Consumer and Managerial Considerations," *Academy of Marketing Science Review* (Volume 1999 No. 02), pp. 4-6.

77 See also Tony Meenaghan, David Shipley: Media effect in commercial sponsorship, *European Journal of Marketing* Volume: 33 Issue: 3/4 Page: 328 - 348, April 1999.

78 "Tata Steel Ranked Best in World by WSD," *The Hindu Business Line* (18 July 2001). "Tata Steel Rated Best in World," *Business Standard* (23 Juni 2005).

79 Sunijb Dutta and K Subhadra, Branding a Commodity: The Tata Steel Way," *ICFAI Center for Managegemt Research (ICMR)*, 2004, p. 2.

80 Ibid., p. 3.

81 The Economic Value Added (EVA) is the difference between return on the capital invested in the business and the weighted average cost of Capital multiplied by the Invested Capital. The cost of capital represents the cost of debt that the company borrows from banks and the expectations of their shareholders in terms of dividends and share prices. The importance and relevance of EVA is primarily based on the appreciation of shareholders and other stakeholders, like employees, customers, suppliers, society and the government. A positive EVA meets the expectations of shareholders and facilitates the satisfaction of the expectations of other stakeholders. A negative EVA on the other hand does not meet the expectations of the shareholder and furthermore can weaken a company from discharging its responsibilities to its various stakeholders.

82 Web site of *Tata Steel Ltd.*, Fort, Mumbai, India, cited October 2005.

83 Sunijb Dutta and K Subhadra, Branding a Commodity: The Tata Steel Way," *ICFAI Center for Managegemt Research (ICMR)*, 2004, p. 4.

84 Arindam Sinha, "Tata Steel's In-House Campaign Stresses Gyan in the New Steelennium," *Financial Express* (27 April 2000).

85 Ibid.

86 "Annual Report 2003." *Tata Steel Ltd.*

87 Source: www.tatasteel.com.

88 Wolfgang Weidner, "Industriegueter zu Marken machen," *Harvard Business Manager* (May 2002), pp. 101-106.

89 Web site of *Tata Steel Ltd.*, Fort, Mumbai, India, cited October 2005; K. Subhadra, Branding a Commodity: The Tata Steel Way," *ICFAI Center for Managegemt Research (ICMR)*, 2004, p. 5.

90 Ibid.

91 "Busting Business Cycles," Business World (23 June 2003).

92 Sunijb Dutta and K Subhadra, Branding a Commodity: The Tata Steel Way," *ICFAI Center for Managegemt Research (ICMR)*, 2004, p. 5.

93 Web site of *Tata Steel Ltd.*, Fort, Mumbai, India, cited October 2005.

94 Ibid.

CHAPTER 6

Beware of Branding Pitfalls

I don't know the key to success, but the key to failure is trying to please everybody.

Bill Cosby

Branding efforts can fail – there is no question about that. Every month, you read about at least one or two companies that lost a good sum of money on some kind of brand communication that just didn't reach or influence the customer.

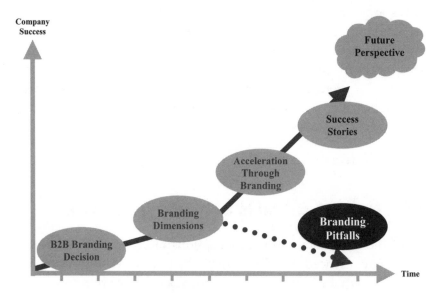

Fig. 65. Guiding principle branding pitfalls

The point is to learn from failed branding efforts of B2B companies that jumped into branding without considering the complete range of important aspects we addressed in previous chapters. In this chapter, we will address the problem of branding pitfalls that B2B organizations must be aware of in order to ensure that branding initiatives will reap results.

Good branding can make a **significant difference** to the **financial health** and **public awareness** of your company. David Aaker, the brand guru, contends that one common pitfall of brand strategists is to focus only on brand attributes and not the whole branding process. Aaker shows how to break out of the box by considering emotional and self-expressive benefits and by introducing the brand-as-person, brand-as-organization, and brand-as-symbol perspectives. The **twin concepts of brand identity** (the brand image that brand strategists aspire to create or maintain) and brand position (that part of the brand identity that is to be actively communicated) play a key role in managing the "out-of-the-box" brand.[1]

A second issue that Aaker emphasizes is to realize that individual **brands are part of a larger system** consisting of many intertwined and overlapping brands and subbrands. We manage a **"brand system" that requires** clarity and synergy, that needs to adapt to a changing environment, and that needs to be leveraged into new markets and products. With the advances of B2B branding knowledge we now know that there are more areas[2] where brand managers may make mistakes.

Here are the five major pitfalls.

Pitfall No. 1: A Brand Is Something You Own

One of the most common misconceptions of branding is that companies are convinced that they "own" the brand. Wrong! A brand is not always what a company wants it to be. It is a promise to your customers, the totality of perceptions about a product, service or business, the relationship customers have with it based on past experiences, present associations and future expectations. No matter what the business and its corporate executives would like their brand to be, brand reality is always defined by the customer's view.

That the reality of a brand only exists in the mind of the customers, we know from day-to-day business and from theories. Starting with the brand name, it is the customers' knowledge and the perceived meaning that determine the understanding of the brand promise. We know that customers have a local or national **pre-understanding** which can affect brand performance dramatically. For *Siemens Automation Systems*, the *SI* prefix to the various automation technologies was a suitable form of product brand classifications: *SI-Numeric* for Numeric Controls. *SI-Matic* for Programmable Controls and *SI-Rotec* for Robotic Controls. Unfortunately, *SI-Rotec* is pronounced in German like "Zero-tec", which was not an accurate description of the sophisticated electronic robot control and this resulted in confusing the customer's perception. Another example of predetermination of brand name is the international marketing approach of the US trade magazine for promoted giftware "Gift". The English name was used as the title around the world, and although in many countries the consumer had the desired associations with the term, the German language translates "gift" as poison, and the **resulting difference in the perception** of this word was enough to sabotage the planned promotion approach.

Kevin Roberts shows many similar examples in his recent publication.[3] The CBBE model supports this notion. According to Kevin Keller's Customer-Based Brand Equity model (described in Chapter 4 of this book) brand knowledge creates in the customer's minds the **differential effect that builds brand equity**. Kevin Keller, the creator of this model, promises to build a Number 1 Rated Brand "in less than a decade" by applying the model.[4] If strength, favorability and uniqueness are recognizable, brand building is possible. With this awareness of the brand in the minds of the customers, multiple brand association will occur and the outcome is the enlargement of the brand equity. The company owns the brand equity but the customer owns the brand.

Pitfall No. 2: Brands Take Care of Themselves

Some companies surprisingly think that brand building has some kind of domino effect – once activated and successful it just keeps on going and going. Unfortunately brands do not take care of themselves. Surely, there can be some kind of domino effect; companies of famous consumer brands experience that their brands start to have a life of their own. This corresponds to the fact that a company doesn't own a brand (Pitfall No. 1) since it is defined by **customers' perceptions** and **associations** which never can be fully dictated by a company.

Your reputation is what you mean to the marketplace – a reputation for delivering on customer needs and wants in a way that is unique. If you have a good reputation why wouldn't you protect it? If not, competitors will undermine it or copy it with the result that new sales reps may not answer to it, prospects may not hear about it, customers may not continue to believe it. You are responsible for shaping perceptions of what you do, what you offer and how you stand behind your reputation. If a brand is an asset, then it must be treated like one – **receiving investment, management** and **maintenance.** A brand is affected by internal and external forces requiring reactions and changes. But this only occurs if the organization clearly understands the brand and how to manage it.[5]

Proactive brand management is the key to success: **Do not react, act**. This can happen **through brand differentiation or pure re-branding** – innovation through re-inventing the brand. With a long term perspective, the business brand can keep its freshness. With the help of digital brand communication, B2B brands are much easier to refresh than B2C brands. Due to the one-to-one relationship, brand messages can be transmitted to the customers more easily than in mass market approaches.

Declining brands could be identified through various means. Brand metrics like **Keyword Search (KWS)** and **Natural Language Processing (NLP)** are very helpful, in addition to press coverage and customer recognition. If you identify a declining situation in your company or brand portfolio, you'd better act.

The glass-ceramic brand *Ceran®* from *Schott* is an interesting example of a brand that was resting on its laurels. Although *Schott Ceran®* is the most important individual product brand in the *Schott* portfolio, the company somehow lost sight of its brand management. During the 80's the company promoted its brand heavily to appliance manufacturers, kitchen designers, retailers, as well as end consumers. In the late 80s *Schott* moved away from its former ingredient brand strategy for *Ceran®*, pushing their corporate brand *Schott* to the fore. Today, *Schott* is only promoting its product to end consumers when entering new markets.

Schott is well-known, respected, and successful in the industrial sector. For consumers in Germany and many other countries, it has become the generic term for glass stove tops. It may be a desired goal for any brand to become an industry standard but only if people still perceive the standard as brand and can relate to it as such. Unfortunately this is not the case for *Ceran* anymore. The reality is that only few people, especially in the United States, even know that *Ceran* is the brand name of the glass-ceramic manufacturer *Schott*. This is not surprising considering that the majority of end product manufacturers abstain from referring to the brand *Ceran®* in their own communications.

This should not imply that the product is not successful, because it is. Its success story already began more than three decades ago and the company has sold more than 50 million glass-ceramic cooking surfaces worldwide since then. This number clearly shows how *Schott Ceran* revolutionized cooking appliances with its invention. In Europe, more than half of all new electric cooking appliances are now equipped with *Ceran®* cook top panels, regardless of the energy sources available. In 2004 *Schott* further optimized its material composition which, along with a modified production process has improved the heat transmission of the glass-ceramic surfaces for the latest generation of *Ceran Suprema®*. The successful result reduced boil-times by up to 16% and therefore reduced energy consumption at the same time.[6]

And here we are back at the problem – do consumers/buyers of cooking appliances for whom this is certainly interesting and relevant know this too? Does anybody care to inform them about the obvious advantages of *Ceran®* cooking panels? The term and product has become so generic that it is seen as self-explanatory although most consumers do not know *Ceran*.

Searching the web on the terms "glass-ceramic" and *Ceran*, you will stumble across many forums handling questions like "What pans for *Ceran* black glass electric cooktop?", "Does it scratch easily?"

Of course you could argue that since all major manufacturers of cooking appliances already have stoves with glass-ceramic panels, it is irrelvant that the brand has lost its power to differentiate and add value. But isn't this also the case with other companies like *Intel*? Today, almost every PC producer in the world is offering products with *Intel Inside* – did this impair their branding success? Obviously it didn't. Therefore we are also recommending a resumption of a holistic brand strategy for *Schott Ceran®*.

Pitfall No. 3: Brand Awareness vs. Brand Relevance

Many businesses make the mistake of vastly overrating the importance of brand awareness. Of course, if customers and stakeholders don't know you or your brand you are completely out of the picture, but to know you does not equal to buy from you. Plastering the streets with your corporate logo does **surely raise brand awareness** but much more is needed to sell your products or services. A brand also has to convey a meaningful and **relevant brand message** effectively targeted to reach customers and stakeholders.

In 2001, *E.ON*, a German utility company (after merging with *VEBA* and *VIAG*) chose to jump on the branding wagon to promote its commodity, electrical power. Millions of Euros were invested in broad-coverage advertising campaigns to develop their brands. Just four months after launching the "Mix it, baby" campaign developed with Arnold Schwarzenegger by the *E.ON* group, the *E.ON* brand achieved an aided recall of an amazing 93% and an unaided advertising recall of 66%. But did the estimated advertising expenditure of EUR 22.5 million pay off? Well, the German press reported in 2002 that the campaign was able to persuade only 1,100 customers to switch to *E.ON* – translating into canvassing costs of an incredible EUR 20,500 per customer. With the average annual turnover of around EUR 600 per customer, it is quite doubtful that this investment will ever pay off over the customer life cycle.[7]

Consider another company, *BASF*. Their slogan "We don't make a lot of the products you buy. We make a lot of the products you buy better". This is the corporate statement that has made the *BASF* corporate advertising campaign the most recognized of any corporate campaign from the North American chemical industry. *BASF* describes itself as "the world's leading chemical company". It is very successful and highly regarded around the world. Based in Europe, they have large operations in North America. *BASF* reported 2005 sales of €42.7 billion (up 14 percent from last year) and income from operations (EBIT) before special items of more than €6.1 billion (up 17 percent). The company's 83,000 employees manufacture thousands of products globally. The fact is they don't make many finished products – virtually all of the 6,000-plus products that they manufacture are ingredients that enhance the finished products consumers buy daily.[8]

It's unusual for a chemical company to run a branding campaign. In fact, Ian G. Heller, the director of branding valuation at Real Results Marketing agencies, accuses North American chemical companies of "shockingly low" levels of expenditures on branding – often less than 0.5 % of sales.[9] *BASF*, as the exception, is proud of its ad campaign along with the numerous benefits it has received from the increased level of awareness about *BASF*. As they point out, in one survey, "Nearly 70 percent of respondents recognized the slogan and 48 percent of all respondents both recognized it and correctly attributed it to *BASF* as part of a measure known as true awareness." The company goes on to say that, "By way of comparison, *BASF's* top three competitors in the U.S. received between 1 percent and 2 percent true slogan awareness."[10]

We don't make the computer screen. We make it sharper.
Paliocolor® liquid crystals from BASF substantially improve the viewing angle and contrast for flat screens. In contrast to other highly developed liquid crystals on the market, Paliocolor can be applied in coat only micrometers thick and polymerized into a hard film that provides high contrast and sharp images at wide angles.

We don't make the sandboard. We make it lighter.
BASF manufactures Terluran® acrylonitrile butadiene styrene (ABS) plastics that are often used as the core of sandboards, snowboards and other sporting goods. Plastic materials are well-known for providing lightweight performance in comparison to other materials.

We don't make the dress. We make it brighter.
BASF manufactures Ultraphor® optical brighteners for finishers of polyester/cellulosic blend fabrics. In addition, the company manufactures dispersion dyes such as Bafixan® that are well-suited to polyester, and are used in microfiber and sports clothing.

We don't make the motorcycle. We make it quicker.
BASF manufactures Ultramid® polyamide nylon, which is replacing metal in more and more automotive part applications. Because Ultramid provides high mechanical strength, rigidity and thermal stability, it performs as well as metals and is lighter in weight. Nylon's light weight helps make vehicles more fuel efficient and quicker. In addition, BASF manufactures polyisobutyleneamine (PIBA) which is a gasoline additive that provides superior intake valve detergency while controlling combustion chamber deposits, making for a cleaner burning, better performing engine.

Fig. 66. *BASF* corporate campaign 2006[11]

Brand awareness is the first layer of the Brand Building Pyramid in Kevin Keller's CBBE Model but it is only a prerequisite for brand relevance. [12] Brand relevance is directly triggered by the brand functions as described in Chapter 2. In the B2B environment, risk reduction, increased information efficiency, and value added through image benefit creation drives the brand functions directly. These factors are widened by the increased importance of the proliferation of similar products and services, increasing complexity, and incredible price pressures. As a result, if you are only looking at brand awareness, the company is missing out on the value driving aspects.

The question is: does this kind of marketing spending create brand relevance? Consumers are not choosing finished goods based on the raw materials used. The audacity and brilliance of *BASF's* advertising campaign is that they are paying to build awareness among a group of people who are not actually their customers. Nevertheless, done right, the campaign hits its mark and achieves relevant awareness in the right target group. Done wrong, it would be like Ferrari running an expensive campaign on Nickelodeon and then claiming success because awareness of their expensive sports cars has increased among 5-year olds. Awareness is not good for its own sake; it must be targeted to the right audience.[13]

In today's environment, unless a brand can maintain its relevance as categories emerge, change, and fade, narrow application preference may not be sufficient. Walter Seufert *BASF* President Europe is very convinced that the campaign was successful: "There are three main reasons, first the competition was real upset, second customers praised it, and third many new customers signed up."

Pitfall No. 4: Don't Wear Blinders

Many businesses mistakenly base their branding strategies solely around their **internal image of their brands**. The problem with this approach is that the internal view can often be quite different from the customer's. Management is quite often too close to a company to remain objective about the role it can realistically play in the marketplace. Arrogance, wishful thinking and office politics often further distort realities. This lack of objectivity needs to be compensated by effective customer analysis. By gaining customer input, they will better determine their current brand image, and also discover what they need to do to make it more relevant.[14]

ITT Industries, Inc. a global engineering and manufacturing company with leading positions in the markets of Fluid Technology Motion and Flow Control, is a great example of a company that successfully revealed and removed its "blinders". One division of the company is the world's premier supplier of pumps, systems and services to move, control and treat water and other fluids. It is moreover a major supplier of sophisticated military defense systems, and provides advanced technical and operational services to a broad range of government agencies. ITT Industries also produces industrial components for a number of other markets, including transportation, construction and aerospace. In 1995, ITT Industries gained independence from ITT Corporation and organized itself around three distinct divisions – Automotive, Defense & Electronics and Fluid Technology.[15] Despite the fact that its market offerings are targeted at relatively small groups of prospects, the company launched a million dollar branding campaign targeted at the general public in 1998. The reason was an identity problem that might not have been effectively uncovered if the company had only taken an internal perspective.

In 1997 the company conducted a study in the financial community to measure awareness of the then two year old company. It revealed both good and bad news. Positive was that people immediately recognized the "ITT" name and associated it with high-quality products. Unfortunately, when it came to ITT Industries, they were unclear on what ITT Industries is, and what it wanted to be. Many – particularly those in the investment community – still associated the ITT brand not only with its engineered products, but with financial services and resort hotels. Two out of every three respondents listed hotels, casinos or telephone equipment as its primary businesses.

The confusion partly stemmed from a mix-up with its former parent company ITT Corporation that was making front-page news in its battle to stave off a hostile take over by Hilton at that time. The research clearly underlined the need for a corporate brand strategy and campaign that would help to clarify ITT Industrial's brand essence by communicating a clear message to its stakeholders. The corporation realized that it needed to set ITT Industries apart from all other ITT's in the minds of investors, prospective customers and employees, and bring together its many strong businesses and brands under one umbrella.[16]

In 1998, the company launched a campaign targeted at the general public. The campaign presented the new corporate logo and the "Engineered for life" tagline. It comprised television and print advertisements. The print ads appeared in leading business publications including The *Wall Street Journal*, The New York Times, Barron's, The Economist, The Financial Times, Forbes, Fortune, Business Week and a number of other publications.[17]

If a company moves away from their internal view, building a strong brand involves a series of logical steps: "establishing the proper brand identity; creating the appropriate brand meaning; eliciting the right brand responses, and forging appropriate brand relationships with customers."[18]

No one knows the branding game better than brand extension guru Scott Bedbury – master of creating living-brands. In his seven years at *Nike*, Scott conceived and directed the worldwide 'Just Do It' branding campaign, increasing *Nike* revenue from US$750 million to US$5 billion by the time he left *Nike* in 1994. He then joined *Starbucks* in 1995, as chief marketing officer, where he was responsible for growing the US$700 million Seattle-based company into a global brand. There he championed the serving of *Starbucks* on all United Airline flights, engaged in a joint venture with *PepsiCo* to market *Starbucks* "Frappuccino" in supermarkets and joined with *Dreyer's Grand Ice Cream* to introduce six flavors of *Starbucks Ice Cream*. *Starbucks* expanded in the three years of his employment from 390 stores to 1,600 stores worldwide. Nowadays they boast 4,435 stores on three continents as well as branded coffee paraphernalia, music, and candy.[19] Bedbury helped *Nike* and *Starbucks* look outside for market opportunities rather than inside at a mirror.

We would put Eric Kim, the new Chief Marketing Officer of *Intel*, in the same club as Bedbury. Together with Chief Executive Paul Otellini, he saw the changes in *Intel's* marketplace and the need to change its strategy. On January 3, 2006, the world's biggest chipmaker scrapped its 37-year-old *Intel Inside* logo as part of a major rebranding that will emphasize its shift away from its core PC business into consumer products. The original *Intel Corp.* logo featuring a lowered "e" will be replaced with one showing an oval swirl surrounding the company's name. The phrase "Leap ahead" will supplant *Intel Inside*, which launched the *Silicon Valley* giant into public awareness and helped it build the world's No. 5 brand, worth an estimated US$36 billion, according to Interbrand 2005 scoreboard.[20]

The company said that although the *Intel Inside* tagline will disappear, it will retain a marketing program with that name in which *Intel* helps PC makers advertise products that use its chips. *Intel* is counting on the consumer appetite for digital media and networking to drive business as the PC market slows and as rival Advanced *Micro Devices Inc.* makes inroads into the markets for laptop and server computers.[21]

The brand overhaul also puts a new face on an internal shift accelerated since the new CEO Otellini took charge of the company in May 2005. The changes take the focus off individual chips and puts it on "platforms" that the company hopes will spur the integration of *Intel*-based computers with digital media and networks in homes, businesses and schools. This takes the brand strategy and aligns it with the business strategy that has been underway at *Intel* for several years. The new campaign also plays down *Intel's* venerable *Pentium* brand while emphasizing its *Centrino* line of laptop chips and a new effort called "Viiv" that aims to integrate PCs into home entertainment such as by recording TV shows and sending them to other devices. *Intel* also for the first time revealed that its new chip for laptop computers will be marketed as Core. That processor, to be a key part of Viiv, is to debut early next year and will be a major product launch as *Intel* seeks to regain ground in the mobile market against *AMD*.

The Santa Clara, California-based company is rolling out the re-branding just weeks after it elevated Eric Kim to the role of Chief Marketing Officer. *Intel* hired Kim away last year from *Samsung Electronics*, where he was credited with helping to forge a savvy consumer brand to take on industry stalwarts such as Japan's *Sony Corp.*

This example shows that *Intel* didn't wear blinders. Instead, they saw the threat from their major rival *AMD* and the newcomer Samsung, and moved aggressively ahead and changed the ingredient brand *Intel Inside* to a master brand with a new logo and the tagline "Leap Ahead". No doubt, we will probably see more changes from that company.[22]

Pitfall No. 5: Don't Let Outsiders Do Your Job

Earlier in this book we recommended enlisting the assistance of professional brand agencies in order to assure a certain degree of objectivity. But that doesn't mean that you should let them do this job alone! A good brand agency can assist in developing a **holistic brand approach** but their foremost intention is to make money. They are not the ones to tell you who you are, and what your company is about. Many businesses fail to acknowledge that they need to be actively involved in the whole process and that it is not enough to hire a branding agency.

A strong and comprehensive brand approach requires a high level of personal attention and commitment from the CEO and CMO and the other senior management if you want to be successful. The branding approach needs to be **elevated into the board rooms**. Corporate branding addresses additional issues concerning all stakeholders (customers, shareholders, media, competitors, governments and many others).[23]

And if you are seeking help, who should you approach, an **ad agency or a consultant company?** There was a time when advertising was indisputably acknowledged to be the highest form of marketing – indeed, for many brand owners, advertising and branding were synonymous. But today, the situation has changed. As Niall Fitzgerald, CEO of *Unilever*, famously said a few years ago: "There is an alarming discrepancy between what our brands are going to need and what agencies are good at."[24]

The concept of "branding" has moved far beyond communicating product differences and building "image". This means that advertising agencies need to shift from creating advertising to providing high-end strategic advice about not only marketing, but the business as a whole. However, personal experience and studies suggest that brand owners do not yet believe that agencies are delivering at that higher level; good news for consultancies providing brand strategy advice. The big networks – *Omnicom, WPP, Interpublic* – all have their feet firmly in both camps, owning both world-renowned advertising agency groups, as well as international brand consultancies.

We suggest a combined approach: strong internal resources and commitment, advice from brand consultants or knowledgeable individuals, like professors, and the use of excellent advertisement specialists. In 1992, *Andersen Consulting* spent approximately US$10 million globally on advertising. ***Accenture* did their successful re-branding that way**.

Accenture is the new name for *Andersen Consulting*, which broke away from *Arthur Andersen* in 2000,[25] after a longstanding feud. The change to *Accenture* was the fastest, most expensive re-branding effort in history as everything was changed to fit the new logo in a matter of days.[26] The name change follows an independent arbitrator's August 2000 ruling in favor of *Andersen Consulting* in its arbitration with *Andersen Worldwide* and *Arthur Andersen*. Under the terms of the ruling, *Andersen Consulting* was excused from any further obligations to *Andersen Worldwide* and *Arthur Andersen* and given until December 31, 2000 to adopt a new name with no explicit or implicit reference to *Andersen*. It was then that *Arthur Andersen* got into so much legal

Fig. 67. *Andersen Consulting* and *Accenture* logos

trouble for allowing *Enron* to cook their books and destroying *Enron's* documents as *Enron* collapsed. Today *Arthur Anderson* is history, but *Accenture* was not affected at all. At the end of 2005 *Accenture* had more than 126,000 (including more than 4,100 senior executives) based in more than 110 offices in 48 countries delivering a wide range of consulting, technology and outsourcing services, with revenues of US$15.55 billion for fiscal 2005 (12 mos. ending Aug. 31, 2005).

Under the leadership of former Chairman and CEO Joe W. Forehan *Accenture* had dedicated its brightest management talents to steer that re-branding exercise: Teresa Poggenpohl; Partner and Director-Global Brand, Advertising, and Research, Jim Murphy Global Managing Director – Marketing & Communications. The task was re-branding, re-positioning and re-structuring. The old *Andersen Consulting* already had set a new standard for marketing a professional services company. *Andersen Consulting* is widely credited as being the first professional services firm to advertise aggressively. As Jim Murphy, Global Managing Director of Marketing & Communications said, "In 1989, *Andersen Consulting* not only created a new management and technology organization, but also created with the help of our communications agency Young & Rubicam, a new advertising category for professional services."

The partners understood marketing in a strategic sense and had the courage to create the brand and invest in it at a time when branding was not a priority for professional services firms. This was a breakthrough approach for transforming the company. The first step was the re-branding. To create the new brand identity they used an inside-out, outside-in approach. Top management used the Business-to-Employee (B2E) Portal to communicate the re-naming task. Out of the 65,000 professionals, 47 teams were formed and 2,700 suggestions were created through a "brand-storming" exercise. "*Accenture* was the only name in our final round of selection that was developed by an employee," Poggenpohl said. "It's a fanciful name that means nothing around the world."

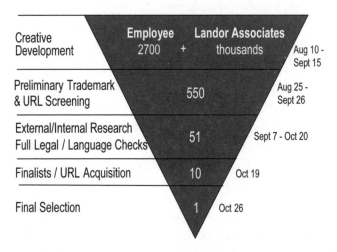

Creative Development	Employee 2700 +	Landor Associates thousands	Aug 10 - Sept 15
Preliminary Trademark & URL Screening		550	Aug 25 - Sept 26
External/Internal Research Full Legal / Language Checks		51	Sept 7 - Oct 20
Finalists / URL Acquisition		10	Oct 19
Final Selection		1	Oct 26

Fig. 68. Naming development in 2000 from *Anderson Consulting* to *Accenture*

With the help of *Landor Associates*, not only was the new brand name was selected but also a distinctive logo created. In addition, intensive market research was conducted to acquire possible client judgments and reaction.

Accenture did much more than simply change its name. Landor Associates was engaged to help reposition the firm in the marketplace to better reflect its new vision and strategy to become a market maker, architect and builder of the new economy by executing a new business strategy and refocusing its capabilities. Moving away from the IT-driven company image to business and technology consulting, *Accenture* aspires to become one of the world's leading companies, bringing innovations to improve the way the world works and lives. The other big task was the integration of 6 WPP agencies in 147 days during the whole exercise:

Landor	Brand strategy, naming consultancy, word mark, visual identity system
Y&R Advertising	Brand strategy, advertising, global launch
Burson-Marsteller	Brand strategy, global launch
Wunderman	Marketing communications, global launch
Luminant	Marketing communications
The Media Edge	Media buying

After a teaser campaign from August to the end of December, the new name was promoted aggressively, accompanied by a major marketing push. All clients and many industry experts were informed through promotion packages. More than US$175 million were spent for a huge marketing push with the help of an advertising campaign, using print and television advertisements. In addition, highly visible events were sponsored such as World Golf Championship, *BMW/Williams Formula 1* and the World Economic Forum in Davos 2001. The biggest single expenditure was the four TV spots during the US 2001 *Super Bowl*. The results were overwhelming. Three months post-launch, the unprompted awareness amongst target audiences reached 29% – eclipsing nearly every competitor. *Accenture* was recognized as a leader in its field in less than 18 months, and the new brand achieves industry recognition such as:

- European Effie
- ACE Award for the launch kit
- WPP Partnership Program Award
- *Accenture's* Jim Murphy voted *PR Man of the Year, Marketer of the Year* by B2B magazine

Besides the task of re-branding and repositioning *Accenture*, a restructuring of the organization was initiated. The first step was the change of the ownership structure from a partnership to a limited company. *Accenture* changed three months later to a public traded company. It had its initial public offering (IPO) at the New York stock exchange in June 2001.

Following a decade of prosperity and growth, *Accenture* staked a new direction and forged a new identity at the turn of the 21st century. After successful arbitration against *Andersen, Accenture* was able to recast itself under a new name, coinciding with the launch of a new positioning. The re-branding and repositioning of *Accenture* was unprecedented in scope and timeframe – the largest re-branding initiative ever undertaken by a professional services firm, being successfully implemented across 47 countries in just 147 days. *Accenture* launched this re-branding and repositioning to its global audience with a multi-phase global marketing campaign that began before the official changeover occurred on January 1, 2001. The challenge was daunting, but the objectives clear: To reposition the company, transfer brand equity to *Accenture,* raise awareness of *Accenture* globally and to eliminate residual confusion with *Arthur Andersen.* Changes in the business climate in 2001 prompted a refinement to their positioning, one that delineated *Accenture's* ability to help companies capitalize on their marketplace opportunities by bringing their ideas to life.

Summary

Pitfalls in B2B branding are unlikely to be anticipated by newcomers to the branding effort. Beware of the following pitfalls in order to ensure that branding initiatives will reap results.

- One of the most common misconceptions of branding is **that companies believe that they "own" the brand**. No matter what the business and its corporate executives would like their brand to be, brand reality is always defined by the customer's view.

- Some companies think that **brands take care of themselves**. If companies let their brand asset deteriorate, the overall company performance can suffer. We recommend proactive brand management through brand differentiation or pure re-branding.

- A company may not have their priorities set if it is **overrating the importance of brand awareness** instead of focusing on brand relevance. Managing touchpoints and messages effectively and targeting the right customers and stakeholders can assure efficient use of funds and management time.

- Many businesses mistakenly base their branding strategies solely around the **internal image of their brand**. This type of wishful thinking may lead to lack of objectivity. By gaining customer input, it can determine the current brand image, and also discover what is needed to do to make the brand more relevant.

- **Advertising agencies and consultants** may do their job by assisting in developing a holistic brand approach but the company should determine its own brand identity.

The essence is to learn from failed branding efforts of B2B companies that jumped into branding without considering the **whole range of brand creation and steering.**

Notes

1   D.A. Aaker, *Building Strong Brands*, (New York: The Free Press, 1996).

2   Dan Morrison, "The Six Biggest Pitfalls in B-to-B Branding," *Business2Busi-ness Marketer* (July/August, 2001).

3   Kevin Roberts from *Saatchi & Saatchi* supports in his outstanding publication *Lovemarks-the future beyond brands* that brands only exist in the customer's mind. He even goes one step further and states that if brands are in the heads of people they could even become Lovemarks. He is mainly talking about consumer brands that are so beloved that they go beyond just being known brands. It is interesting to note that some B2B brands such as *FedEx, IBM, Siemens, Segway*, or *Zwilling* made it on to his Lovemarks list.

4   Paul Rittenberg, "Building a #1 Rated Brand in Less than a Decade," *The Advertiser* (October 2002).

5   Dan Morrison, "The Six Biggest Pitfalls in B-to-B Branding," *Business2Business Marketer* (July/August, 2001).

6   "Annual Report 2003/2004," *Schott AG*, p. 6, 41.

7   McKinsey, *Marketing Practice*, p. 12.

[8]   Web site of *BASF Corporation*, Florham Park, NJ, cited January 2006.

[9]   "Making Specialty Chemicals Special Again," *Chemical Week* (Annual 2003), p. 12.

[10] Ian G. Heller, "When Good Companies Do Bad Branding," *Real Results Marketing* (March, 2004).

[11] Source: www.basf.com, cited February 2006.

[12] Keller, K.L., *Strategic Brand Management*, 2003.

[13] Ian G. Heller, "When Good Companies Do Bad Branding," Real Results Marketing, (March, 2004).

[14] Dan Morrison, "The Six Biggest Pitfalls in B-to-B Branding," *Business2-Business Marketer* (July/August, 2001), p. 1.

[15] Web site of *ITT Industries, Inc.*, White Plains, NY, cited August 2005.

[16] „Evolution of a Brand," *In Our Hands – ITT Company Magazine* (Fall 1998), pp. 7-8.

[17] „ITT Industries Launches New Corporate Ad Campaign," *In Our Hands – ITT Company Magazine* (Fall 1998), pp. 13-14.

[18] Paul Rittenberg, "Building a #1 Rated Brand in Less than a Decade," *The Advertiser* (October 2002).

[19] Cameron Dart, "Brands Are Alive!" *brandspa* (February 2002), p. 14.

[20] Robert Berner and David Kiley, "Global Brands," *Business Week* (July 2005), pp. 86-94.

[21] Web site of *Intel Corporation*, Santa Clara, CA, cited January 2006.

[22] Ibid.

[23] Ibid.

[24] "Ad Agencies Vs. Consultancies: Weighing the Differencies," *Brandchannel.com (2001).*

[25] A very detail description of the situation could be found in: Kevin Keller, "Best Practice Cases in Branding", "Accenture: Rebranding and Repositioning a Global Power Brand," Prentice Hall, August 2003 and Richard Girard, "Accenture Profile", Polaris Institute, June 2003. http://www.polarisinstitute.org/corp_profiles/public_service_gats_pdfs/Accenture.pdf.

[26] Kaikati, Jack (2003), "Lessons From Accenture's 3Rs: Rebranding, Restructuring, and Repositioning," *Journal of Product and Brand Management*, Volume 12, Issue 7, 2003.

CHAPTER 7

Future Perspective

The art of prophecy is very difficult, especially with respect to the future.

Mark Twain (1835-1910)

During the last two decades, most industries around the world have had to face major structural changes. The development of new technologies, globalization, and diminishing regulatory environments has had significant impact on business strategies and practices of many companies.[1] In some cases the directions of the changes were obvious long before they effectively came, in others not.

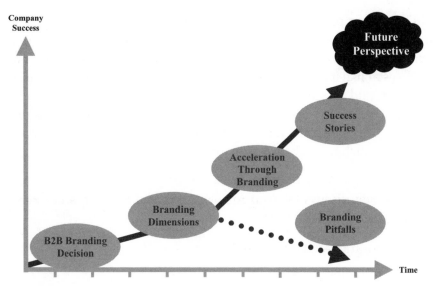

Fig. 69. Guiding principle future perspective

In our opinion, B2B branding and brand management will become increasingly significant. Some even argue that the future of brands **is the future of business** and that sooner or later, the brand will become the only major sustainable competitive advantage in many B2B areas. How this brand future will be constituted is the question. We agree with Scott Bedbury and his Principle No. 8 from *A New Brand World:*[2]

> Relevance, simplicity, and humanity
> – not technology –
> will distinguish brands in the future.

A brand should no longer simply be seen as a logo or icon. Rather, it is a holistic experience in which all activities of a company must be aligned and integrated to gain maximum competitive advantage. Although more than half of the 50 most valuable brands in the world were created more than 50 years ago, age is not a deciding factor for brand success. Even the strongest brands today can get stuck in a complacent time warp, resting on their old laurels and thereby missing out new and important market trends.

Old and once prestigious company brands being overtaken by new and baggage-free competitors is a common phenomenon.[3] The real challenge for businesses is therefore to **maintain their position**, not just to establish it in the first place. It is essential to check the relevance of your brand message regularly and improve and adapt to new circumstances and trends, while keeping the heart of the brand untouched. Companies must be able to constantly deliver on their brand promise, which has to be relevant, meaningful and valued by customers.

Here we will discuss the four major trends that all companies need to recognize and respond to.

- Corporate Social Responsibility
- Branding in China
- Design and Branding
- Lovemarks and Brand Leadership

7.1 Corporate Social Responsibility

There is a continuous debate about whether corporations owe anything more to society than to satisfy customer needs and make money in the process. At one extreme are groups that attack and dislike corporations. In the middle are groups that believe corporations owe something back to society. At the other extreme are groups that see corporations with no obligations to contribute to social welfare.

Let's examine the first group. In 2004, the documentary *The Corporation* based on the homonymous book *The Corporation: the Pathological Pursuit of Profit and Power* by Canadian law professor Joel Bakan attracted considerable attention. Beginning with the nineteenth-century US Supreme Court decision granting the corporation status as a "person", the film proceeds with anthropomorphizing the corporation by wondering what type of "person" it would be. By applying the *Diagnostic and Statistical Manual of Mental Disorders* to the corporate "personality," they conclude that it would be clearly judged as "psychopathic" because it effectively has no **moral or social obligations**. This "pathology" gimmick is employed throughout the film, but actually does nothing to clarify the essential features of the entity. By being provocative and emotional, the film mainly appeals to those young people involved in the anti-globalization and other social protest movements, yet lacks any serious critique of contemporary social and economic life. Fundamentally confused, the work can be seen as both backward and reactionary. Their recommendations at the end are mere band-aid solutions, generally pleading for state regulation.[4]

Anti-globalization protestors attacking multinational companies and their brands as "bullies" is not really a new phenomenon. An activist crying for better social behavior of the so-called "bullies" can be compared to beauty pageant candidates pleading for world peace. Both are not taken too seriously and their wishes are unlikely to be realized any time soon. Companies are not here to make the world a better place but to provide us with what we need in order to make our lives more comfortable and to make money in the course of doing this. If we would like to see more social awareness

from these companies, it is the employees, customers, and stakeholders who have to initiate the demand. And this is where the
power of the brand comes in.

Those in the middle see today's corporations surrounded by a word-
processed, all-seeing digital world. Companies have no choice but to
behave well. The strongest incentive comes from their desire to have
a positive global brand. To protect the reputation of its brand, a
business has to acknowledge that its success demands a holistic approach to promoting its product or service, including more social
responsibility.

Brands of the future will have to stand not only for **product quality**
and a **desirable image** but will also have to signal something whole-
some about the company behind the brand. "The next big thing in
brands is social responsibility," says Mr. Olins, "It will be clever to
say there is nothing different about our product or price, but we behave well. Far from being evil, brands are becoming an effective
weapon for holding even the largest global corporations to account. [5]

Brands actually function to protect consumers, create prosperity, to
bind people together internationally, and they have the potential to
bring enormous benefits to the developed – and developing –
worlds. They are central wealth creators to businesses and economies and they can only play a positive role.

More corporations now understand and have witnessed the positive effects of implementing cause-marketing campaigns, but how
much more is there to corporate philanthropy? And how can corporations wishing to help the community, as well as the bottom line,
profit from the experiences of their peers?

Branding and social responsibility seek to create a just and sustainable world by working with companies to promote more responsible
business practices, innovation and collaboration. Company reputation and corporate citizenship often affect a company's ability to
operate overseas or influence consumer purchase behavior. According to the 2001 Corporate Social Responsibility Monitor, forty-

two percent of North American consumers reported having punished socially irresponsible companies by not buying their products.[6]

Companies that do business in a manner that is responsive to the concerns of their multiple stakeholders have a strategic business advantage. A company's brand image can be enhanced when it is identified with issues that strongly appeal to its customers and employees. Out of this favorable identity, businesses can build strong loyalty among employees and customers and position themselves favorably in the marketplace.[7]

Many American companies are now discovering what their international counterparts have known for years: that **reputation as a good corporate citizen matters** and that transparency and accountability for corporate citizenship can enhance brand image and good will. The institutionalization of such practices is evidenced by the fact that the number of companies reporting on corporate citizenship has climbed from 200 five years ago to over 4,000 today.[8]

Companies are expressing corporate social responsibility in at least six ways:[9]

1. **Cause promotions** support a cause by increasing community awareness and contributions to the cause.

2. **Cause-related marketing** ties donations to a cause to the corporation's performance, most typically to product sales volume.

3. **Corporate social marketing** focuses on campaigns to influence positive behavior change.

4. **Community volunteering** involves employee and retail/franchise partner donation of their time in support of a cause.

5. **Corporate philanthropy** entails writing a check, giving a grant or in-kind contribution of corporate services and resources.

6. **Corporate socially responsible business practices** relate to the adoption of discretionary business practices and investments that contribute to improved environmental and community well-being.

Through these actions and those of their intermediaries – companies reflect the understanding that they are an integral part of the social and economic world in which they operate. This is why corporate managers need to bring society into the company; why they need to turn their brands into citizen brands.

In the emerging networked, post-industrial world, managing that relationship is one of the most important challenges that companies face. And companies that understand and embrace this are likely to be the ultimate winners in the future.

7.2   Branding in China

With a branding industry that grossed a staggering US$13 billion in advertising spending in 2003, and US$30 billion in 2005, China presents a whole new frontier in the global race for mindshare and market share. Although China is better known as the world's manufacturing base, branding and innovation have started to appear more frequently in the ambitious blueprints of an increasing number of Chinese companies. The long-term benefits and strengths generated from the branding strategies of many international companies are now more visible to local enterprises. While many Chinese companies have been competing on price and the struggle for immediate benefits, international players have been increasing the presence and reputation of their products and companies on the China market. Branding, which has yet to be mastered by the majority of local companies, has been a major contributor to their success, just as it has been on the international market. The investment that these overseas companies have made in terms of building a long-term image for their products is finally paying off.[10]

Twenty three years ago, Theodore Levitt published his provocative classic, "**The Globalization of Markets**," in the *Harvard Business Review*. He saw global corporations exploiting the "economics of simplicity and standardization" to price their global products far below the local competition. "No one is exempt and nothing can stop the process," he proclaimed, "everywhere everything gets more and more like everything else as the world's preference structure is re-lentlessly homogenized."[11]

His argument seemed irresistible to executives. In the 1980s, for in-stance, Japanese companies like *Toyota* and *Panasonic* applied excep-tional production quality controls and scale efficiencies to market standardized products across the globe at prices that tempted even the most patriotic consumer. During the late 1980s and the 1990s, scrambling to establish beachheads in some new country markets, global companies had no time-or apparently any need-to worry about local adaptation.[12]

In March 2000, *Coca Cola's* CEO Douglas Daft announced the com-pany's new "**think local, act local**" marketing strategy. Having em-braced Levitt's vision for decades, global-brand owners started to listen more closely about how to adapt product attributes and ad-vertising messages to local tastes. However, it didn't mean that Levitt was so wrong about the global standardization of markets and brands. Two forces will drive its return: the rebound of the global economy and China's emergence as a player on the world economic stage[13]. Just as the global economic downturn led con-sumers around the world to focus locally, a rebounding world economy will revive the appeal of global brands. In an up-cycle, consumers feel more optimistic and extravagant and are eager to participate in an international marketplace; the pace of China's eco-nomic and industrial growth ensures that China will become the twenty-first century's factory to the world; any company anywhere in the world will be able to outsource the production of anything to China. Yet, already, China itself is emerging as a source of global brands. Chinese brands like *Lenovo* in computers, *Haier* in appli-ances, *TCL* in mobile phones, and Tsingtao in beer are extending internationally. And there will be more. The more or less virgin status of branding industrial products or services can be compared to the status of general branding in China.

For decades, China has enjoyed a dominant place in world manufac-turing because of its low-cost labor. Chinese businesses were satisfied with the role of being OEM's, supplying the world's biggest brands and retailers' private labels with a huge diversity of product. Today, the wind has changed and even China's government has explicitly stated that it sees "branded commodities" as their way towards world success.[14] It is now urging some of China's largest companies to brand their products globally. This is a logical strategy – China is after all the world's biggest potential consumer market. The market is growing internally and externally, with GDP increasing 9.2 percent year one year to 14.753 trillion Yuan US$1.833 trillion (2005 est.) in July 2005. This continued stable and rapid growth is alluring for all businesses.[15] As the Chinese economy grows and diversifies, customer preferences and behaviors will inevitably change.

Competitive pressures in the Chinese home market put constant pressures on prices, underlining the importance of branded products that can be much more profitable than those of mere OEM's. The foreign competition moreover puts tremendous pressures on companies to constantly improve and innovate, thus providing the chance to move away from the image as producers of cheap goods. Market research and marketing information systems are still in their infancy in present day China. Nonetheless, the market is strongly characterized by rapidly growing brand awareness and preference of consumers. In order to exploit these trends, companies have to invest heavily in product innovation and quality. Businesses have to move away from constantly tapping into severe price wars with competitors as this has almost become a national passion. On the road to internationalization, Chinese companies must convert their domestic advantages into international ones. The actual marketing management in China though, shows many areas that need further improvement. The United States still has the strongest marketing engine in the world, while China has just started to build its own. If Chinese businesses continue to apply the science of modern marketing management, the years to come will undoubtedly show a narrowing of this difference.[16]

According to the professional assessment organization *Beijing Famous-Brand Evaluation Co., Ltd.* the Chinese *Haier* group is on top of the most valuable Chinese brands. This producer of household appliances is the most valuable brand with more than 100 billion Yuan (US$12 billion) assets. In 2004 the group reported exports of more than US$1 billion. Reasons for this huge success are seen in the further opening of the market and the following increase in competition in this special sector.[17] *Haier* is now one of the world's biggest refrigerator brands. Some argue that this is partly due to the "borrowed" belief among customers that the brand is of German origin. More than 20 years ago, the company bought the production-line technology from *Liebherr*, a German industrial conglomerate. They obviously made a decent attempt to borrow the name ("-herr" pronounced to the best of their linguistic ability as *Haier*) as well as the technology.[18]

In the research report Brands in 2004 on the most valuable Chinese brands, there are 43 brands listed. The average sales scale of the brands in 2004 is RMB 11.885 billion Yuan (US$1.478 billion), increased by 24.7% compared with that in the last year, and the brand value has grown by 14% in average. The average ratio of brand value to sales income is 0.84 to 1. Most companies of the list are selling to end-user; B2B companies have not made it to the list, only six supply to industrial clients.

Table 7. Most valuable brands in China

Brands	Company	Main products	Brand Value in RMB billion Yuan
Haier	Haier Group Company	All types of household appliances	61.600
Hongtashan	Yuxi Hongta Tobacco (Group) Co., Ltd.	Cigarettes	46.900
Legend	Legend Group Co., Ltd.	Computers	30.700
TCL	TCL Group Stock Co., Ltd.	TV sets and mobile phones	30.569
Changhong	Sichuan Chonghong Electronic Group Co., Ltd.	TV sets	27.016
Midea	Guangzhou Midea Group Stock Co., Ltd.	Air conditioners and microwave ovens	20.118

These brands are in 24 industries, and 18 provinces and regions. Guangdong ranks the first and owns 9 brand companies, Sichuan owns 6, Jiangsu owns 4, Zhejiang, Shandong, Jilin, and Beijing own 3 each. According to the total value of brands, Guangdong still ranks the first, and then Sichuan, Shandong, Jilin, Yunnan, and Beijing in sequence.

The Chinese government is now urging some of China's biggest companies to sell branded products abroad. The home market is fiendishly competitive and puts constant pressure on prices. Branded products can be more profitable than those of OEMs, and competing in foreign markets forces companies to innovate and improve, thus helping them to move away from their image as producers of cheap goods.

Here we describe three Chinese companies – *Galanz Group, Haier,* and *TTI* – each of which has taken a different route to expansion and branding. Then we will describe B2B Chinese companies.

Galanz Group – Taking OEM Route

Most Chinese companies seeking to expand abroad have pursued an OEM strategy, enabling them to build scale quickly without the need for corresponding investments in marketing. Information technology has made it feasible to construct global networks that seamlessly link production in China to marketing and design operations in developed markets. Conversely, manufacturers in developed markets can outsource what would otherwise be high-cost production, in turn creating greater price flexibility.

Cost and quality leadership and the ability to support a number of global customers and to acquire the needed technology and capabilities are the key success factors in this model. Low costs, which are necessary to secure the initial contracts, must be accompanied by excellent skills in supply chain management and sourcing. A number of customers are required to minimize dependence on any one of them and to gain scale. But while this strategy demands the lowest level of additional skills from Chinese companies, it also offers the lowest upside from the market. Returns can come only through expanding scale to achieve a position of global dominance in components and assembly.

Galanz Group Co. Ltd, a Guangdong-based home appliance company is an example of globalization through an OEM strategy. Founded in 1978 as a textile company with 200 employees, in 1992 it started making microwave ovens, which it soon began manufacturing for OEM customers, targeting those keen to lower their manufacturing costs but not yet ready to set up operations in China. The company is now the world's largest producer of **microwave ovens**, with almost 30 percent of the global and 70 percent of the Chinese market.

Galanz maintained cost leadership while integrating itself into its customers' networks and lowering prices to gain market share and scale; industry average pricing dropped by 18 percent a year in the late 1990s. Since then *Galanz* has signed more than 80 contracts with OEMs. The strategy has paid off. By 2005, sales to OEMs represented over 60 percent of the company's revenue, and annual production had reached 15 million–plus units. Total sales had risen to more than 5 billion renminbi (over US$600 million) and net profits to more than 450 million renminbi. *Galanz* is now introducing branded products for markets in South America and rolling out an OEM approach for other home appliances.

Haier and CSSC Case – The Build-up Step-by-Step Approach

In B2B many Chinese companies are just at the beginning of branding. An interesting example is *Haier*. *Haier* is seen as a role model for the next Chinese industrial giants. *Haier* is a diversified manufacturer of more than 80 products ranging from refrigerators, washing machines, and air conditioners to cell phones and televisions and the world's fifth largest maker of white goods. Since the end of the last century, *Haier* has been enjoying leading domestic market shares in washing machines (25 %), refrigerators (22 %), vacuum cleaners (20 %), and air conditioners (12 %).[19] Figure 70 summarizes the three stages of development through which *Haier* passed.

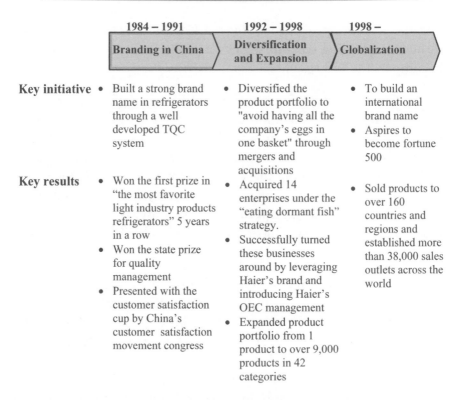

Fig. 70. Development stages for branding in China

In 2005, the company had worldwide sales of more than US$10 billion, a 15 percent increase since 2001. Long dominant in China as one of the first truly nationwide brands, *Haier* now aggressively pursues a globalization strategy on several international fronts, now selling its products in 160 countries and owning 13 factories outside China:

- **Japan** – *Haier* executes sales of nine appliance products through Sanyo Corporation at prices 10-20% lower than Japanese competitors.

- **United States** – A US$40 million Camden, South Carolina production facility went on-line in 2000, producing large volume refrigerators.

- **Europe** – *Haier Europe*, founded in 2000, coordinates sales and marketing of customized product lines across 13 countries. The company also purchased a Padova, Italy factory for localized white goods production

- **India** – *Haier* is in talks with *Tata Group* to outsource part of the manufacturing as labor cost in China is already higher than in India.

Haier's global branding approach is to extend *Haier's* strong domestic brand reputation into the West by introducing innovative products for niche consumer markets and then expanding into bigger ones. Such strategy enables the company to enjoy the higher margins that come with brand sales instead of slugging it out as a low-cost supplier to Western companies.

TTI and TCL Case – Buying Your Way in

The alternative to entering a market step-by-step is to buy into it through **mergers and acquisitions**. Suitable targets would be companies with valuable assets—brands, customer bases, technology, or channels—as well as products that have become overpriced as a result of management's failure to monitor costs, to move production offshore to low-cost locations (such as China), or to extract the best prices from overseas factories or offshore OEMs.

A buyer could move the bulk of the acquired company's production to China and retain the brand name, distribution channels, and some of the local talent. Over time, it could co-brand the product with its own name to build consumer awareness of its Chinese brand. Once the association and awareness had been firmly established, the buyer could phase out the target brand. The biggest obstacle for a Chinese company would be locating qualified turnaround managers for its typically distressed targets, since it would be unlikely to have post merger-management and marketing skills in-house.

Techtronic Industries Co. Ltd. (*TTI* or the Group) is a world-class supplier of superior home improvement and construction tools with a powerful portfolio of trusted brands and a strong commitment to innovation and quality. *TTI's* acquisition spree started 2000.

In August they acquired *Ryobi* brand in North America for power tools. In August 2001 *TTI* acquired *Ryobi Europe* for power tools and outdoor products. In November of the same year they bought the *Homelite* brand of lawn and garden equipment. In March 2002 they also integrated *Ryobi Australia* and *Ryobi New* Zealand power tool and outdoor power equipment businesses. April 2003 *TTI* acquired *Royal Appliances Mfg. Co.*, and January 2004 they added *Ryobi* brand in North America for outdoor power equipment. Finally January 2005 they acquired *Milwaukee®* and *AEG®* electric power tools and *DreBo®* carbide drill bits. Run by a strong management team, the brands are kept separate, but the production facilities are integrated and run cost efficiently. Branding is on the mind of the business leaders. More brands are on their shopping list, but financial restriction could hinder the expansion. But this brand expansion model may soon spread more over China.

Fig. 71. Brand portfolio of the *TTI Group*

A leading Chinese electronics maker is pursuing a variant of this approach. *TCL International Holdings* purchased an insolvent German television maker, *Schneider Electronics*, for US$8 million in September 2002 in an attempt to break into the European market. Included in the acquisition price were *Schneider's* plants; its distribution network of chain stores, hypermarkets, and mail order; and trademark rights to a series of brands, including *Schneider* and *Dual*. *TCL*, hoping to avoid European quotas on the importation of Chinese TV sets, expects to continue production in Europe. A professional management team is helping *TCL* understand the local market and sales networks, and some *Schneider* employees have been rehired to oversee production. If the strategy is successful, *TCL* could one day introduce the *TCL* brand to the European market. Electronics products bearing the name are already exported to Australia, the Middle East, Russia, South Africa, and Southeast Asia. In a twist, *TCL* is using its *Schneider* brand to position its mobile telephones in the high-end segment of the Chinese market. More recently, *TCL* bought *GoVideo*, of Scottsdale, Arizona, which makes DVD players.

In July 2004 *TTE Corporation* ("TTE"), the biggest global TV manufacturer, jointly set up by *TCL* and Thomson, officially started operation in ShenZhen, China, which its business covers all major markets in the world.

Thomson owns two leading television brands, Thomson in Europe, and RCA in the US. The RCA brand is respected as one of the oldest brands in televisions in the US, and commands a 13 percent market share. The two companies have manufacturing facilities in China, France, Mexico, Poland, Thailand and Vietnam, and it is likely that there will be some consolidation of manufacturing facilities. Major US retailers have put unrelenting pressure on makers to cut their prices, and that has benefited manufacturers with major facilities in China, which benefit from a large domestic market.

For *TCL*, the deal represents an opportunity to transform from a Chinese company to a global company. Chinese companies take advantage of their manufacturing expertise and huge domestic market to build presence; now more want to stretch their wings and become global companies.

The traditional route would have been to focus on certain foreign markets, and build brand recognition. This is a long, slow and expensive process, especially when the newcomer has to fight established brands. For a business challenged by low margins, such as television manufacture, a brand-building strategy would have quickly forced it into the red. As a result, *TCL* opted instead to partner with Thomson as a way to quickly expand into major international markets.

Also, in April 2004, *TCL Mobile* has signed memorandum of under-standing (MOU) with *Alcatel* to form a joint venture which is engaging in mobile phone development, production, sales and relevant services in the world. *Alcatel* intends to grant to the joint venture company a license to use the *Alcatel* brand name for handsets sales and distribution, building on the brand's strength in the telecom-munications industry globally.

Many of China's appliance and consumer electronics manufacturers have little choice but to go global. Born into an industry that is essentially open to worldwide competition, they must gain scale in the only place they can—the home turf of the world's multination-als. Just getting into the branding game, though, will require a combination of attractively priced products, good service, and first-rate technology. To stay there, the Chinese will have to build or buy a wide range of new skills. But if standards of quality and service remain high, a number of Chinese companies will earn shelf space for their branded goods in developed markets and, one day, might even capture the price premiums that some of their Japanese and South Korean competitors enjoy.

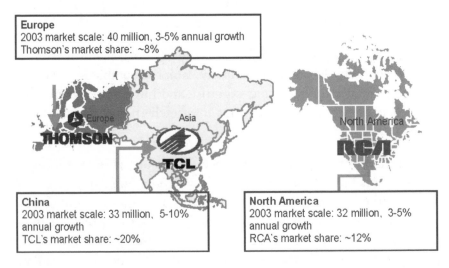

Fig. 72. *TCL* global brand coverage

Chinese B2B Companies

In the B2B world, a few outstanding Chinese companies can be identified today. On the list of the top 25 Chinese brands are the *Jiefang* brand for commercial trucks from *FAW Group Company*, the plastic pipe manufacturer *Guangdong Goody Plastic Stock Co., Ltd.*, and the *Jinde Pipe Industrial Group Co., Ltd.* Most of the former state owned industrial conglomerates are not known to the public, but also working on their brand improvements. As a typical example, consider the *China State Shipbuilding Corporation (CSSC)*. The new *China State Shipbuilding Corporation* is a state-owned conglomerate of 58 enterprises engaged in shipbuilding, ship-repair, shipboard equipment manufacturing, marine design and research. The workforce of 95,000 is located in East China, South China and Jiangxi Province. Major enterprises include *Jiangnan Shipyard, Hudong Shipbuilding, Guangzhou Shipyard* and *China Shipbuilding Trading Company.*[20] CSSC had delivered 5 million dwt (deadweight tons) ships in the year, accounted for 40% of the overall output of China, and 7% of the world output, which symbolized that *CSSC* had achieved its goal of stepping into the top five shipbuilding corporations in the world.

Its brand is recognized by the users and buyers of vessels in China, and now is also in some parts of the international markets, like fish trawler or merchant ships. The holding company has a visible logo and even a tag line *Shipbuilding for Tomorrow*, but the marketing power lies in the operating companies, and often they compete with each others.

China presently builds about 15 percent of the world's total tonnage of ships and holds 17 percent of all the global orders. Currently they are No. 3 and their goal is to beat the Korean and Japanese competition and to become No. 1 world wide. Brand will play an important role in that process.

Fig. 73. Brand portfolio of *CSSC*

"Made in China" today is what "made in Japan" was in 1960s. Twenty years from now or even sooner, China will be the new Japan in terms of economic power.

7.3   Design and Branding

Design is an increasingly important tool for differentiation. "Mankind has always used symbols to express fierce individuality, pride, loyalty, and ownership. The power of symbols remains elusive and mysterious – a simple form can instantaneously trigger recall and emotions.

Competition for recognition is as ancient as the heraldic banner on a medieval battlefield."[21] To take just one example, a precursor of brand design can be found in the work of Herman Miller, Inc., a leading global provider of office furniture and services that create great places to work.

The founder developed a unique design, signature and brand and what set his products apart was his recognizable editorial style, covering everything from product to corporate identity (CI). Through problem-solving research and design, the company seeks to develop innovative solutions to real needs in working, healing, learning, and living environments. Net sales of US$262,000 in 1923 grew to US$25 million in 1970, the year the company went public; net sales in fiscal year 2004 were US$1.34 billion.[22]

From a historical perspective, it is fascinating to consider parallels between the worlds of fine arts and branding. We could identify

Fig. 74. *Herman Miller* design

great cultural leaders, such as Rembrandt or even Warhol, as the inspirers of their own powerful brands because, ultimately, the key to their success lay in their unique ability to echo the cultural values of their societies. Today, however, the underlying principle of branding has to do with the nature of customer needs, and it is simply not enough to be flexible and responsive to that needs. What is required is a deeper level of insight, one that enables us to become a driver of change by anticipating the emerging values in business and society.

Siemens, one of the world's oldest and largest electrical companies, can boast of more than 100 years of product and brand design history and business success. This colorful past vividly illustrates the fact that design has played a more important role in electrical engineering than in any other technology-related or -based field. *Siemens* maintained its leadership position in business for a very long time, and the design orientations supported that superiority. Over the years *Siemens* moved more and more out of the consumer business, took their household appliances into a joint venture with *Bosch*, and in 2005 sold off their mobile phones business to the Taiwanese competitor *BenQ*. Now they are concentrating only on business solutions. Nevertheless, *Siemens* maintains its multifaceted picture of design culture which influences the specific exigencies of "electrical design" during the 20th century and stays ahead of competition.[23]

Design language and brand identity of a company goes together. While brands speak to the mind and heart, brand identity is tangible and appeals to the senses. Brand identity is the visual and verbal expression of a brand. Identity supports, expresses, communicates, synthesizes, and visualizes the brand. It is the shortest, fastest, most ubiquitous form of communication available. You can see it, touch it, hold it, hear it, watch it move. It begins with a brand name and a brandmark and builds exponentially into a matrix of tools and communications. On applications from business cards to websites, from advertising campaigns to fleets of planes and signage, brand identity increases awareness and builds businesses.[24]

A similar success story could be seen at *Philips*.[25] Beginning in 1991, Stefano Marzano, CEO and chief creative director of *Philips Design*,

Siplace X-Series

Fig. 75. Classic *Siemens* electrical and electronic components[26]

has been developing a new role for design, based on a simple but challenging ideal – to anticipate and create preferable and sustainable futures through design[27]. This thinking matured into the notion of High Design. According to High Design principles, design is a multidisciplinary synthesis enriched by diverse and complementary bodies of knowledge from human sciences, technology, and materials expertise to aesthetics and communication sciences. Such a vision of design led *Philips Design* to the definition of Strategic Futures, a methodology that facilitates the alignment of business roadmaps, technology trends, and global/regional cultural forecasts and sociological insight to creatively support actionable solutions.

The fundamental starting point of High Design is its ability to focus on the emerging values and needs of people. Over the past decade,

Philips Design has built up a multicultural team of researchers (including ethnographers, cultural anthropologists, sociologists, popular-culture "cool hunters," and long-term-sustainability strategists) with one goal – to study different societies and develop ways of feeding the knowledge gathered into the design and brand process. The final aim is to leverage design as an agent of change and, in so doing, to enable more sustainable relationships among people, artifacts, and environments. In order to extend this philosophy, the High Design principles were translated into the dedicated brand design process currently in use at *Philips Design*.

Philips Heart Care Telemedicine Services (PHTS) provides an appropriate demonstration of the way in which brand design supports human-focused, and technology-based businesses. *Philips Medical Systems* is a leader in the B2B healthcare industry, directly targeted to end users. The result is a brand positioning based on the deeper values and preferences of European end users. The *PHTS* launch anticipates a fundamental shift in health management, from therapy to prevention, from hospitals to on-site treatments, from cure to care, and it represents a new vision of "connected care" relevant to Europeans. In summary, *Philips's* brand design process offers a unique design management approach to delivering a strategic brand direction.

Design and brand identity is about real passion, strong emotions and deep attachments. For a growing number of companies, design has become a professional obsession. Beginning in 1999, the *International Design Magazine (I.D.)* has been publishing a list of the 40 "most design-driven" companies that push innovation. **In** 2005, *Nike* was number one. But also on that list are and were industrial companies like *Caterpillar, Federal Express, Bloomberg* and *John Deere*. *John Deere* produces farm and earth moving equipment. Farm implements are "cool", farmers love the company's machines and service. Lucky are also the American mechanics who work on European cars. *Hazet Tools*, a major German tool manufacturer with many special tools for European cars offers a product line, *Ingenious Tools* which pleases both eyes and hands.

Design goes far beyond the beauty of a product or service. Customer involvement and employee participation is necessary to incorporate various aspects of "design products". When the designers follow the basic principles of industrial design – **form follows function** – success is possible and design awards are granted. In 2005, *Hilti,* producers of saws for demolition, general construction and masonry trades, won the *Red Dot* award. This amazing power tool cuts through anything. The saw is equipped with the technique *Smart Power* which is an innovation incorporating a motor with variable power control and an intelligent sensing system. Design, technology and practicability are coming together.

One arena where design matters most – and is the least considered – is in the creation of essential enterprise systems. Systems are typically invented when problems arise, such as customer service, maintenance, and supervision of all sorts of activities: transportation, production, even marketing. "Beautiful Systems" are simple and straight to the point. They fulfill their purpose without hesitation. We do not want system overload, we want results. Again look at *FedEx*, study the supply chain of *General Electric* and draw your conclusions. Tom Peters phrases it this way in his *Essential* mini book: "We need fewer techies and more poets in our systems design shop, and more artists … and more jazz musicians … and more dancers." [28] He even wants to place the designer"… at the CEO's immediate right at the boardroom table." Design has the opportunity to capture the soul of an enterprise. B2B companies such as *Bombardier, Caterpillar, FedEx IBM,* and *Microsoft* are on the list of the most design-driven companies in America.[29] Design relevance related to corporate and product design is an essential part of corporate success. Bob Lutz, the head of *General Motors North America,* says that he thinks that *General Motors* is in the art business. It's art, entertainment and mobile sculpture that coincidentally happens to provide transportation. Well, if *General Motors* is in the art businesses, then all of us in some fashion are in the art business.

The direction is about increased corporate and product design strategy to create brand identity through thorough alignment and

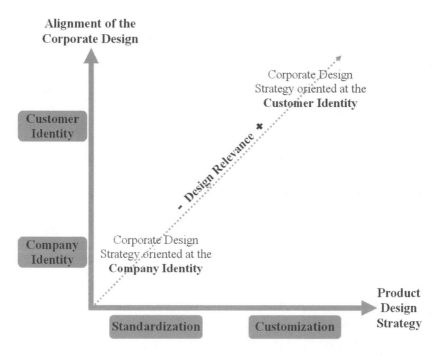

Fig. 76. Design relevance related to corporate and product design

customization. A litmus test could easily be applied at any corporate document or product. Does your design show simplicity, clarity, grace and beauty? If your customer confirms your findings, you have a chance to beat the competition. By creating uniqueness you have the chance to create an emotional connection, and make a difference.

For readers looking for some help in designing brand identity, we recommend using the following steps of the time-tested method from Alina Wheeler's Designing Brand Identity.[30]

Research and Analysis: Create a core team, define members, and communicate project kick-off, purpose, and team to the rest of the company, schedule meetings, clarify the vision, strategies, and goals of the leadership, research stakeholders' needs and perceptions, conduct an internal, competitive, technology and legal audit, interview key management, and evaluate existing brands and brand architecture.

Brand Strategy: Clarify brand strategy, develop a positioning platform, co-create brand attributes, present brand brief document, create a naming strategy, evaluate sub-brands.

Design Concept: Visualize the future, design brand identity, finalize
brand architecture, examine applicability, present visual strategy.

Brand Expressions: Finalize identity solution, initiate trademark
protection, prioritize and design applications, design identity program, apply brand architecture, asset management strategy, build
synergy around new brand, develop launch strategy and plan,
launch internally first, launch brand externally, develop standards
and guidelines, nurture brand champions, support the legacy,
monitor brand quality and performance.

Creating a new brand identity may take 2-3 months, depending on
the size of the organization, complexity of business, number of
markets served, type of market (global, national, regional, local),
nature of the specific problem, research required, legal requirements, decision-making process, number of decision makers, and
number of brand applications. There are no shortcuts to this process, developing an effective and sustainable brand takes time.
There are no instant answers, and a commitment to a responsible
process is imperative. When a new brand is created, it will be easier for salespeople to sell, customers to buy, and for the company's
brand to build equity.

"In the last 40 years, design has really been liberated from the cultural discrimination between developed and developing countries
and has become truly global. Today, no matter where you go – the
United States, Europe, Asia, Latin America, the Middle East, Russia
– customers want the best possible product, and they want world-
class design. Tokyo, Seoul and Singapore are now as sophisticated
as Milan, New York and London. Hong Kong, Shanghai and Kuala
Lumpur lead in urban architecture. The most beautiful modern
bridges are in Tokyo, Istanbul and Denmark. And India is taking
the lead in software development. "[31]

7.4 Lovemarks and Brand Leadership

As consumers, we are all surrounded by so-called Lovemarks[32] – brands that have managed to reach far beyond mere brand recognition and loyalty. They are essential parts of our lives today. People would sorely miss *Coca Cola*, *McDonald's*, and *Starbucks* if they were no longer available. These brand can more easily survive negative headlines – e.g. product defects – or other similar tough times that would heavily damage other brands. This is because the consumers "do care about them" and have internalized the brand message completely.[33]

A great B2C example is the *Apple iPod* with its irreplaceable batteries. After two self-professed *Apple* junkies made a film called "iPod's Dirty Secret" and launched a protest Web site, *Apple Computer Inc.* addressed and eliminated the problem. The fascinating part is that the protest was an act of love: "We made that film because we believe in the brand so much." Instead of being disappointed in it and changing to another brand they "invested" in it to assure a better brand performance in the future.

Is there a potential for industrial Lovemarks? What in the B2B world could customers love? What about consumers wearing *Caterpillar* licensed boots or CEOs' alter ego, their *Lear Jet*?

Yes, B2B brands could be loved, even take on a new level of insistence by the customers. Just imagine you expect a needed spare part and *FedEx* or *DHL* delivers it on time over and over again. This carrier becomes a part of your daily life; it is your emotional rescue. But again it is the customer who brings **your brand to a new level**.

This insight means that expectations are the essence of branding and they need to be managed efficiently. In a complex world with sophisticated technology and multiple relations, the task is to keep your operations and offerings as simple as possible. Coordination and collaboration with the various share- and stake-holders is required, just as important is leadership from the top.

B2B companies need to move from product and system to more attention to service. Large corporations like *IBM* and *GE* have more then 60% of their turnover created by services. *Tata Steel's* premium pricing became possible because they adopted a holistic branding approach covering everything from the development, design, to the implementation of marketing programs, processes, and activities. Marketing and brand management is an essential ingredient in business success.

> *Regardless of age, regardless of position, regardless of the business we happen to be in, all of us need to understand the importance of branding. We are CEOs of our own companies: Me Inc. to be in business today, our most important job is to be head marketer for the brand called you.*

Tom Peters in Fast Company, 1997

Summary

In our constantly changing business environment of new technologies, globalization and market liberalization, alert companies are presented with great opportunities. Winning companies will disrupt old practices and initiate new ones to exploit major trends. The following trends should be watched and incorporated into your company's thinking and business action:

- **B2B branding and brand management** will become increasingly important, and the future of brands is the future of business, probably the only major sustainable competitive advantage. Companies that are going in this direction are on the right track.

- **Branding and social responsibility** seeks to create a just and sustainable world by favoring companies that promote more responsible business practices, innovation and collaboration.

- **Branding in China** is in a stage of leap-frogging into the world market. For decades, China has enjoyed a dominant place in world manufacturing because of its low-cost labor. Chinese businesses today are pursuing aggressive branding strategies involving internal growth or acquiring foreign brand icons and managing them. Both approaches could lead to world success.

- **Design and branding** are increasingly important tools for differentiation. Relevance, simplicity, and humanity – not technology – will distinguish brands in the future.

- **Lovemarks go beyond branding** – brands that have managed to reach far beyond mere brand recognition and loyalty. Their customers "do care about them" and have internalized the brand.

To be successful in the B2B world, a holistic branding approach is required. It should cover everything from the development and design, to the implementation of marketing programs, processes, and activities that are intersecting and interdependent. Marketing and brand management will be critical to a company's success in the future.

Notes

1 Duane E. Knapp, *The Brand Mindset*, 2000, p. 182.

2 Scott Bedbury, *A New Brand World*, 2002, p. 183.

3 Ibid.

4 Joanne Laurier and David Walsh, "The Corporation: A Reformist Plea for State Regulation," *WSWS* (25 August 2004).

5 "Who's Wearing the Trousers," *The Economist* (8 September 2001), pp. 26-28.

6 Jenny Rayner and Walter Raven, *Corporate Social Responsibility Monitor,* 2002.

7 Philip Kotler and Nancy Lee, *Corporate Social Responsibility,* 2004.

8 "Branding and Corporate Citizenship," *WinWinPartner.com, 2002.*

9 Philip Kotler and Nancy Lee, *Corporate Social Responsibility: Doing the Most Good for Your Company and Your Cause* (Wiley 2005).

10 Wang Pei, "Building a Global Brand in China," *China International Business* (February 2006).

11 Theodore Levitt, "The Globalization of Markets," *Harvard Business Review* (Vol. 61, May-June 1983), pp. 92-102.

12 Kong Lihua, "Making Brands Go Global: Chinese Companies' Brand Management," 2006.

[13] John Quelch, "The Return of the Global Brand," *Harvard Business Review* (August 2003).

[14] Rita Clifton and John Simmons, *Brands and Branding,* London, 2003, Introduction, p. 1.

[15] Central Intelligence Agency (CIA), "The World Factbook 2006," (10 January, 2006).

[16] Waldemar A. Pfoertsch, Oliver Kong and Amber Xu, "Branding in China: Haier & TCL Building Their World Wide Consumer Recognition," 2005, pp. 2-6.

[17] "Haier Ranked Most Valuable Chinese Brand," *China Internet Information Center* (4 December 2002); "Haier Listed in World's Top 100 Recognizable Brands," *China Internet Information Center* (3 February 2004).

[18] Rita Clifton, "The Future of Brands," in: *Brands and Branding,* Rita Clifton and John Simmons (eds), 2003, p. 232.

[19] In 1984 Qingdao General Refrigerator Factory was on the verge of bankruptcy. It was collectively owned by 820 workers with an accrued deficit of RMB 1.47 million, and sales of less than RMB 4 million annually. Today, renamed *Haier*, the company employs nearly 20,000 workers, sells its products in 31 countries, and turns over $US 10 billion, predominantly in the sale of white goods. Zhang Ruimin, Chairman and CEO of the *Haier Group* won 2006 the 26th place in the list of "world's most respected business leader", becoming the only Chinese entrepreneur on the list of the Financial Times. He became famous in China through is pursue of quality; the story goes that he go so outraged in a meeting that he destroyed with a sledge hammer a faulty refrigerator, and all the fore worker had to do the same. This story is portrayed in the move **CEO Mi Ji I** from LIAO ZHU and helped to introduce *Haier* to the Japanese market.

[20] According to a statistic, during the period of "Tenth-five Plan"(2001-2005), *CSSC*'s output, with an annual increase of 24.4%, had been growing from 2.09million dwt in 2001 up to 5million dwt in 2005. With an overall amount of only 1.43million dwt, year 2000's total output was only equivalent to 3 months' in 2005. By the end of November 2005, *CSSC* had won 95 new ships orders in 2005, amounting 7.54million dwt, which was 2.94million dwt more than the whole year's amount of 2004. In the mean time, there were 285 ships order in hand, totally 15.86 million dwt, which was 3.21million dwt more than the beginning of the year. For more information see http://www.globalsecurity.org/military/world/china/cssc.htm.

21 Alina Wheeler, *Designing Brand Identity*, 2003, p. 1.

22 Herman Miller follows even in its web design the branding principles Who are we? What we believe? What we do? Where we are? Where we've been? available at http://www.hermanmiller.com/CDA/SSA/ IP/0,1776,a10-c11,00.html.

23 Christoph Hoesch, *Siemens Industrial Design* (Hatje Cantz Publishers, 2005).

24 Alina Wheeler, *Designing Brand Identity*, 2003, p. 4.

25 Marco Bevolo and Reon Brand, "Brand Design for the Long Term," *Design Management Journal* (Vol. 14 No. 1, 2003), pp. 33-39.

26 This circuit board surface mounting equipment is characterized by its maximum user-friendliness with the implementation of vision technology. Use on the portal side and improved monitoring is now possible thanks to a lower construction height and a transparent visual access. As a high end product, this new range has been consistently designed in accordance with the corporate design of the "Si-place" product family. designafairs 2005 for Siemens, Germany.

27 Stefano Marzano, *Creating Value by Design*, 1998.

28 Thomas J. Peters, *Design*, 2005, p. 61.

29 "Top 40 North America's Most Design-Driven companies," *I.D. Magazine*, (January/February 1999); *I.D. Magazine (International Design)* is America's leading critical magazine covering the art, business and culture of design.

30 Alina Wheeler, *Designing Brand Identity*, 2003.

31 Hartmut Esslinger, "The Riveting Head of Frog Design Talks About Business Before and After the Bubble," *I.D. Magazine* (June 2003).

32 Kevin Roberts, *Lovemarks*, 2004.

33 Tom Asacker, A Clear Eye for Branding. *On Business, Brands and Marketplace Success*, Paramount Market Publishing, Ithaca, N.Y. 2005.

About the Authors

Philip Kotler is the S.C. Johnson & Son Distinguished Professor of International Marketing at the Kellogg School of Management, Northwestern University, Evanston, Illinois. He received his Master's Degree at the University of Chicago and his PhD Degree at MIT, both in economics. He did postdoctoral work in mathematics at Harvard University and in behavioral science at the University of Chicago.

Professor Kotler is the author of *Marketing Management: Analysis, Planning, Implementation and Control*, the most widely used marketing book in graduate business schools worldwide; Principles of Marketing; Marketing Models; Strategic Marketing for Nonprofit Organizations; The New Competition; High Visibility; Social Marketing; Marketing Places; Marketing for Congregations; Marketing for Hospitality and Tourism; The Marketing of Nations; Kotler on Marketing, Building Global Biobrands, Attracting Investors, Ten Deadly Marketing Sins, Marketing Moves, Corporate Social Responsibility, Lateral Marketing, and Marketing Insights from A to Z. He has published over one hundred articles in leading journals, several of which have received best-article awards.

Professor Kotler was the first recipient of the American Marketing Association's (AMA) "Distinguished Marketing Educator Award" (1985). The European Association of Marketing Consultants and Sales Trainers awarded Kotler their prize for "Marketing Excellence".

He was chosen as the "Leader in Marketing Thought" by the Academic Members of the AMA in a 1975 survey. He also received the 1978 "Paul Converse Award" of the AMA, honoring his original contribution to marketing. In 1989, he received the Annual Charles Coolidge Parlin Marketing Research Award. In 1995, the Sales and Marketing Executives International (SMEI) named him "Marketer of the Year".

Professor Kotler has consulted for such companies as *IBM*, *General Electric*, *AT&T*, *Honeywell*, *Bank of America*, *Merck* and others in the areas of marketing strategy and planning, marketing organization and international marketing.

He has been Chairman of the College of Marketing of the Institute of Management Sciences, a Director of the American Marketing Association, a Trustee of the Marketing Science Institute, a Director of the MAC Group, a former member of the Yankelovich Advisory Board, and a member of the Copernicus Advisory Board. He has been a Trustee of the Board of Governors of the School of the Art Institute of Chicago and a Member of the Advisory Board of the Drucker Foundation. He has received honorary doctoral degrees from the Stockholm University, University of Zurich, Athens University of Economics and Business, DePaul University, the Cracow School of Business and Economics, Groupe H.E.C. in Paris, the University of Economics and Business Administration in Vienna, Budapest University of Economic Science and Public Administration, and the Catholic University of Santo Domingo.

He has traveled extensively throughout Europe, Asia and South America, advising and lecturing to many companies about how to apply sound economic and marketing science principles to increase their competitiveness. He has also advised governments on how to develop stronger public agencies to further the development of the nation's economic well-being.

Waldemar Pfoertsch holds the position of Professor for International Business at the Pforzheim University, and he is visiting lecture at the Executive MBA Program of the Liautaud Graduate School of Business, University of Illinois at Chicago. In addition he is an Online Tutor for MBA Program International Management University Maryland College Park and at the Steinbeis University in Berlin.

He received two Master Degrees (economics & business administration) and his Doctorial Degree in social science at the Free University Berlin. He did his post-doctoral work in industrial planning at the Technical University Berlin.

His latest publication in German covers the areas of B2B marketing, Brand Management and Ingredient Branding. He also published: Living Web and Internet Strategies. In preparation is Blogs: The new business language. He also published several articles in German, Chinese and English language on international management issues.

Professor Pfoertsch has consulted for such companies as *Daimler-Chrysler*, *HP*, *IBM*, and many medium size corporations in Europe, Asia and North America in the areas of international marketing and brand management. He is on the advisory board of various companies and non profit organizations.

His other teaching positions had been at the University of Cooperative Education Villingen-Schwenningen, Visiting Associate Professor at Kellogg Graduate School of Management, Northwestern University and Lecturer for Strategic Management at Lake Forest Graduate School of Management.

Prior to his teaching appointments, he was a Management Consultant for international consulting companies. In this position, he has traveled extensively throughout Europe, Asia and North America working with companies in developing international strategies. His earlier positions include being an Economic Advisor to the United Nations Industrial Development Organization (UNIDO) where he worked as an advisor to the government on how to develop internationally competitive industries. He also worked for many years in the automation industry, serving automotive companies.

Contact him at:

Pforzheim University, Tiefenbronnerstrasse 65, 75175 Pforzheim
Tel.: +49-171-536 8998
E-mail: waldemar@pfoertsch.com
Skype: wapskype

Bibliography

"A New Era in Asian Shipping," *Asia Times* online (2 September 2000), available at http://www.atimes.com/se-asia/BI02Ae04.html.

"Ad Agencies Vs. Consultancies: Weighing the Differencies," *brandchannel.com* (2001), available at http://www.brandchannel.com/forum.asp?bd_id=4#.

"Annual Report 2004," *NOL Ltd.*, available at http://www.nol.com.sg/investor/ar2004/download.html.

"Another Great Year: Annual Report 2004," *Cemex Corporation*, available at http://www.Cemex.com/ar2004/eng/pdf/cx04eng.pdf.

"APL Web Site Makes Hot 100 For Fourth Year Running," *APL Ltd. Press* release (18 September 2003), available at http://www.apl.com/press_releases/html/press_release_hot100_09182003.html.

"Branding and Corporate Cititzenship," *WinWinPartner.com 2002*, available at http://www.winwinpartner.com/Expert%20Resources/Branding/index.html.

"Building for Future Generations – Cemex 2003 Sustainablility Report," *Cemex Corporation* (26 January 2005), available at www.cemex.com/sr2003/eng/pdf/SR03english.pdf.

"Cemex Provides Guidance for the Fourth Quarter of 2005," *Cemex Corporation* (16 December 2005), available at http://www.cemex.com/qr/mc_pr_121605.asp.

"Cemex to Acquire RMC," *Business Wire* (27 September 2005), available at http://www.panapress.com/newswire.asp?code=2515.

"Changing Markets and the Importance of Brand Relevance," *AME Info* (8 November 2004) available at http://www.ameinfo.com/56527.html January 20, 2006.

"Cover Story: Game On," *Eventmarketer* (4 May 2004).

"EU, U.S. Duel over Plane Subsidies," *USA Today* (30 May 2005), available at http://www.usatoday.com/news/washington/2005-05-30-us-eu-air-bus_x.htm.

"Flugzeug mit Doppelbett und Schoenheitsfarm," *Frankfurter Allgemeine Zeitung* (19 January 2005, No. 15).

"GDP up 9.5% in First Half," *China Internet Information Center* (20 July 2005) available at china.org.cn.

"Is Big Blue the Next Big Thing?" *The Economist* (21 June 2003).

"Making Cement a Household Word," *Los Angeles Times* (January 2000).

"Recognition of Signs and Logos," Analysis for the Olympic Committee 1995, *Today* (20 July 1995).

"SIA Reveals the "First To Fly" Logo for Its A380," *Singapore Airlines Ltd.* News release (5 January 2005), available at http://www.singapore-air.com.

"Siemens warnt vor Hoerschaeden durch Handy-Ausschaltmelodie," *heise mobil* (26 August 2004), available at http://www.heise.de/mobil/newsticker/meldung/50410.

"Tata Steel Ranked Best in World by WSD," *The Hindu Business Line* (18 July 2001), available at http://www.thehindubusinessline.com/businessline/2001/07/19/stories/0219614k.htm

"Tata Steel Rated Best in World," *Business Standard* (23 Juni 2005), available at http://www.businessstandard.com/search/storypage_new.php?leftnm=lmnu1&leftindx=1&lselect=1&autono=192372

"Technology Product Life Cycle," White Paper, *Myxa Corporation*, available at http://www.myxa.com/wp_tplc.htm.

"Top 40 North America's Most Design-Driven Companies," *I.D. Magazine*, (January/February 1999).

"Toronto Crash Is First for Airbus' A340," *USAToday* (2 August 2005), available at http://www.usatoday.com/news/world/2005-08-02-air-bus-safety_x.htm.

"Who's Wearing the Trousers," *The Economist* (8 September 2001).

Aaker, D.A. and Joachimsthaler, E., *Brand Leadership* (New York: The Free Press, 2000).

Aaker, D.A., *Brand Portfolio Strategy* (New York: The Free Press, 2004).

Aaker, D.A., *Building Strong Brands*, (New York: The Free Press, 1996).

Anderson, J.C. and Narus, J.A., *Business Market Management: Understanding, Creating, and Delivering Value*, 2nd edn (New Jersey: Pearson Prentice Hall, 2004).

Ante, S.E., "The New Blue," *Business Week* (17 March 2003).

Armstrong, D., "A Whole New Magic Carpet Ride: SFO up and Ready for 2006 Arrival of Airbus A380," *San Fransisco Chronicle* (27 January 2005), available at http://www.sfgate.com/cgi-bin/article.cgi? file=/chronicle/archive/2005/ 01/27/BUGLBB0UL01.DTL.

Backhaus, K. and Voeth, M. (eds), *Handbuch Industrieguetermarketing: Strategien-Instrumente-Anwendungen*, 1st edn (Wiesbaden: Gabler, 2004).

Backhaus, K., *Industrieguetermarketing*, 7th edn (Munich: Franz Vahlen, 2003).

Backhaus, K., Schroeder, J. and Perrey, J., "B2B-Maerkte – Die Jagd auf Markenpotenziale kann beginnen," *Absatzwirtschaft*, pp. 18-54.

Ball, B. and Monoghan, R., "Redefining the Sales and Marketing Relationship," *Potentials in Marketing* (October 1994), pp. 19-20.

Balmer, J.M.T. and Greyser, S.A., "Managing the Multiple Identities of the Corporation," *California Management Review* (Vol. 44 No. 3, 2002), pp. 72-86.

Baumgarth, C., Freter, H., Schmidt, R., *Ingredient Branding*, Working paper, University Siegen, Marketing (Siegen: 1996).

BBDO, "Ingredient Branding in the Automotive Industry – Telematics and CRM," *Point of View 3* (January 2003).

Bedbury, S., *A New Brand World* (New York: Viking Penguin, 2002).

Belz, C. and Kopp, K-M., "Markenfuehrung fuer Investitionsgueter als Kompetenz- und Vertrauensmarketing", in: *Handbuch Markenartikel*, Band 3, Manfred Bruhn (ed) (Stuttgart: Schaeffer-Poeschel, 1994): pp. 1577-1601, available at http://www.imh.unisg.ch/org/imh/web.nsf/0/415cbb227d222b2cc1256d6b0050c1c8/$FILE/B2BBrand-11Nov02-chr.pdf.

Berner, R. and Kiley, D., "Global Brands," *Business Week* (August 2005).

Bevolo, M. and Reon Brand, "Brand Design for the Long Term," *Design Management Journal* (Vol. 14 No. 1, 2003), pp. 33-39.

Blackett, T., *Trademarks* (Basingstoke: Macmillan Press, 1998).

Bloomenkranz, L., "Evolving the UPS Brand," *Design Management Review,* vol. 15, no. 2 (Spring 2004), pp. 68-73.

Brondoni, S.M., *Brand Policy and Brand Equity*, Symphonya, Emerging Issues in Management (Milano: Istituto di Economia d'Impresa, 2002).

Brown, S.L. and Eisenhardt, K.M., *Competing on the Edge* (Boston: Harvard Business School Press, 1998).

Bruhn, M. (ed), *Handbuch Markenartikel*, Band 3 (Stuttgart: Schaeffer-Poeschel, 1994).

Bruhn, M., *Marketing, Grundlagen fuer Studium und Praxis,* 6th edn, (Wiesbaden: Gabler, 2002).

Butterfield, L., *Icon of a Passion – The Development of the Mercedes-Benz Brand*, Wiley, 2005.

Bugdahl, V., *Marken machen Maerkte* (Munich: CH Beck, 1998).

Callahan, S., "Look What Brown Has Done for UPS," *BtoB's Best 2004* (25 October 2004): p. 26.

Caspar, M., Hecker, A. and Sabel, S., "Markenrelevanz in der Unternehmensfuehrung – Messung, Erklaerung und empirische Befunde fuer B2B-Maerkte," Working Paper, *Marketing Centrum Muenster (MCM) and McKinsey & Company.*

Central Intelligence Agency (CIA), "The World Factbook 2006," (10 January 2006) available at http://www.cia.gov/cia/publications/factbook/index.html.

Clancy, K.J. and Krieg, P.C., *Counterintuitive Marketing Achieving Great Results Using Common Sense* (New York: The Free Press, 2000).

Clegg, A., "The Myth of Authenticity," *brandchannel.com* (15 August 2005).

Clifton, R. and Simmons, J., *Brands and Branding*, (London: Profile Books, 2003).

Clifton, R., "The Future of Brands," in: *Brands and Branding*, Rita Clifton and John Simmons (eds) (London: Profile Books, 2003): 227-241.

D'Aveni, R.A., *Hypercompetition* (New York: The Free Press, 1994).

Dart, C., "Brands Are Alive!" *brandspa* (February 2002), p. 14, available at http://www.agcd.com/docs/betterbrandarticles/brands_are_alive.pdf.

Davis, S., "Brand Metrics: Good, Bad and Don't Bother," *The Canadian Marketing Report* (26 January 2004).

Davis, S.M., "The Power of the Brand," *Strategy & Leadership* (28 April 2000, Vol. 28, No. 4): pp. 4-9.

De Chernatony, L. and McDonald, M., *Creating Powerful Brands in Consumer, Service and Industrial Markets*, 3rd edn (Oxford: Butterworth Heinemann, 2003).

Deane, D.H., "Associating the Corporation with a Charitable Event Through Sponsorship: Measuring the Effects on Corporate Community Relations," *Journal of Advertising* (Winter 2002).

Douglas, S.P., Craig, C.S. and Nijssen, E.J., "International Brand Architecture: Development, Drivers and Design," *Journal of International Marketing* (Vol. 9 No. 2 2001), available at http://pages.stern.nyu.edu/~sdouglas/rpubs/intbrand.html.

Dreznder, D.W., "Bottom Feeders," *Foreign policy* (2000).

Dunn, M., Davis, S.M., "Creating the Brand-Driven Business: It's the CEO Who Must Lead the Way," in: *Handbook of Business Strategy* (Vol. 5 No. 1, 2004), pp. 241-245.

Einemo, U., "AP Møller-Maersk and P&O Nedlloyd in Merger Talks," *Bunkerworld.com* (10 May 2005), available at http://www.bunkerworld.com/news.

Elkin, T., "Branding Big Blue," *Advertising Age* (28 February 2000).

Ellwood, I., *Essential Rand Book: Over 100 Techniques to Increase Brand Value* (London: Kogan Page, 2002).

Esch, F.-R. et al, *Corporate Brand Management: Marken als Anker strategischer Fuehrung von Unternehmen* (Wiesbaden, Gabler, 2004).

Esch, F-R. (ed), *Moderne Markenfuehrung – Grundlagen – Innovative Ansaetze – Praktische Umsetzungen*, 1st edn (Wiesbaden: Gabler, 1999).

Esch, F-R., *Strategie und Technik der Markenfuehrung*, 2nd edn (Munich: Vahlen, 2004).

Esslinger, H., "The Riveting Head of Frog Design Talks About Business Before and After the Bubble," *I.D. Magazine* (June 2003).

Farrell, G., "Building a New Big Blue," *USA Today* (22 November 1999).

Ferrer, C., "Branding B2B Technology Companies – An Investment for Success," *Techlinks: Community Publishing* (18 October 2000) available at http://www.techlinks.net/articleNew.cfm?articleurl=101700164131.

Fites, D.V., "Make Your Dealers Your Partners," *Harvard Business Review* (March-April 1996).

Freter, H. and Baumgarth, C. "Ingredient Branding – Begriff und theoretische Begruendung," in: *Moderne Markenfuehrung – Grundlagen – Innovative Ansaetze – Praktische Umsetzungen,* 1st edn, Franz-Rudolf Esch (ed) (Wiesbaden: Gabler, 1999).

Gentry, C.R., "Building on Brand Awareness, " *Chain Store Age* (July 2003), pp. 36-37.

GEO, *Imagery 2 – Innere Markenbilder in gehobenen Zielgruppen* (Hamburg: Gruner und Jahr, 1998).

Ginter, T.,Dambacher, J., "Markenpolitik im B2B-Sektor," in: *Handbuch Industrieguetermarketing: Strategien-Instrumente-Anwendungen,* 1st edn, Klaus Backhaus and Markus Voeth (eds) (Wiesbaden: Gabler, 2004): pp. 53-69.

Godefroid, P., *Business-to-Business-Marketing* (Ludwigshafen: Kiehl-Verlag, 2000).

Goettgens, O., Gelbert, A. and Boeing, C. (eds) *Profitables Markenmanagement: Strategien – Konzepte – Best Practices,* 1st edn (Wiesbaden: Gabler, 2003).

Gorrell, C., "Quick Takes," *Strategy & Leadership,* Oct 2002, Issue 30, p. 5.

Graham, S., *Build Your Own Life Brand! A Powerful Strategy to Maximize Your Potential...* (New York: Free Press, 2001).

Griffin, R., "Associate Partner the Custom Fit Communications Group," available at http://www.customfitonline.com/news/branding001.htm.

Hague, P. and Jackson, P., *The Power of Industrial Brands* (Maidenhead: McGraw-Hill, 1994).

Hague, P., "Branding in Business to Business Markets," White Paper, *B2B International Ltd.,* available at http://www.b2binternational.com/whitepapers.html.

Hague, P., Hague, N., and Harrison, M., "Business to Business Marketing," White Paper, *B2B International Ltd.,* available at http://www.b2b-international.com/whitepapers.html.

Hamel, G., *Leading the Revolution* (Boston: Harvard Business School Press, 2000).

Heller, I., G., "When Good Companies Do Bad Branding: How to Know if You Should Do Brand Advertising," *Real Results Marketing,* (March, 2004), available at http://federaldirect.com/RealResultsBranding.pdf.

Hill, C.W.L., *International Business: Competing in the Global Marketplace*, 4th edn (New York: McGraw-Hill/Irwin, 2003).

Hochstadt, H.R., "Chairman's Letter," *NOL Review 1998*, available at http://www.nol.com.sg/investor/anreport98/chairman98.pdf.

Hoepner, A., "Siemens hat bei Handys den Anschluss an die Weltspitze verloren," *heise mobil* (6 June 2005), available at http://www.heise.de/mobil/newsticker/meldung/60308.

Hoesch, C., *Siemens Industrial Design – 100 Years of Continuity in Flux* (Hatje Cantz Publishers, 2005).

Kapferer, J-N, *Strategic Brand Management – Creating and Sustaining Brand Equity Long Term* (London: Kogan Page, 1997).

Keller, K.L. and Sood, S., "The Ten Commandments of Global Branding," *Asian Journal of Marketing*, vol. 8, no. 2 (2001): 97-108.

Keller, K.L., "Building Customer-Based Brand Equity," March 2001, Amos Tuck School of Business, Dartmouth College, published in *The Advertiser*, October 2002.

Keller, K.L., *Strategic Brand Management*, 2nd edn (Upper Saddle River, NJ: Prentice-Hall, 2003).

Keller, K.L., "Manager's Tool Kit," The Brand Report Card, *Harvard Business Review* (February, 2000),

Kleinaltenkamp, M., „Ingredient Branding: Markenpolitik im Business-to-Business-Geschaeft", in: *Erfolgsfaktor Marke*, Koehler, R. Majer, W., Wiezorek, H. (eds.) (Munich: Franz Vahlen, 2001).

Knapp, D.E., *The Brand Mindset* (New York: McGraw-Hill, 2000).

Koehler, R. Majer, W. and Wiezorek, H. (eds.): *Erfolgsfaktor Marke* (Munich: Franz Vahlen, 2001).

Kotler, P. and Keller, K.L., *Marketing Management*, 12th edn (Upper Saddle River, NJ: Prentice Hall, 2006).

Kotler, P. and Lee, N., *Corporate Social Responsibility – Doing the Most Good for Your Company and Your Cause*, 1st edn (Hoboken: Wiley & Sons, 2004).

Kumar, N., *Marketing as Strategy: Understanding the CEO's Agenda for Driving Growth and Innovation* (Boston: Harvard Business School Press, 2004).

Laforêt, S. and Saunders, J., "Managing Brand Portfolios: How the Leaders Do It," *Journal of Advertising Research* (September/October 1994), pp. 64-76.

Lamons, B., "Brick Brand's Mighty – Yours Can Be, Too," *Marketing News* (22 November 1999): p. 16.

Lamons, B., *The Case for B2B Branding: Pulling Away from the Business-to-Bursiness Pack*, 1st edn (Mason, OH: Thomson/South Western, 2005).

LaPointe, P., "The Picture of Brand Health," *CMO Magazine* (December 2005), available at http://www.cmomagazine.com/read/120105/brand_health.html.

Laurier, J. and Walsh, D., "The Corporation: A Reformist Plea for State Regulation," *WSWS* (25 August 2004), available at http://www.wsws.org/ articles/ testdir/aug2004/corp-a25.shtml.

Legge, P. de, "The Brand Version 2.0: B2B Brands in the Internet Age," *Marketing Today – The Online Guide to Marketing in the Information Age*, available at http://marketingtoday.com/marketing/1204/brand_v2.htm.

Letelier, M.F., Flores, F. and Spinosa, C., "Developing Productive Customers in Emerging Markets," *California Management Review* (Summer 2003).

Levin, A., "Jet Burns, but All Aboard Escape in Toronto," *USA Today* (2 August 2005), available at http://www.usatoday.com/news/world/2005-08-02-airbus-safety_x.htm.

Levitt, Theodore, "The Globalization of Markets," *Harvard Business Review* (Vol. 61, May-June 1983), pp. 92-102.

Lihua, K. "Making Brands Go Global: Chinese Companies' Brand Management," Working Paper, *Pforzheim University of Applied Science* (2006).

Lindstrom, M., "B2B = Boring to Branding," *ClickZ Network* (19 February 2002), available at http://www.clickz.com/experts/brand/brand/article.php/975631.

Machnig, M. and Mikfeld, B. "Erweiterte Markenfuehrung. Stakeholder-Kommunikation im politisch-oeffentlichen Raum," in: *Profitables Markenmanagement: Strategien – Konzepte – Best Practices*, 1st ed, Olaf Goettgens, Adel Gelbert and Christian Boeing (eds) (Wiesbaden: Gabler, 2003).

Maddox, K., "IBM's Strategy Keeps it in and on Demand," *BtoBonline* (25 October 2004), available at http://www.btobonline.com/article.cms?articleId=22239.

Malaval, P., *Strategy and Management of Industrial Brands: Business to Business Products and Services* (Norwell, Massachusetts: Kluwer Academic Publishers, 2001).

Manning-Schaffel, V., "UPS & FedEx Compete to Deliver," *brandchannel.com* (17 May 2004) available at http://www.brandchannel.com/ features_effect.asp?pf_id=210.

Markides, C.C., *All the Right Moves: a Guide to Crafting Break-Through Strategies* (Cambridge, MA, 1999).

Marzano, S., *Creating Value by Design* (Bussum: V + K Publ, 1998).

Morrison, D., "The Six Biggest Pitfalls in B-to-B Branding," *Business2Business Marketer* (July/August, 2001).

Pandey, M., "Is Branding Relevant to B2B?," *brand features – brandspeak* (27 January 2003), available at http://www.brandchannel.com/brand_speak.asp?bs_id=53.

Pei, W. "Building a Global Brand in China," *China International Business* (February 2006), available at http://www.cityweekend.com.cn/en/beijing/cib/2006_02/building-a-global-brand-in-china.html.

Pepels, W., *Produktmanagement: Produktinnovation, Markenpolitik, Programmplanung, Prozessorganisation*, 3th edn (Oldenbourg: 2001).

Peters, T.J., *Design: Innovate. Differentiate. Communicate*, (London: Dorling Kindersley, 2005).

Petromilli, M.,Morrison, D. and Million, M., "Brand Architecture: Building Brand Portfolio Value," *Strategy and Leadership*, Vol. 5, 2002.

Pettis, C., *TechnoBrands: How to Create & Use Brand Identity to Market, Advertise & Sell Technology Products*, (American Management Association, 1994).

Pfoertsch, W. and Mueller, I., *Ingredient Branding* (forthcoming2007).

Pfoertsch, W. and Schmid, M., *B2B-Markenmanagement: Konzepte – Methoden – Fallbeispiele*, (Munich: Franz Vahlen, 2005).

Pfoertsch, W., Kong, O. and Xu, A., "Branding in China: Haier & TCL Building Their World Wide Consumer Recognition," Working Paper, *Pforzheim University of Applied Science and CEIBS China Europe International Business School* (2005).

Pierce, A. and Moukanas, H., "Portfolio Power: Harnessing a Group of Brands to Drive Profitable Growth," *Strategy & Leadership* (Vol. 30 No. 5 2002), pp. 15-21.

Pierce, A., Moukanas, H., and Wise, R., *Brand Portfolio Economics – Harnessing a Group of Brands to Drive Profitable Growth* (Mercer Management Consulting Inc., 2002).

Podmolik, M.E., "FedEx Campaign Touts New Unit," *BtoB Online* (25 October 2004) available at http://www.btobonline.com/article.cms?articleId=22275.

Prodhan, G. and Li, B., "BenQ to Take over *Siemens'* Mobile Unit," *Reuters.com* (7 June 2005), available at http://www.reuters.com/newsArticle. jhtml?type=businessNews&storyID=8721097.

Quelch, J., "The Return of the Global Brand," *Harvard Business Review* (August 2003).

Rayner, J. and Raven, W., *Corporate Social Responsibility Monitor* (London: Gee, 2002).

Ries, A. and L., *The Fall of Advertising & the Rise of PR* (New York: Harper Collins, 2001).

Rittenberg, P., "Building a #1 Rated Brand in Less than a Decade," *The Advertiser* (October 2002), available at www.knowledgenetworks.com/info/press/news/2002/10-02%20(Brands)%20The%20Advertiser.pdf.

Roberts, K., *Lovemarks* (New York: powerHouse Books, 2004).

Robinson, P.J., Faris, C.W. and Wind, Y., *Industrial Buying and Creative Marketing* (Boston: Allyn & Bacon, 1967).

Rossiter, J. and Pfoertsch, W., *Blogs: The New Language of Business* (Paramount Market Publishing, 2006).

Schlender, B., "How Big Blue Is Turning Geeks into Gold," *Fortune* (9 June 2003), pp. 133-140.

Schmitz, J.M., "Understanding the Persuasion Process Between Industrial Buyers and Sellers," *Industrial Marketing Management* (Vol. 24), pp. 83-90.

Slywotzky, A.J. and Morrison, D.J., "Concrete Solution – Company Operations," *The Industry Standard* (28 August 2000), available at http://www.findarticles.com/p/articles/mi_m0HWW/is_33_3/ai_66682402.

Smith, F.W., "Federal Express: The Supremely Packaged Warehous in the Sky," in: *Brand Warriors: Corporate Leaders Share Their Winning Strategies*, Fiona Gilmore (ed) (London: HarperCollinsBusiness, 1997).

Strauss, G., "The Corporate Jet: Necessity or Ultimate Executive Toy?," *USA Today* (25 April 2005), available at http://www.usatoday.com/money/companies/management/2005-04-26-corp-jets-cover_x.htm.

Temporal, P., "What Is Positioning?" *brandingasia.com* (April/May 2000).

Turley, J., "Silicon 101," *Embedded Systems Programming* (27 January 2004), available at http://www.embedded.com/showArticle.jhtml? articleID= 17501489.

Turpin, D., "Brand Management," *IMD Perspectives for Managers,* vol. 105 (November 2003), available at http://www02.imd.ch/documents/pfm/persp_2003/pfm_105.pdf.

Vitale, R.P. and Giglierano, J.J., *Business to Business Marketing: Analysis and Practice in a Dynamic Environment*, Thomson Learning, 2002.

Webster, F.E. and Wind, Y., *Organizational Buying Behavior* (Upper Saddle River, NJ:, Prentice Hall, 1972)

Wentz, L., "Brand Audits Reshaping Images," *Ad Age International* (September 1996), pp. 38-41.

Wheeler, A., *Designing Brand Identity: A Complete Guide to Creating, Building, and Maintaining Strong Brands* (New Jersey: John Wiley & Sons, Inc., 2003).

Whitmyre, R., "The 5 Deadly Sins of B2B Marketing", White paper, *Tiziani Whitmyre*, May 2005.

Willmott, M. *Citizen Brands: Putting Society at the Heart of Your Business* (Hoboken: Wiley & Sons, 2001).

Yee, P.H., "Rebranding Pays off for UPS," *thestar online* (17 May 2004), available at http://biz.thestar.com.my/news/story.asp?file=/2004/5/17/business/7911971&sec=business.

Internet Adresses

Accenture, www.accenture.com.

Acme Brick Company, www.brick.com.

Advanced Micro Devices, Inc., www.amd.com.

BASF Corporation, www.basf.com.

British Airways Plc., www.britishairways.com.

Caterpillar Inc., www.cat.com.

Covad Communications, www.covad.com.

FedEx Corp., www.fedex.com.

Herman Miller, www.hermanmiller.com.

IBM Corporation, www.ibm.com.

Infineon Technologies, www.infineon.com.

Intel Corporation, www.intel.com.

Klueber, www.klueber.com.

Lapp Cable, www.lapp.de.

Magna International Inc., www.magna.com.

MTU Aero Engines GmbH, www.mtu.de.

Online Encyclopedia, www.answers.com.

SAP AG, www.sap.com.

Singapore Airlines Ltd., www.singaporeair.com.

Swarovski AG, http://business.swarovski.com

United Parcel Service of America, Inc., www.ups.com

Wal-Mart Stores, Inc., www.walmartstores.com

Company and Brand Index

Subject Index

Subbrand 74, 212, 237, 265, 278

Supplier evaluation and selection
  29

Supplier structure 47

Supplies and services 21

Synergy 235, 236, 270, 320

Synergy effects 81, 82, 178, 234

Synergyeffects 247

T

Tagline 31, 92, 101, 102, 135, 170,
  199, 213, 237, 263, 287, 289

Think global, act local 247

Think local, act local 303

Three C'sof branding 162

Time pressure 25, 30, 39, 40

Trade show 116, 122

Trade shows 110, 114, 115

Transformational Strategy 186

Transnational brand strategy 89,
  226

U

User 24, 26

USP 94

V

Value added 8, 44, 46, 94, 285

Value creation 67

Value delivery 67

Value exploration 67

Value opportunities 67

Visibility 47, 162, 163

Visual identity 92, 99, 198

Visual identity code 92

Volatile demand 23

W

Word-of-Mouth 146–48, 184